Social Movements in ⌣_

Social Movements in Global Politics

David West

polity

First published in 2013 by Polity Press

Polity Press
65 Bridge Street
Cambridge CB2 1UR, UK

Polity Press
350 Main Street
Malden, MA 02148, USA

ISBN-13: 978-0-7456-4959-7
ISBN-13: 978-0-7456-4960-3(pb)

A catalogue record for this book is available from the British Library.

Typeset in 10 on 11.5pt Palatino by
Servis Filmsetting Ltd, Stockport, Cheshire
Printed and bound in Great Britain by T.J. International Ltd, Padstow, Cornwall

The publisher has used its best endeavours to ensure that the URLs for external websites referred to in this book are correct and active at the time of going to press. However, the publisher has no responsibility for the websites and can make no guarantee that a site will remain live or that the content is or will remain appropriate.

Every effort has been made to trace all copyright holders, but if any have been inadvertently overlooked the publisher will be pleased to include any necessary credits in any subsequent reprint or edition.

For further information on Polity, visit our website: www.politybooks.com

For Paul

We must resolutely reject all discourses that try to convince us that we are powerless. (Alain Touraine, *Beyond Neoliberalism*, p. 116)

Contents

Acknowledgements

I would like to thank undergraduate students in my courses on New Social Movements and Global Social Movements over the last two decades for their critical feedback, insightful questions and, on occasions, justified incomprehension. For their insightful comments on an earlier draft of this book, I am grateful to Barry Davies, David Eden, John Hart, Michael Leininger-Ogawa, Marian Sawer, Ryan Walter and Paul Davies. I would also like to thank two anonymous reviewers who, from their very different perspectives, offered a number of constructive suggestions. Melbourne University's School of Social and Political Sciences generously provided me with a room and facilities as a Visiting Fellow during 2011–12. The Australian National University allowed me sabbatical leave during the same period, without which writing this book would not have been possible.

A Political Preface: Social Movements, Global Crisis and the Failure of Institutional Politics

Outline

As its title suggests, this Political Preface sets the topic of social movements in the context of current events and emerging crises. It is prefatory in the sense that its content is not part of the more systematic exposition of subsequent chapters. The nature of politics and social movements is considered in chapter 1 and the rest of the story unfolds from there. The following sketchy remarks are designed instead to throw light on the importance of social movements and extra-institutional politics as a topic that is more than academic. Our understanding of politics both within and beyond existing political institutions influences both how we think and, more importantly, how we act politically. If the following remarks are themselves more political in a certain sense – more controversial and more reflective of a substantive political position – that fact is, to adapt Heinrich Böll's phrase, neither intentional nor accidental but unavoidable.[1]

1 The Crisis of Institutional Politics

In coming decades, the world faces intractable and, in some cases, potentially catastrophic problems. There are longstanding problems such as widespread poverty, untreated disease and insecurity in developing countries, endemic regional conflicts, wars and the growing

---

[1] Herbert Marcuse added a Political Preface to his *Eros and Civilization: A Philosophical Inquiry into Freud* (London, Allen Lane, 1969). I have adapted Heinrich Böll's epigraph to *Die Verlorene Ehre der Katherina Blum* (Munich, DTV, 1976).

dangers of nuclear proliferation. More recently, a series of environ-mental problems threatens to push the world towards crisis. World population has grown exponentially from around 2 billion at the beginning of the twentieth century and has recently exceeded 7 billion. It is expected to reach (and possibly stabilize at) somewhere between 9 and 10 billion people. At the same time, rising population is accompa-nied by continuing economic growth in affluent countries and rapidly rising living standards and consumption in a number of developing countries including the BRICS – Brazil, Russia, India, China and South Africa. Although much of this economic development is obviously to be welcomed, to the extent that it increases the living standards of pre-viously impoverished people, it still implies a rapidly increasing and ultimately unsustainable ecological burden on the planet.

The most prominent environmental threat is surely global warming, which threatens to transform the world's climate in undesirable and possibly uncontrollable ways. A severe and intensifying impact on non-human species and biodiversity is already occurring. The avail-ability of arable land and fresh water is threatened by population growth and climate change. On most predictions, rising sea levels will inundate low-lying areas of the world, including major cities inhabited by tens of millions of people. Some islands in the Pacific and Indian Oceans are already becoming uninhabitable.[2] If human habitats are significantly degraded by such changes, then large-scale movements of population, which are likely to dwarf existing migration flows, are unavoidable. It is hard to predict how climatic changes and large-scale movements of people across borders will impact on fragile nation-states, but they will surely contribute to instability, insurrection, terrorism and other forms of conflict.[3] Even wealthy liberal democra-cies are potentially vulnerable under plausible scenarios of resource shortages, 'peak oil' and global financial crisis. It seems that we have entered what has been called, in geological terms, the 'anthropocene age'.[4] This term refers to the fact that for about the past 10,000 years – and for the first time in the four and a half billion years of the Earth's existence – the world's ecology and climate are being determined not only by geological and astronomical events but increasingly by human

---

[2] See M. L. Parry, O. F. Canziani, J. P. Palutikof, P. J. van der Linden and C. E. Hanson , eds., *Contribution of Working Group II to the Fourth Assessment Report of the Intergovernmental Panel on Climate Change* (Cambridge and New York, Cambridge University Press, 2007) and www.ipcc-wg2.gov/publications/Reports/index. html#AR. (All URLs cited were last accessed on 8 April 2013.)

[3] See P. K. Conkin, *The State of the Earth: Environmental Challenges on the Road to 2100* (Lexington, University Press of Kentucky, 2007).

[4] The term was coined by ecologist Eugene F. Stoermer and popularized by climate scientist Paul Crutzen: see J. Goodell, *How to Cool the Planet* (Boston and New York, Houghton Mifflin Harcourt, 2010), pp. 15–16.

activities as well. Human impact on the world is the by-product of the growth of human population and the spread of agriculture and then industry. The anthropocene age is characterized by an unprecedented and exponential acceleration of the rate of environmental change. Climatic changes that previously took place over thousands or millions of years are now occurring over centuries and even decades. Ironically, despite the clear human imprint on the anthropocene age, it is unlikely to benefit the human beings who are now exerting such large effects, let alone non-human species and ecosystems.

We might expect that governments would be able to solve these problems, particularly the democratic and liberal governments now established in more developed countries. But in the face of the momentous threats just outlined, current responses from national and global political institutions are clearly inadequate. There is no sign that intractable problems such as poverty, untreated disease, inequality and war will be resolved. In response to global warming, liberal democracies appear unable to adopt policies that might be able to deal with the problem in a timely way, in part because these policies are unpopular with electorates who are focused on short-term and largely material goals. Governments have successfully regulated some forms of pollution and instituted measures such as environmental impact reviews. But they have so far proved unable to make sufficiently radical changes. Developing countries, which are more often governed by authoritarian regimes less directly constrained by popular opinion, place understandable emphasis on achieving rapid economic growth even at the cost of environmental damage. They are unwilling to make material sacrifices before they have even begun to enjoy the benefits of industrial society. However justified this position, with about 6 billion of the world's 7 billion population, developing countries are therefore set to contribute very substantially to global warming. Finally, although there are international forums like the United Nations, which in theory transcend the limited perspective of individual nation-states, these institutions are only dubiously democratic, weak and unable to bring about international consensus. There is currently no single institution with the authority required to enforce just and effective solutions to environmental and other global problems in the common interests of all. As a result, nuclear proliferation continues apace. World poverty and hunger persist. In the case of global warming and despite achievements like the Kyoto Protocol, individual nation-states have so far failed to agree on common action of sufficient scale and urgency. Rich states, which have contributed by far the most to global warming until now, are still waiting for other states to act first, hoping to benefit as 'free-riders' from the sacrifices of others and gain an advantage in the ongoing competition for wealth and power. All the signs are that both national and international efforts to address climate change will be far too little, too late.

The inadequate responses of nation-states are to some extent a symptom of, and are certainly exacerbated by, a widely observed crisis of institutional politics in the developed world.[5] There is widespread dissatisfaction with politics and politicians even in affluent liberal democracies and, associated with that, rising levels of apathy, at least as far as formal politics is concerned. Party membership is in secular decline. Where voting is voluntary, levels of participation are falling. But beyond these easily quantifiable tendencies, there is increasing concern about the *quality* of politics and political participation. A variety of processes is undermining the capacity of institutional politics to achieve collective goods. This 'depoliticization' assumes a variety of forms.[6] Politicians seem increasingly self-interested and pragmatic, focused on electoral success and sometimes personal gain rather than ideological goals or political visions in the national interest. Political parties more and more resemble electoral machines dedicated simply to winning power, devoid of ideals and ideology. Growing cynicism in the electorate corresponds to falling levels of trust and participation. Both tendencies combine to undermine the pursuit of long-term and collective goals as opposed to short-term objectives and the immediate self-interest of citizens. The egalitarian 'democratic moment', which to some extent tamed corporate power and inaugurated social democratic welfare states after the Second World War, seems to have passed.[7] Pursuit of broader egalitarian goals and common interests *beyond* the confines of the nation-state seems even less likely. If we had nothing to rely on but existing political institutions, then our prospects would indeed be bleak.

In what follows, however, I shall suggest that this bleak and pessimistic outlook can be avoided. In fact, such pessimism reflects an incomplete conception of politics, which ignores significant avenues for social and political change through *extra*-institutional forms of politics. Whereas a narrow view of politics confined to institutional forms only serves to reinforce our sense of powerlessness in the face of intractable global problems, the view of politics canvassed in this book focuses on political activities that take place largely outside of these institutional domains, giving rise to new forms of politics, inspiring institutional reforms and sometimes leading to regime change and even revolution. The extra-institutional dimension of politics exists alongside (although it is often ignored by) the regular politics of established institutions.

[5] See, for example, C. Crouch, *Post-Democracy* (Cambridge and Malden, MA, Polity Press, 2004); G. J. Mulgan, *Politics in an Antipolitical Age* (Cambridge and Malden, MA, Polity Press, 1994); C. Hay, *Why We Hate Politics* (Cambridge and Malden, MA, Polity Press, 2007).

[6] For a thorough analysis of 'depoliticization' in this sense, see Hay, *Why We Hate Politics*, esp. chs. 2–4.

[7] Cf. Crouch, *Post-Democracy*, esp. ch. 1.

Focusing on this dimension of politics will reveal many alternative futures that are not apparent if we focus only on the likely permutations of institutional politics. Politics and society can change in all kinds of unforeseen ways as a result of the activities of social movements. So problems that seem at present to be insoluble, catastrophes that appear inevitable, may be able to be resolved by political means after all. It is important to note, at the same time, that although recognizing the importance of extra-institutional politics helps to dissipate the pessimistic conviction that global crises and endemic social problems are insoluble, it does not sit happily with a naïve optimism either. Optimism in the face of the current global situation is just as unhelpful as pessimism. Optimism encourages apathy as well: not because nothing can be done but, on the contrary, because nothing *needs* to be done. Both optimism and pessimism are opposed to what can be described as an *activist* perspective on politics, which insists that solutions to global problems are neither impossible nor inevitable. Political problems always depend on the decisions, ingenuity and actions of citizens. Another future certainly *is* possible, but that future is up to us.

In order to understand the extra-institutional dimension of politics, we shall focus in this book on the activities of social movements. Social movements can be defined as enduring patterns of collective activity that take place outside and often in opposition to official political institutions.[8] As we shall see in more detail in future chapters, they take a variety of forms: they can be progressive, radical or conservative, secular or religious, short-lived or longstanding. In their progressive and radical manifestations, they challenge and seek to reform or transform existing institutions. Conservative movements seek to preserve the same institutional order, and reactionary movement may even try to reinstate an order that has already been superseded. Important examples of social movements that have played a decisive role in the formation of current political institutions are the nineteenth- and twentieth-century workers' movements and the several waves of the women's movement. Contemporary green movements respond directly to environmental crisis and have, in a number of countries, given rise to new green parties. In recent decades, social movements have contested the terms of neoliberal globalization. The important point at this stage is that social movements offer a range of possibilities for political action and social change in addition to those offered by the institutional political system.

However, as we shall see in more detail in the next chapter, this is not, of course, to say that institutional politics is not important or indeed essential. An emphasis on social movements should not be taken to

---

[8] Cf. J. Pakulski, *Social Movements: The Politics of Moral Protest* (Melbourne, Longman Cheshire, 1991), p. xiv.

imply that our political institutions cannot be made to work better; on the contrary, that is precisely the goal of many movements. A number of political scientists concerned about the crisis of institutional politics make interesting suggestions for reform. In the face of widespread cynicism and depoliticization, Colin Hay holds out the possibility of a less cynical politics of the common good, which would refrain from attributing a 'narrowly instrumental conception of human nature' to all political actors.[9] Others have proposed more practical (and in some countries already tried) remedies such as proportional representation, citizens' juries and forums, neighbourhood assemblies, 'television town meetings' and extended civic education.[10] What remains critical in the present context, though, is the relationship between democratic institutions, however reformed, and extra-institutional political forces. Describing the relationship between institutional and extra-institutional politics in terms of 'parties' and 'causes', Crouch makes the point that:

> we cannot rest content with working for our political goals solely by doing so *through* a party. We also have to work *on* a party from outside by assisting those causes that will sustain pressure on it. Parties which are not under pressure from causes will stay rooted in the post-democratic world of corporate lobbying; causes which try to act without reference to building strong parties will find themselves dwarfed by the corporate lobbies.[11]

The relationship and tension between movements and institutions is reflected in other proposals for deepening or radicalizing democracy by, for example, extending democratic practices further into the public sphere and civil society, where social movements are most active. John Keane recognizes and welcomes the rise of 'monitory democracy', which 'is defined by the rapid growth of many different kinds of extra-parliamentary, power-scrutinizing mechanism'.[12]

An understanding of extra-institutional social movements acting alongside, with and against the official institutions of politics should, by drawing attention to the many and diverse links between individual political actors and the various levels of institutional politics, allow a more comprehensive account of politics. Individuals act politically

---

[9] Hay, *Why We Hate Politics*, p. 161.
[10] Cf. B. Barber, *Strong Democracy: Participatory Politics for a New Age* (Berkeley and London, University of California Press, 2003), 2nd edn, esp. ch. 10.
[11] Crouch, *Post-Democracy*, pp. 111–12.
[12] J. Keane, 'Monitory Democracy and Media-Saturated Societies', *Griffith Review*, 24, 2009, accessed at https://griffithreview.com/edition-24–participation-society/monitory-democracy-and-media-saturated-societies, and cf. J. Keane, *The Life and Death of Democracy* (New York and London, Simon & Schuster, 2009).

not only by voting in elections, lobbying their elected representatives, joining political parties and so on. They can also be active in a variety of other ways by participating in social movements: as activists or more loosely affiliated supporters; by contributing ideas, help and resources; as members of associated organizations; and, more distantly, by altering their behaviour, attitudes and language in accordance with the movement's ideals. Social movements offer alternative and, in some ways, more immediately accessible avenues of action for individuals. As a result, it also becomes easier to conceive how our own actions and the collective actions of citizens can have significant effects. The connections between individual initiatives and any eventual outcomes may be complex and uncertain, but it is at least possible to think that we can make a difference. To have a more complete understanding of politics, both institutional and extra-institutional, is to understand all the many ways in which we can act upon the world.

The fact that ordinary citizens can make a difference is reinforced by the very unpredictability of extra-institutional politics. Prediction is notoriously difficult in all human affairs. Even when political scientists confine their attention to the institutional domain of politics, it is difficult, if not impossible, to foresee future events: whether in the form of the results of elections or the actions of leaders. This uncertainty is significantly compounded when we turn to social movements. As some of the examples already mentioned make clear, social movements often emerge unexpectedly and sometimes succeed in transforming seemingly well-entrenched regimes. The collapse of the communist states of the Soviet Union and Eastern Europe after 1989, the fall of Indonesia's Suharto regime in 1998 and the disintegration of a number of Arab dictatorships of North Africa and the Middle East from 2011 are striking examples. In the West, the rapid shifts in attitudes to women, homosexuality and racial minorities from the 1960s offer less dramatic but no less significant ones, demonstrating that the actions of a small group and even a single individual can have dramatic effects. The 2011 rebellion in Tunisia was sparked by the self-immolation of a market trader who had been badly treated by the authorities. The fall of communist Rumania's Ceauşescu regime began with a rowdy outburst at one of his usually staid and stage-managed public appearances.

This perspective on a future that is always open to political intervention is further reinforced by consideration of our past. An examination of earlier extra-institutional movements shows us that the world we know and the political institutions we have inherited are themselves the products of past struggles. Liberal rights and freedoms, democratic institutions and universal citizenship would not exist without the actions of radical social movements in the past. Anti-slavery, working-class and democratic activists helped to extend the rights of citizenship to all men. The first wave of feminism extended those same rights to women. At the same time, it is important to recognize that those liberal democratic laws and institutions which, with all their imperfections, currently protect our individual rights and freedoms are always vulnerable to future threats and challenges. They are maintained only by the habits, beliefs, values and, above all, the potential actions of citizens. There can be no guarantee, for example, that our current rights and liberties will survive the challenges of global warming and 'peak oil', international terrorism, nuclear proliferation and nation-state rivalries. And the problem is not just that external forces might destroy our liberal democratic institutions: it is rather that we may be tempted to sacrifice our rights and liberties for the sake of security and survival in the face of such external threats. Extra-institutional politics, in other words, is concerned with the preservation of existing institutions as well as with their reform or transformation.

At the heart of the activist conception of politics outlined in this book is thus the recognition that 'we' have in the past made, and can in the future again make, a significant difference to the societies we live in. Who 'we' are, how we can act and what we should do are some of the questions that will be addressed in the following chapters. Some things, of course, may just be beyond our control. We cannot quickly or easily reverse two centuries' accumulation of carbon dioxide; we cannot put coal, gas and oil back into the ground. But beyond such obvious practical constraints are a number of political and potentially solvable challenges. How can we persuade other people to recognize environmental degradation, world poverty and nuclear proliferation as serious problems? How can people who may agree about what needs to be done act together effectively in order to influence the decisions of government? How can we transform our values and patterns of consumption and redirect economic activities to more sustainable goals? Such political challenges are obviously considerable. But there is no doubt that in the past actors just like us have made a difference in similarly challenging circumstances.

2 Plan of the Book

This book focuses on the activities of extra-institutional political actors and social movements. Part I provides a more detailed picture of the nature and importance of extra-institutional politics. Chapter 1 examines the differences between institutional and extra-institutional politics. After a brief look at the conventional understanding of official or institutional politics, we explore in a preliminary way the nature of social movements as extra-institutional actors and their relations to institutional politics. Chapter 2 provides a brief historical overview of the contributions of some social movements to the formation of our current political institutions. Religious, nationalist and bourgeois movements are associated with the rise of the modern nation-state and capitalism. Working-class activism, the anti-slavery and women's movements for suffrage and moral reform played an essential role in establishing current principles of universal and equal citizenship for all.

Part II considers some of the main features of contemporary extra-institutional movements and their associated ideas, strategies and tactics. In chapter 3 we turn to the recent upsurge in western liberal democracies of what have been called new social movements, which have been highly influential for a number of reasons. In the first place, they first appeared in affluent liberal democracies, which were not thought to be in need of reform. Their surprising emergence encouraged both a revised understanding and revaluation of extra-institutional politics. Chapter 4 examines the ideas of culture and identity, oppression and liberation in the context of some contemporary movements, particularly anti-racist, women's and gay and lesbian movements. Race, ethnicity, gender and sexuality have become key bases of identity and engagement. Chapter 5 turns to the ideas, strategies and tactics associated with environmental and green movements. For the first time these movements have politicized nature, animal welfare and species diversity, contributing related and novel ideas of political action and organization. Chapter 6 considers the renewed focus on material and economic concerns in the alter-globalization movement from the 1990s, which has – in a sometimes perplexing variety of ways – advocated alternatives to corporate or neoliberal globalization. Contradicting some new social movement enthusiasts who claimed that economic issues are no longer significant, the alter-globalization movement practises what can be described as a new politics of exploitation.

Part III examines some theoretical approaches that can usefully be applied to the study of social movements. Chapter 7 examines normative and formal approaches to social movements. The upsurge of social movement activism in western societies has led to a significant normative shift, so that social movement activism is no longer seen as immoral or pathological but rather as an essential and legitimate dimension of politics. Sociologists and political scientists are now able to investigate extra-institutional activism not as an abnormal and dysfunctional outburst of collective behaviour but as a potentially rational mode of collective action. Chapter 8 considers a series of theoretical approaches that seek to explain the substantive goals and characteristics of specific movements. These theories focus less on how social movements function and more on the context in which they emerge and what they aim to achieve in contemporary society. Chapter 9, finally, brings together the overall argument of the book by presenting in outline the limits and potential role of a critical theory of social movements.

Further Reading

For a determinedly non-apocalyptic yet sobering review of looming environmental crises, see Paul K. Conkin, *The State of the Earth: Environmental Challenges on the Road to 2100.* The limitations of institutional politics and the potential role of social movements are explored by Colin Crouch in *Post-Democracy.* An alternative notion of democracy is charted in John Keane's *The Life and Death of Democracy.* More detailed suggestions for readings about particular social movements and the activist conception of politics defended in this book will be provided in subsequent chapters.

Part I

Foundations

1

Introduction:
What Are Social Movements?

Outline

The current agenda of formal or institutional politics represents only part of politics. Equally essential to the political domain are issues and agents currently excluded from formal politics. As much as it is about the workings of existing institutions, politics is about the emergence of new issues, new agents and constituencies. The extra-institutional actions of these agents contribute to the reform and sometimes replacement of institutions. By the same token, a narrowly institutional conception of politics ignores potentially important issues and constituencies and obscures potentially oppressive power relations. It leaves us ill-equipped to address through political action intractable local and global problems. By contrast, an emphasis on the extra-institutional politics of social movements leaves the field of politics open to emerging issues, agents and constituencies and thus offers a perspective that encourages broader political awareness and action. In order to understand the nature of extra-institutional politics, we need to start with a clear understanding both of the nature of politics in general and of the narrower domain of institutional politics. Extra-institutional politics is, in the first place, everything political that takes place outside of institutions.

1.1 What is Politics? The Scope of Social Power

Politics is concerned with the actions of politicians and governments, elections and voting, political parties, interest groups, pressure groups and campaigns, parliaments and the making of laws. But, as the topic of this book implies, an exclusively institutional view of politics is limited in ways that narrow our understanding of politics and restrict our capacity for political action. As we shall see throughout the rest of this chapter, if we focus too much on official or institutional forms of politics, we risk neglecting or ignoring the important contribution of social movements and extra-institutional politics. A related limitation is to confine our view of politics to problems, decisions and processes that are conventionally defined as political or what amounts to the conventional agenda and day-to-day realities of politics. Crucially, this is to ignore the fact that what is counted as political is itself a contentious issue and one routinely contested by social movements. In fact, defining something as political is in a sense the first political act. Establishing new political issues and advancing the interests of excluded social groups typically involve people acting together outside of existing institutional channels or, in other words, extra-institutionally. By the same token, a narrowly institutional view of politics leads us to see many events and developments as things that just happen to us rather than as political problems that we are potentially able to solve. So critical global problems – some of which were briefly explored in the previous chapter – are seen as insoluble. In order to be able to address and solve such problems, on the other hand, we need to adopt a much broader perspective on both the nature of politics and the possibilities of political action.

It will help us to locate this broader perspective if we start from an initially abstract view of the nature of politics and political problems. Although it is obviously only the starting point for an understanding of politics and political action, this abstract view helps us to focus on what is distinctive about political problems and to see why pessimism is not inevitable. We can identify this preliminary perspective by asking ourselves, when we look at the world and its many challenging problems, which of these problems can *in principle* be solved by human actions alone and which cannot. This preliminary definition is deliberately broad. It allows us to exclude as *non*-political only those problems that cannot under any circumstances be solved by human actions. Hurricanes and volcanoes, earthquakes and tsunamis and a future asteroid impact are natural events that cannot presently be controlled by human actions.[1] Even in the case of natural disasters we can do many things to mitigate the *consequences* of such events, consequences which to that extent belong to the category of political problems. Governments and aid organizations can help those affected by natural disasters to rebuild destroyed buildings, to repair water and

---

[1] With enough advanced warning and further development of missile technology, it might be possible to divert approaching meteors. The human ability to intervene would in that case require considerable resources, making it clearly a political issue.

electricity supplies, to mend roads and treat contagious diseases. By the same token, it is a failure of politics when governments do not respond adequately to natural disasters, as occurred with the US Federal Government's response to Hurricane Katrina in 2005.

From the abstract and deliberately broad perspective that we are considering, it becomes apparent that many seemingly 'insoluble' problems are in fact soluble, at least in principle, by political means. Burgeoning human population, regional poverty and growing inequality, increasing environmental degradation of the planet, rising carbon emissions threatening catastrophic climate change – all of these are problems that could be solved by human actions. For these problems, the actions required are well known and do not depend on novel technologies, although technological advances (such as new and more efficient forms of renewable energy, carbon sequestration and food production) would obviously help. In these cases, the fundamental difficulties are essentially political, because their solution depends on the actions of people and governments. A central feature of political problems is their intrinsically collective or social nature: their solution depends on eliciting decisions and co-ordinating the actions of a plurality of people. Problems that can be solved by a single individual, a private couple or a family, such as where to find work, what to eat and where to live, are accordingly not political.[2] The political challenge is to get people to agree on the necessary actions, to persuade people to act and, when people are willing to act, to co-ordinate their actions effectively. These challenges are made more difficult by the fact that different people often have diverse and conflicting interests, values and beliefs, which they are determined to pursue.

The peculiar difficulty of political problems becomes obvious, once we abandon the abstract perspective and regard them, as we are more often inclined to do, from our subjective perspective as individuals. Looking at the world and its problems from that perspective, we are immediately susceptible to feelings of pessimism and powerlessness. How can I, as a single and isolated individual, make any difference, when faced with the indifference or even opposition of so many other people? How can so many people with their diverse interests, beliefs and values ever be persuaded to think, let alone to act, in the ways I would like? Such feelings of powerlessness are likely to increase as an individual's political awareness expands. Information available from newspapers, mass media and the internet makes us aware of the range and depth of intractable local and global problems. The broader our awareness, the less easily we can imagine that our own actions might make a difference. Indeed, it would be worrying if any single

---

[2] Whether *all* collective and in-principle-soluble problems are in fact political is a more complicated issue that we shall address in what follows.

individual really could make a significant difference to the world on their own. After all, many people have (to others) unattractive or even repugnant views. Some people are selfish, evil or destructive, some are irrational or even insane. Dictators like Julius Caesar, Napoleon, Stalin and Hitler vie as world-historical individuals with social movement leaders such as Martin Luther King, Nelson Mandela and Aung San Suu Kyi. Crucially, even supposedly powerful individuals, whether dictators, presidents or social movement leaders, are powerful only because they are able to influence the actions of many other people by virtue of their political office, financial resources, persuasive talents or charisma. Dictators depend on their control of government officials and armies. Social movement leaders must be able to inspire others to act. In other words, leadership depends on 'followership'.[3]

Political action thus typically depends on the collective efforts of many people or what can be called *social power*. Individual problems can be solved through the actions of individuals by their own means, resources and capacities or their individual power. Political problems depend on the deployment of collective or social power: the resources, capacities and actions of many people. This obviously has a positive aspect. Human beings acting together are able to achieve things far beyond the capacities of any single individual, even the most powerful and resourceful. Many individuals acting together are able to generate social power in order to achieve collective goals for their common benefit. This is evidently a fundamental condition of the flourishing of human societies.

Collective action is, however, something that is particularly difficult to achieve, because the conflicting wills and interests of many people must be reconciled. So how do human societies actually achieve social power? As the notion of constitution implies, societies achieve social power by setting up – or constituting – institutions of government. The state's founding constitution serves, in that sense, to constitute the state as a collective agent.[4] Social power depends on some form of authoritative rule or governance, which resolves the problem of co-ordinating the views and actions of many people. In most states, social power thus results from the *power* of government *over* its subjects or citizens. Whether the system is presidential or parliamentary, monarchical or dictatorial, the government is able to control the actions of the rest of society. But, except in the most violent dictatorships, the government's ability to exert control also depends on much more than brute coercive

---

[3] See J. M. Burns, *Leadership* (New York and London, Harper & Row, 1978), and G. Little, *Political Ensembles: A Psychosocial Approach to Politics and Leadership* (Oxford and New York, Oxford University Press, 1985).

[4] For an account of the US Constitution in these terms, see H. Arendt, *On Revolution* (Harmondsworth, Penguin, 1973), ch. 4, esp. section I.

force. Brute force is the kind of power that leaders of criminal organizations exert over their members and victims.[5] In most ordered societies, on the other hand, social power takes the form of authoritative governance, whereby the power of leaders and government is recognized by the governed as legitimate. Forms of governance regarded as legitimate within a particular society constitute that society's political institutions. Political institutions in this sense are evidently at the heart of any plausible view of politics, although as we proceed it will emerge that they by no means account for the entire field of politics.

1.2 The Institutional View of Politics: Social Power as Authoritative Governance

The standard view of politics focuses on social power as embodied in the authoritative institutions of particular states, as well as governance bodies at both national and international levels.[6] Political institutions constitute social power by determining and co-ordinating the actions of many individuals according to agreed rules and procedures. These institutions are authoritative because the powers they accord to government are regarded as legitimate. Citizens obey their government because they think they should, rather than simply out of fear or physical necessity. To that extent, the government's power over its citizens amounts to authority rather than merely coercive power or force. Authoritative political institutions are clearly at the heart of any systematic study of politics. In common with other social sciences, the established discipline of political science or political studies is concerned not simply with individual human behaviour but with the social interactions between people. However, politics differs from other social sciences such as social psychology, anthropology, sociology and criminology, because it focuses on authoritative political institutions and associated beliefs, values and actions. In the western context, the discipline of politics thus studies such things as governments and elections, politicians and political parties, alternative policies and legislation, the working of state bureaucracies, opposing party ideologies and so on.

Those institutions that make up the government of a state are

---

[5] In fact, even criminal organizations like the Mafia only survive in virtue of their own idiosyncratic but rigorously enforced codes of honour.

[6] For a classic account of politics in these terms, see D. Easton, *The Political System: An Inquiry into the State of Political Science* (New York, Knopf, 1971), 2nd edn, which defines the political system as 'the authoritative allocation of values' for a society: pp. 128–9 and 135. For discussion of a variety of definitions, see A. Leftwich, ed., *What is Politics? The Activity and its Study* (Oxford, Polity Press, 2004).

obviously of central importance in the field of politics. In a dictatorship or monarchy, government may be exercised by one individual,
although other people will play an essential role as advisers, admin-
istrators and enforcers of the ruler's will. In a constitutional regime,
government is made up of a series of institutions and procedures
which, along with the powers and responsibilities of various officers,
are set out in a state's constitution. A constitution may exist in written
form, as in France, the USA and Australia, or as a set of unwritten
conventions, as in the UK. The government in the narrow sense is the
executive branch or, in other words, those bodies and individuals that
make decisions and propose laws on behalf of society as a whole. The
executive includes the various departments of state including president
or prime minister, cabinet and ministers of various departments. The
executive also includes public bureaucracies with their public or 'civil'
servants and officials, who administer and implement government
policies. In constitutional systems, the executive is constrained by the
rule of law. Laws are enacted by legislative bodies such as parliaments
and houses of representatives and their members. The legislative role
is shared with upper houses or senates and their members or senators.
Another important branch of government in the core institutional
sense is the judicial system or system of justice. Courts and judges
interpret the laws passed by parliaments and adjudicate between
contending parties, settling disputes over the interpretation of the
law. Sometimes they interpret the state's constitution and may be able
to overturn laws or actions deemed to be unconstitutional. Courts
determine when laws have been infringed and impose appropriate
penalties and punishments. The judicial system depends on agencies
of enforcement and their officers as well. Police, prison and probation
services administer the punishments and penalties determined by the
courts.

The issue of enforcement points to another fundamental feature of
political institutions: they necessarily include a variety of means of
coercion and force. Max Weber famously defined the state as that entity
which 'upholds the claim to the monopoly of the legitimate use of
physical force in the enforcement of its order'.[7] Governments and legislatures take decisions, implement policies and make laws, but what
is distinctive about authoritative political institutions is their sovereign
status within a particular country or territory. The state is the ultimate
source of laws in its territory. Even though organizations and individuals in society have the ability within certain limits to make their own
decisions, those limits constraining their freedom of action are set by

---

[7] See M. Weber, 'The Profession and Vocation of Politics' ['Politik als Beruf'] (1919)
   in *Max Weber: Political Writings*, ed. P. Lassman and R. Speirs (Cambridge and
   New York, Cambridge University Press, 1994), pp. 310–11.

the state. Crucially, however legitimate or popular they may be, the laws and decisions of the government must ultimately be enforceable. A state that is unable to enforce its decisions is a weak state and, at the extreme, a failed state that is no longer recognized as the legitimate authority either by its citizens or by other states. The sovereignty of the state contrasts with the status of religious and other bodies within society, whose rights and powers are subject to the ultimate authority of the state. The components of the state responsible for the enforcement of its authoritative decisions include, as we have seen, police and prison systems. In states of emergency, when the survival of the state is threatened, police and armed forces may be called upon to restore civil order. More conventionally, armed forces are called upon to defend the state's territory from acts of terrorism or foreign aggression and invasion by other states.

The relations of one state both with other nation-states and with threatening non-state actors such as terrorists belong to the realm of international relations. In the international domain, organized and institutional politics is primarily concerned with inter-state relations. These include the conduct of diplomacy, negotiations between governments and the making of alliances and treaties. There are also a number of significant institutions of international governance. International bodies such as the United Nations (UN), International Monetary Fund (IMF) and the World Trade Organization (WTO) are examples of such institutions. A fundamental feature of international politics is the fact that there is no sovereign global authority with the power to enforce its decisions. Although there are powerful states such as the USA and China, there is no sovereign world state able to adjudicate between states and enforce international law. Even when powerful states claim to enforce international law, they do so without recognized legitimacy or authority. In international relations, states can only agree to set up, and declare their intention to abide by, international treaties and instruments of law. So international law has a fundamentally different status from the domestic laws of any sovereign nation-state. However persuasive and justified they may be, international laws lack the backing of any global body with, in Weber's terms, a 'monopoly of the legitimate use of physical force'.

Returning to relations within the nation-state, the institutional view of politics is also concerned with a wide range of organizations that play important roles in relation to the central institutions of government. Most well known in electoral democracies are political parties, which compete for government office in periodic elections. The study of political parties, their ideologies and policies, internal dynamics, electioneering tactics, sources of electoral support and styles of leadership, are all central topics of the mainstream study of politics. The relationships between political parties and government obviously vary according to differing constitutional arrangements and electoral systems. In liberal democracies, political parties usually represent broadly opposed coalitions of interest, values and ideology. This was not always the case. Before the nineteenth century in Europe, political parties were more likely to represent different stances on the monarchy and opposing religious affiliations. In the nineteenth century, the predominant conflict was between the 'landed interest' of aristocracy and land-owning gentry on the one hand and commerce on the other. Today ideological differences seemingly play a decreasing role in the era of 'catch-all' parties and 'presidential', media-driven elections.[8] But in western democracies, party differences still have some relation to differences of wealth and property. Major parties have stronger links either with business and 'capital' or with the working class, labour and trade union organizations. Other differences, of ethnicity and religion, gender, sexuality and ecology, relate to competing parties in more complex and varied ways.

Still further from the formal institutional core of politics and political authority are a variety of other organizations, including interest groups and pressure and lobby groups, which exert influence on the central political institutions and actors. In pluralist societies, interest groups are formally constituted organizations which, as their name suggests, represent the interests of their constituency through legally recognized or tolerated forms of action such as lobbying, public communication and education. Some interest groups have close relationships to political parties. For example, business organizations have ties with parties of capital, trade union organizations with parties of labour. Interest groups are also able to voice the concerns of a wide variety of other groups and interests, which would otherwise not be directly represented by any of the existing two or three major parties. Lobby and pressure groups are similar to interest groups in being formally constituted organizations but differ in that they represent particular opinions, values or single issues rather than a constituency of interest in the narrower sense. People organize to protect the environment, ban smoking or abolish the death penalty without having any personal interest in these issues. Citizens often assume moral stances that have no connection with, and are sometimes even opposed to, their own interests. In a pluralist society, political issues are typically played out between a variety of interest and lobby groups as well as through major electoral parties. So, for example, campaigns concerned with smoking and health are conducted by groups representing

[8] On 'catch-all' (also known as 'big tent') parties, see O. Kirchheimer, 'The Transformation of the Western European Party Systems' in *Political Parties and Political Development*, ed. J. La Palombara and M. Weiner (Princeton, NJ, Princeton University Press, 1966).

the victims of lung cancer and medical practitioners; they may be opposed by organizations representing the tobacco industry and its workers.

The foregoing brief sketch of institutional politics represents the core subject matter of political science as conventionally understood. It might be thought that this constitutes the entire field of politics and the proper subject matter of political science. This would also imply that institutional politics is the only place for the solution of political problems. For a number of reasons, which will be explored in the following section, it is essential that politics is understood more broadly to encompass the extra-institutional domain of social movements. A more inclusive account of politics will have the additional advantage of putting in a more hopeful light the intractable political problems considered in the Preface.

1.3 Beyond Institutional Politics: The Challenge of Social Movements

Why, then, should we look at politics beyond the confines of authoritative political institutions? In the first place, because the denial that legitimate forms of politics can exist beyond political institutions is not so much a factual claim as a normative or ideological one. Conservatives typically see no valid role for extra-institutional politics, because they are opposed to institutional change. The conservative opposes institutional change either on the grounds that our current institutions are already as good as they can possibly be in an imperfect world or because change is fraught with danger. But the conservative position implicitly favours currently privileged groups and vested interests, who have no need for, and would not benefit from, institutional change. The claim that politics is equivalent to the sum of activities occurring within existing political institutions excludes from the beginning the possibility that these institutions might have serious inadequacies and that extra-institutional movements might be required and might legitimately seek to remedy them. The conservative position assumes that any defects within current institutions can be corrected by actions from within them, whereas historical experience shows that necessary reforms often occur only as a result of an extra-institutional challenge.[9]

Until the 1960s, this conservative position largely prevailed within the social and political sciences. Social movements were associated

---

[9] For a historical overview of the contribution of social movements, see chapter 2. *Political* conservatives endorse current institutions; *moral* or *social* conservatives aim to preserve traditional norms and 'family values'.

with mass movements of fascism in Italy and Germany and with revolutionary communism in the Soviet Union and China. The successes of these totalitarian threats to free and democratic institutions were explained as manifestations of collective irrationality, if not hysteria. National Socialist rallies in Hitler's Germany, Stalin's 'cult of personality' in the Soviet Union and the excesses of China's Cultural Revolution are typical phenomena in this sense. Crowds, rumours and panics were studied as similar manifestations of collective irrationality – of what happens when individual common sense is overcome by collective emotions. Social movements within western societies were regarded in the same way as irrational outbursts of frustration, as threats to law, order and the proper processes of government.[10] This attitude to social movement politics began to change from the 1950s and 1960s with the arrival of an array of extra-institutional challenges, which have achieved significant reforms of both western and non-western institutions. The African-American Civil Rights movement in America, the 'second-wave' women's movement and feminism, the gay and lesbian liberation movements, green and environmental movements are prominent examples. The democracy movement in Eastern Europe and the Soviet Union helped to dislodge seemingly well-entrenched communist regimes, which rapidly collapsed after 1989. More recently, the alter-globalization and Occupy movements combine these concerns with economic issues and conflicts. These movements have brought about – and continue to bring about – significant changes to what had been regarded as already legitimate liberal and democratic institutions.[11]

A second reason why we should be concerned with extra-institutional politics is in order to understand the formation of current institutions. The conservative identification of politics with contemporary institutions implies a paradoxical attitude to their history. Conservatives condemn extra-institutional challenges to institutions which owe their present form to earlier phases of extra-institutional challenge. From the history of European states as well as from the existence of tyrannical and despotic states today, it is apparent that the institutions of the state cannot simply be equated with social power. The collective power of states often begins life as the social power of a small minority, which conquers and exploits its subject population. Most European states can be traced to such acts of conquest and usurpation. It is only after a long history of resistance and rebellion that western states can plausibly be represented as expressions of citizens' social power. Their institutions are (imperfectly) liberal and democratic only as a result of protracted,

---

[10] For more on theories of social movements as irrational collective behaviour , see below: chapter 7, pp. 158–62.

[11] These movements will be discussed in chapters 3–6.

often violent, struggles. Civil wars were fought in order to limit the absolute powers of monarchs and to secure the rights of parliament. The fight against monarchy was fought by middling classes, the emerging merchants and traders of what Marx famously dubbed the 'bourgeoisie', as well as by disgruntled aristocrats, religious minorities and rebellious peasants. A later wave of conflicts emancipated slaves, extended the franchise beyond the propertied few and eventually to women as well as men. Although many factors undoubtedly played a role in these changes, it is impossible to understand fully these crucial stages of western institutional history without considering the essential contribution of extra-institutional social movements.[12]

When we consider the historical formation of contemporary political institutions, it becomes clear, thirdly, that the scope of both the state and institutional politics is itself a central issue of political contention. In common parlance, politics is concerned only with public as opposed to private matters. As conventionally understood today, politics is concerned with government and law, with the organization of the police and the judicial system, with taxation, public infrastructure, welfare and the legal framework of private property in the capitalist economy. Other things are considered to be private matters which are beyond the proper concern of the state and law. Crucially, however, the distinction between public and political versus private affairs is clearly variable, contentious and, indeed, itself intrinsically political. Much of politics has been concerned precisely with including or excluding particular matters from the public and political domain. Historically, one major issue of contention has been religion. Western societies in their present form emerged from the protracted series of religious struggles and wars between Protestants and Catholics that began with the Reformation. The solution to these conflicts advanced by John Locke was a limited form of religious toleration that excluded Catholics and atheists. The principle of religious toleration, which was gradually extended to include all religious persuasions, has become a fundamental tenet of liberalism. Liberalism removes differences of religion from the main public and political agenda, relegating them largely to the private domain of individual conscience and choice.[13] That there was nothing inevitable about this way of defining the public sphere is confirmed by the fact that the separation of religion and politics has become contentious once again. In the United States, religious conservatives campaign for legislation to enforce traditional morality, family values and Christian teachings on abortion, gay and lesbian

---

[12] See chapter 2, esp. sections 2.3–4.

[13] See J. Locke, *An Essay Concerning Toleration, and Other Writings on Law and Politics* (Oxford, Clarendon Press; New York, Oxford University Press, 2006), ed. J. R. Milton and P. Milton.

marriage and evolutionary science. In a number of predominantly Islamic societies, political Islamists are attempting to enforce sharia law and Islamic modes of governance.

The distinction between public and private has more recently been contested by a number of social movements in rather different ways. Until the 1970s in the West, domestic relationships within families were regarded as purely private affairs. At the same time, paradoxically, people were prosecuted for homosexual acts, even though they affected only consenting adults and took place mainly in private. In recent decades, both the women's and gay and lesbian movements have challenged these practices. As a result, issues such as gender equality, sexism and domestic violence, childcare and parental leave, the rights of gays, lesbians and transgender people, and now gay and lesbian marriage have been recognized as legitimately public and political concerns. In these cases, social movements serve to politicize and in that sense to make public previously excluded or private issues and concerns. As a result, the interests of the corresponding constituencies are more effectively represented within the political system as well. The institutions of western states increasingly (although obviously incompletely) reflect the demands and values of these movements.

The exclusively institutional view of politics diverts attention, fourthly, from the fact that the state (however legitimate or illegitimate) is not the *only* centre of social power in society. Social power is centred on a variety of independent social entities, which may be less powerful than the state but which are nonetheless capable of exerting significant influence.[14] Both the social power of these bodies and the conflicts between them impinge directly and indirectly on the formal institutions of the state. Independent centres of social power may restrain and sometimes neutralize the social power of the state. To consider a concrete example, both within liberal democratic capitalist societies and globally, considerable social power is exerted by both national and transnational corporations. By such actions as threatening disinvestment, mounting media campaigns and donating to politicians and parties, corporations are able to influence, resist and sometimes reverse government policy. Indirect influence is exerted when government officials take account of corporate interests in anticipation of direct pressures. The democratic will of the people is, in these cases, modified and sometimes negated by corporate power. Even if Marxist theories of the 'bourgeois state' tend to exaggerate the influence of capital, there

---

[14] Andrew Gamble refers to this as the 'politics of power': see A. Gamble, *The Conservative Nation* (London and Boston, MA, Routledge and Kegan Paul, 1974), ch. 1.

can be little doubt that liberal democratic states are significantly – and surely unduly – influenced by corporate interests.[15]

The plurality of centres of social power means that we cannot assume that the formal equality and democracy, formally equal rights and liberties of liberal democracies guarantee that all groups, interests and issues are fairly represented within the political system. The undue influence of one form of collective power implies the partial or complete exclusion of other interests and constituencies. If state institutions give favourable access to certain interests, then by the same token they tend to exclude others. The disenfranchisement of workers and legal prohibition of trade unions during the nineteenth and early twentieth centuries was associated with the relegation of many issues relating to employment, work practices and contracts to the non-political realm of private affairs. Before the advent of feminism and the women's movement, the exclusion of women from full participation in public political life corresponded to a similar privatization of issues such as marital rape, domestic violence and discrimination on the basis of gender.

However, it is a mistake to regard social power as a given commodity which, once distributed and in place, is forever entrenched and unchallengeable. Social movements of workers and women fought against their exclusion from institutional politics and eventually achieved both greater representation within the state and more effective rights. In that sense, these movements have advanced the social power of workers and women. Social power is not just a feature of visible and already established social constituencies and interests, whether these are within or outside of the formal institutions of the state. Equally important is social power *in formation*, and social power is formed through the emergence and activities of social movements. An important implication is that the limitations and biases of established social power – whether institutional or extra-institutional – are not beyond remedy. Inequalities of social power and problems stemming from those inequalities can be addressed through the formation of rival centres of power. Institutions may be reformed and extra-institutional social power combated through the activities of extra-institutional agents and social movements. In this context, the upsurge from the 1960s of so-called 'new social movements' represents a recent manifestation of new and newly self-conscious constituencies. These emerging centres of social power have brought about substantial changes to western societies and political institutions. Their successes have also led to greater recognition of the importance and legitimacy of extra-institutional politics. Social movements are no longer invariably

---

[15] See R. Miliband, *The State in Capitalist Society* (London, Weidenfeld & Nicolson, 1969) and *Capitalist Democracy in Britain* (Oxford and New York, Oxford University Press, 1982).

dismissed as either sources of authoritarian rule or irrational responses to social deprivation. More often, they can now be understood in the context of a broader and more historically informed understanding of social power and politics in all their variety.

1.4 Extra-Institutional Politics: A Preliminary Survey

At this stage it will be useful to consider in a preliminary way some of the basic features of social movements. Social movements, according to Jan Pakulski, are 'recurrent patterns of collective activities which are partially institutionalized, value oriented and anti-systemic in their form and symbolism'.[16] We have already alluded to some of the features of extra- and anti-institutional politics. Once we focus on the extra-institutional dimension of political activism, it is also clear that political agents are not necessarily organized in ways familiar from institutional politics. The focus on social movements leads us to recognize that there are various levels and degrees of organization and disorganization in politics.

At the formative stage of politics, in particular, formal organizations either do not exist or are in the process of being formed. Formal political organizations typically have a constitution, rules of membership, procedures to elect officials and leaders, a common agenda and ways to decide on future policies and actions. By contrast, social movements are diffuse and often unorganized. Movements do not have rules of membership or agreed procedures to elect officials or leaders. Membership is largely informal – a matter of people identifying with, supporting or being active in the movement. Movements are made up of the actions of individuals, informal groups or 'affinity groups' and networks, as well as occasional or transient coalitions of individuals and groups forming in response to particular occasions or events. The ongoing life of the movement may be maintained by these diverse and complex 'ensembles' as much as by any prominent organization, political party or interest group.[17] Movement leaders are widely recognized as influential figures, but they are not elected and, indeed, there may be rival and competing figures. There may also be competing proposals and policies, even sharply divergent ideologies. For example, the women's movement has included liberal, radical, socialist and postmodern feminisms. Environmental movements include those who reject modern urban industrial society altogether and those who seek simply to make that societal form sustainable.

---

[16] Pakulski, *Social Movements*, p. xiv.
[17] The term 'ensemble' is used by Jean-Paul Sartre in *Critique of Dialectical Reason* (London, New Left Books, 1991), trans. A. Sheridan-Smith.

Social movements are, of course, often associated with particular organizations, including organizations of the type discussed above as interest and pressure groups.[18] The working-class movement has been closely associated with socialist, social democratic and labour parties, trade unions, educational associations and co-operative societies. The green movement is associated with Greenpeace and the World Wild Fund for Nature. The women's movement has given rise to a plethora of organizations, rape crisis and women's health centres and domestic violence refuges, electoral lobby groups and feminist publications. But a movement is never completely identified with any particular organization or set of organizations, even at its most mature and fully formed. As examples like the collapse of communism in Eastern Europe after 1989 and the Arab Spring of 2011 demonstrate, movements have a life of their own quite apart from any particular organization. Much happens 'in' a movement – riot and revolution being only the most dramatic examples – that is beyond the control of any of its associated organizations. The movement may give rise to organizations, and organizations sometimes inspire movements, but in both cases the movement extends beyond the boundaries of its organizations. Indeed, much of what is distinctive about the formative and anti-institutional politics of social movements takes place outside of organizations.

Just as social movements challenge the conventional boundaries and organized models of politics, they also pursue alternative modes of political practice, different political strategies and tactics. Social movements do not always follow recognized models of political action such as voting, canvassing support for political parties, lobbying parliament and government officials. They are as – if not more – likely to demonstrate, organize protests and present petitions. Women campaigning for universal suffrage – Suffragists or Suffragettes – broke the law and risked their own lives in order to win votes for women. Gandhi's strategy of 'active non-violence' and 'truth force' involved peaceful but sometimes violently suppressed campaigns of civil disobedience against British rule in India. But the extra-institutional activities of social movements are not always illegal. The women's and gay movements have practised forms of personal and identity politics, cultural activism and campaigning which occur outside normal institutional channels but are within the law. These strategies aim for personal and cultural change as much as for institutional reforms.

As should be obvious from some of the examples cited already, extra-institutional politics assumes a wide variety of forms, which may be judged either constructive or destructive, desirable or undesirable, to be supported or opposed depending on one's values and ideology. Social movements tend to be described according to terms that reflect

[18] See above, pp. 10–11.

the eighteenth-century European Enlightenment, and then widespread, belief that history advances inevitably and irreversibly in a particular direction, which is variously described as improvement, progress or development. This conception of history became more popular with the French Revolution of 1789, which saw monarchical rule swept away by new, seemingly more modern and rational forms of republican government. The terms 'left' and 'right', as political labels referring to advocates of greater or lesser social equality, are derived from the seating arrangements of delegates at the French Revolutionary convention.[19] Although difficult to avoid entirely, terms such as 'progressive', 'radical', 'reactionary' and 'conservative' characterize ideologies and social movements according to their relationship to the supposed direction of history on the dubious assumption that it is possible to know what that direction is.

From the eighteenth century, social movements have been described as *progressive* and *radical* when they represent groups of people and corresponding interests and issues previously excluded from institutionalized politics. Progressives see themselves as on the side of history, encouraging its advance. Radicals are more enthusiastic and impatient for change. The inclusion of new constituencies and interests was seen as an inevitable result of the further development of society along already visible paths of urbanization, industrialization and the development of capitalism. In the eighteenth century, these groups included merchants, traders and manufacturers who were excluded from institutions dominated by the monarchy and aristocracy. From the early nineteenth century and with the advance of industrialization, the inclusion of workers seemed similarly inevitable. Radical social causes have sometimes given rise to *revolutionary* movements which seek change not by working within the existing framework of laws and constitution, nor even by adding new issues and constituencies to the body politic, but by overturning the state altogether.[20] Marxism reflects Enlightenment assumptions in seeing revolutionary transformation as the inevitable by-product of historical development.

Even *conservatism* and conservative social movements can ultimately be understood only in relation to the presumed direction of progress. Conservatives seek to preserve the benefits of established institutions and tradition in the face of progressive and radical challenges. Conservatism only becomes a self-conscious ideology once institutions and tradition are seen to be threatened. A founding conservative

---

[19] See chapter 2, pp. 37–8.

[20] As the word suggests, revolution originally meant the return to, or restoration of, originally pure institutions. It is only in the context of the eighteenth century's progressive view of history that revolution comes to refer to an abrupt transition to a radically new social order: see Arendt, *On Revolution*, ch. 1, esp. pp. 42–7.

text in that sense is Edmund Burke's *Reflections on the Revolution in France* (1790), which defends the *ancien régime* or 'old order' in France against the threatening tides of revolution and radical reform.[21] In that sense, conservative movements are typically defensive or reactive. A movement or ideology is described as *reactionary* when its aim is to reverse progressive or radical changes that have already been achieved. Reactionary social forces in the nineteenth century sought to restore the monarchy in Republican France. Today, conservative campaigns for moral and family values have arisen largely as reactions to reforms and legal changes achieved or advocated by women's and sexual liberation movements, and press for a return to Christian, Jewish and Islamic teachings.

Since the twentieth century, the categories of reactionary, conservative, progressive and radical have come under further strain. Fascist movements in Italy, Germany and Spain reacted to the perceived danger of revolutionary communism and Soviet hegemony. Fascist movements are often described as right-wing and reactionary, since they seek to reinstitute hierarchical, authoritarian and anti-democratic values. However, although these values are shared by monarchical and aristocratic regimes of the old order, twentieth-century fascism aimed for, and for a time realized, a form of society that was strictly without historical precedent.[22] The barbarities of fascist tyranny and genocide contradict in the starkest possible way any assumption that history must inevitably advance. More recent events cast doubt on Enlightenment assumptions of the inevitable decline of religious belief and further secularization of society. At the turn of the twenty-first century, religious revivals and fundamentalist religious movements seeking to overthrow secular states cannot be ignored. These movements advocate either direct rule by priests and clerics or, at least, imposition of the sacred laws of Islam, Judaism or Christianity. Fundamentalist movements are sometimes described as reactionary, because they seek to undo the separation of Church and state identified with the Enlightenment and modernity.

To paraphrase Jean-François Lyotard, the grand meta-narratives of post-Enlightenment thought are no longer credible.[23] Technology continues to advance, population increases and world economic production grows. But the destruction wreaked by wars and repressive regimes only seems to increase in scale as well. Fascism and genocide

---

[21] E. Burke, *Reflections on the Revolution in France*, ed. F. M. Turner (New Haven, Yale University Press, 2003).

[22] See H. Arendt, *The Origins of Totalitarianism* (London, Allen & Unwin, 1967), 3rd edn.

[23] See J.–F. Lyotard, *The Postmodern Condition: A Report on Knowledge* (Manchester, Manchester University Press, 1984), trans. B. Massumi.

cannot be reconciled with any kind of progressive historical teleology. We are approaching closer and closer to absolute environmental limits to ever-increasing growth, consumption and pollution. It is correspondingly less useful and less valid to characterize ideologies and social movements according to their relationship to the supposedly inevitable direction, goal or *telos* of history.[24]

1.5 Be Realistic, Demand the Impossible! Between Realism and Utopianism

Once we become aware of the importance and variety of extra-institutional politics, we are in a better position to understand the nature of politics and what can be achieved by political means. Politics is concerned with the self-conscious regulation of the collective arrangements of a society, on the assumption that human beings consciously decide to organize their common life in one way rather than another.[25] Values and ideals play a significant part in the political choices of a society. In modern societies, we argue and make decisions on the basis of values such as freedom, equality, justice and fairness, often disagreeing both about which values to pursue and about what particular values imply. Political philosophy and theory examine these values in more detail and sometimes seek to ground them in more basic assumptions. Politics, however, is not just about the pursuit of conflicting political values. Politics involves a complex balance of moral or ethical principles and pragmatic considerations of effectiveness, interests and power. This means that there may be a large gap between what is desirable and what is politically possible.

A strong insistence that political goals should be feasible encourages a *realist view* of politics, which insists on the pragmatic dimension of politics. It implies that our political goals should be confined to what can be achieved by political means within a particular society at a particular time. Before we undertake action to achieve any goal, we should establish the facts of the situation, what that situation allows or makes feasible. What is feasible will depend critically on the array of divergent interests at stake in any issue. In politics there are often winners and losers, with outcomes favouring one group at the expense of others. In fact, politics has been defined as the business of 'who gets what,

---

[24] For the implications of these developments for conservatism, see below, section 9.4, esp. pp. 220–1.

[25] Because politics involves choosing between conflicting alternatives, some would argue that politics has not always existed. In societies strictly regulated by ancient rituals, taboos and divine laws, there is little room for politics.

when, and how'.[26] Certainly, the allocation of resources and goods, the distribution of wealth and power, and appointment to positions of authority are all pre-eminently political matters. Because interests are at stake, political outcomes depend on the relative power of different constituencies and interest groups. Where there are conflicts of interest between them, it is likely that more powerful groups will prevail. Realism thus reflects the important insight that political thought must be more than mere wishful thinking; it must be concerned with actual or, at least, achievable social arrangements. So, for example, although religious ideals of the perfect life may be spiritually inspiring for individuals or small communities, they are not strictly political ideals since they cannot be realized at a societal level. Political thought needs not only to propose a better world but also to explain how a better world can be brought about and thrive.

Political proposals that are simply unrealistic or unfeasible are often described as *utopian*. The latter term derives from Thomas More's book *Utopia* (1516), which is an eloquent portrayal of a perfect society free from all poverty, greed and conflict. In fact, More derives the term 'utopia' from a scholarly play on ancient Greek words signifying a 'good place' and 'no place', a merely imaginary place.[27] As a species of political thinking, utopian thought is certainly inadequate and may sometimes be dangerous or counter-productive. If an image of the perfect society does not suggest any feasible action, we risk merely comforting ourselves with fantasies of perfection whilst failing to take those smaller steps that might actually improve society. In the wrong hands, utopian ideals have inspired tyrannical attempts to impose perfection on always imperfect human beings, who are then condemned and sometimes killed as recalcitrant or evil obstacles to a better society.[28]

However, although political realism captures an important truth, it is itself counter-productive when narrowly interpreted. Political realism tends to encourage a form of pragmatism that limits political aspirations to what is considered feasible within the existing rules and anticipated outcomes of the political system, ignoring the much wider range of possibilities that extra-institutional action potentially offers. This kind of pragmatism is implicitly conservative as well, because it favours existing interests and the 'powers that be', who are

---

[26] See H. D. Lasswell, *Politics: Who Gets What, When, How* (1936) (New York, P. Smith, 1950).

[27] T. More, *Utopia* (Cambridge and New York, Cambridge University Press, 1989), trans. R. M. Adams, ed. G. M. Logan and R. M. Adams. The Greek words are *eu-topos* (good place) and *ou-topos* (no place).

[28] K. R. Popper, *The Open Society and its Enemies* (London, Routledge & Kegan Paul, 1966), 2 vols., associates the dangers of utopian thought with Plato, Hegel and Marx.

benefiting from the current state of affairs. At worst, political realism leads to political expediency, justifying the pursuit of short-term and usually self-interested goals without regard for moral principles and the common good, which are dismissed as the stuff of idealistic and utopian dreaming.[29] By the same token, political realism ignores the possible benefits of utopian thought, which serves both to high-light what is wrong with existing society and to preserve, at least at an imaginative level, the possibility that we might lead a better life.

A more fundamental problem with political realism is the impos-sibility of really distinguishing reliably between feasible and utopian goals. To do so in more than an intuitive way would require an unat-tainable degree of knowledge of social and political reality. The view that political and social sciences can reveal objective truths about social and political phenomena inspires continuing efforts to formu-late a reliable and generalizable method for political science akin to methods employed in the natural sciences. Modelling itself on suc-cessful sciences like astronomy, physics and chemistry, a predictive political science aims to identify causal relationships between iden-tifiable variables within the established field of politics.[30] If we could predict what will happen under certain circumstances – including the circumstance in which people choose to act in certain ways – then we would indeed be able to determine which goals are feasible and which merely utopian. Ironically, the ambitious ideal of a predictive science of politics, which would deliver reliable knowledge of the future effects of present actions, itself turns out to be utopian. Whether or not all human phenomena are causally determined and in principle predictable, prediction would require a highly improbable degree of knowledge of every aspect of human existence.[31] In any case, even if such knowledge is theoretically possible, it has little relevance for the current practice of politics. In more concrete terms, social movements and extra-institutional politics fatally undermine any such predictive aspirations. For prediction of political events to be possible, there must not only be reliable causal relationships between different elements

---

[29] On the imaginative contribution of utopian thought to politics, see E. Bloch, *The Principle of Hope* (Oxford, Blackwell, 1986), 3 vols., and H. Marcuse, *Five Lectures: Psychoanalysis, Politics and Utopia* (London, Allen Lane, 1970), trans. J. J. Shapiro and S. M. Weber.

[30] David Hume announces the project of a 'science of man' in *A Treatise of Human Nature* (1739–40), ed. L. A. Selby-Bigge (Oxford, Clarendon Press, 1888), p. xx. Cf. B. R. Crick, *The American Science of Politics: Its Origins and Conditions* (London, Routledge & Kegan Paul, 1959). See also Leftwich, *What is Politics?*

[31] A classic critique of the predictive ideal, which he idiosyncratically associates with the term 'historicism', is outlined by K. R. Popper, *The Poverty of Historicism* (London, Routledge & Kegan Paul, 1961), 2nd edn.

of the political system, but the scope and limits of that system must themselves be clear and fixed. But social movements contest both the definition and scope of politics, making it impossible to demarcate 'the' political system in clear and unambiguous terms. The boundaries of politics are always contestable and often in flux. By implication, any assumptions about what is and what is not politically feasible, what is or is not compatible with existing political realities, will always be contestable as well. Social movements have in the past transformed society in substantial and quite unexpected ways, and there is no reason to believe that they will not transform society again in the future.

In sum, although consideration of what is feasible in a particular society has an important place in political thought, judgements about the realities of the political situation are always at best tentative and provisional. What is politically achievable is always relative to the possible actions of social movements and these, as we have seen, can never be fully determined in advance. A crucial implication for the large range of political problems we have identified as in principle political is that neither optimism nor pessimism are appropriate attitudes for us to adopt towards them. We may be optimistic or pessimistic (however irrationally) about the outcome of a bet, because it is a matter of chance clearly beyond our control. In the absence of exact astronomical predictions reaching far into the future, we may be more or less fearful of the prospects of a disastrous collision between Earth and a meteor. But for the solution of problems we have identified as political, it is not properly a question of optimism or pessimism, because their solution depends on human action. It is rather a question of whether we decide to take the necessary actions to solve them. In other words, it is up to us.

Although they are inappropriate attitudes in politics, both optimism and pessimism have a strong hold on many actual and potential political agents. This is because, in the modern period, the dominant ideologies of liberalism, socialism, social democracy and Marxism have been founded on the assumption that history has a built-in direction and goal. The intellectual revolution of the eighteenth-century European Enlightenment and the associated rise of science, technology and industrial capitalism helped to inspire a widespread faith in 'improvement' and 'progress'. There was a widely held assumption that everything would inevitably get better, whether this meant increasing levels of wealth and consumption, improving standards of health and longevity, or greater access to education and information. To the extent that people are more likely to act if they think their actions are likely to lead to success or are 'on the side of history', the optimism underlying this assumption undoubtedly inspired action on behalf of 'progressive' causes. But optimism can also lead to apathy, when people relax in the complacent belief that things will get better whether they act or not. To be confident that things will in the end turn out for the best makes us less inclined to take action now.[32]

Optimism is also dangerous, when agents are not aware that political actions often have unwelcome unintended consequences. The Russian Revolution was captured by a 'new class' of party bureaucrats and Stalin's cult of personality.[33] Successful revolutions are often captured by new elites or, like the French, Russian and Cambodian Revolutions, descend rapidly into despotism. Optimism also blinds us to the possibility that things might actually get worse. Most observers of the Weimar Republic in 1920s Germany did not anticipate its imminent destruction at the hands of Hitler and National Socialism. Less dramatically, many social democrats and socialists critical of 1970s' European welfare states did not anticipate their dismantling by neoliberal and new right governments in the ensuing decades. In the face of environmental collapse, there is no guarantee that our political institutions will not be undermined or overthrown by authoritarian forces. Responses around the world to global terrorism after September 11 2001 have involved abandoning or restricting long-held and fought-for rights and liberties. The assumption that things cannot get any worse is dangerous, when it makes us complacent and obscures the need to take action in order to preserve existing institutions with the rights, liberties, security and welfare that they guarantee.

When progressive and radical activism are based on optimism, however, they are vulnerable to the sudden waning of optimism. Belief in the inevitability of progress has suffered some severe blows in the last century: from the unprecedented destruction and loss of life of the First and Second World Wars to Nazi and communist genocides, concentration camps, nuclear weapons and pervasive fears of nuclear war. More recently, looming environmental crises and the threat of catastrophic global warming appear to justify pessimism about the prospects of the Earth and the human societies it sustains. National governments and international bodies are failing to act, national electorates are not prepared to make the necessary adjustments to production and consumption. But pessimism of this kind again encourages apathy, in this case as the correlate of feelings of powerlessness and despair. What is the point of acting, if nothing can change and disaster is inevitable? And in that case, of course, pessimism is self-fulfilling. If we do nothing, then a negative outcome will undoubtedly occur.

---

[32] Marxism in its most popular and simplified forms was a radical variant of this kind of optimism. Revolutionary change – the overthrow of capitalism and advance towards socialism and communism – was judged to be inevitable, inspiring confident activism but also complacency.

[33] See M. Djilas, *The New Class: An Analysis of the Communist System* (New York, Praeger, 1957).

History also demonstrates that pessimism deters action in situations where success may be possible. Social movements typically aim for and often achieve goals that are beyond the accepted range of 'realistic' or feasible options. Few in the eighteenth century thought it possible that Britain and other colonial powers would abolish slavery or that women would eventually be elected to public office. At the beginning of the nineteenth century, it was unthinkable to most people that ordinary labourers could be equal citizens and even members of the government. In the first half of the twentieth century, it was almost unimaginable that former slaves and indigenous peoples would gain equal constitutional rights. The collapse of communism in the Soviet Union and Eastern Europe after 1989 was not thought to be possible by observers at the time. We need to escape from apathy, whether it stems from complacency and optimism or from pessimism and hopelessness. But, as we have seen, optimism and pessimism not only are unhelpful, they also rest on dubious epistemological foundations: however likely certain outcomes may seem, we can never really *know* what will happen in the future, because the future ultimately depends on the actions we decide to take in the present.

Crucially, these insights are reinforced by awareness of the extra-institutional dimension of politics. If we do *not* pay attention to social movements, then we ignore the creative or formative dimension of politics – the issues and identities that are becoming political and that may eventually lead to new or reformed political institutions. We are left with a narrow view of political possibilities and hence more vulnerable to either optimism or pessimism. By contrast, when we *do* focus on the activities of social movements, we become aware of new and previously unanticipated possibilities for political action. We realize that the future is not just something to wait for passively but rather something that we can actively make ourselves. This activist perspective opens up the possibility that seemingly intractable global problems might, after all, be successfully addressed by political action. At the same time, the realist critique of utopian thought reminds us of the considerable difficulties and sometimes tragic outcomes of political action. As Antonio Gramsci observed, we require a combination of 'optimism of the will', which is resolutely committed to political action, and that 'pessimism of the intellect' which alerts us to all the potential obstacles and pitfalls in its path.[34] That combination is only possible within an understanding of politics that encompasses both its institutional and extra-institutional manifestations.

---

[34] The phrase is originally from Romain Rolland. Cf. A. Gramsci, *Selections from the Prison Notebooks*, ed. Q. Hoare and G. Nowell Smith (London, Lawrence & Wishart, 1971), p. 175 and note.

Further Reading

A range of definitions of politics can be found in Adrian Leftwich's edited collection, *What is Politics? The Activity and its Study*. Classic institutional definitions of politics are provided by Harold Lasswell in *Politics: Who Gets What, When, How*, and David Easton, *The Political System: An Inquiry into the State of Political Science*. Broad accounts of social movements include Jan Pakulski, *Social Movements: The Politics of Moral Protest*, Paul Wilkinson's *Social Movement* and, from a more historical perspective, Charles Tilly, *Contention and Democracy in Europe: 1650–2000*. For a variety of theoretical approaches to social movements, see chapters 7–9 and the suggestions for further reading included there. Bernard Crick's classic *In Defence of Politics* and Hannah Arendt's more philosophical *The Human Condition* offer accounts of politics emphasizing the active participation of citizens. The dialectic between realism and utopianism in politics is a prominent theme in Marxism and the critical theory of the Frankfurt School: for an overview, see David Held's *Introduction to Critical Theory: Horkheimer to Habermas*.

2

The Role of Social Movements in the Making of Modern Politics

Outline

A historical perspective illuminates the many contributions of social movements to both the formation of contemporary political institutions and the changing shape of the extra-institutional domain of politics itself. Social movements have played a significant role in the formation of modern nation-states, in the emergence of capitalist liberal democracy and in overcoming exclusions from citizenship based on social status, gender, race and ethnicity. For a number of reasons, which derive from both conservative and radical perspectives, this historical contribution has been underestimated and sometimes ignored altogether by students of politics. By the same token, more recent social movements (to be discussed in the following chapters) are important not only for their social and political effects but also for their impact on our understanding of the nature and scope of both institutional and extra-institutional politics.

2.1 Social Movements and the Formation of Contemporary Institutions

If politics is concerned, above all, with how we act in order to preserve and improve our world in the present and for the future, then why should we first turn to the past? The main aim of the following brief survey is to focus on the formative dimension of politics identified in the previous chapter. A historical perspective shows us, in other words, in what ways contemporary institutional forms of politics, which we are sometimes tempted to take for granted, have in fact been formed by, or as a result of, the activities of earlier extra-institutional agents.

What is more, a further by-product of their activities is the transformation of the context in which later social movements now operate. In
other words, both the institutions of politics and the distinctive forms
of extra-institutional politics in today's world are what they are partly
as a result of earlier waves of activism. Examination of the formative
contributions of earlier social movements reinforces, finally, the important point that present institutions are always liable to change again
in the future. Present institutions may be improved by political action
undertaken both within and from outside them. Equally important, if
engaged citizens do not actively sustain these institutions, they may be
undermined or eventually even collapse under the pressure of adverse
circumstances and impending crises.

A brief examination of some important social movements, which
have contributed to both current political institutions and modes of
extra-institutional politics, is designed to serve a number of purposes.
In the first place, it will help us to identify more clearly the main characteristics of social movements by providing us with a more concrete
picture of social movements as a particular mode of politics. Historical
movements share some common formal features whilst pursuing quite
different substantive goals. Different social movements share formal
features relating to their particular style or mode of extra-institutional
activism. These formal features are, at the most abstract level, what distinguish all forms of extra-institutional from institutional politics. Some
features obviously stem from the fact that movements are excluded
from institutionalized ways of acting, so that they must rely on extra-
institutional, disapproved and sometimes illegal tactics. But the formal
characteristics of social movements themselves also change over time.
Particular 'repertoires' of political action are possible only in certain
kinds of society. Different tactics occur, for example, in urban societies
with large concentrations of population and rapid communications as
compared to sparsely populated rural societies with limited communications. The study of past social movements and activism makes us
aware that politics, both institutional and extra-institutional, is affected
by its changing historical context. This applies not only to institutionalized political forms, which we are used to seeing in the context of
political, constitutional and legal history, but also to extra-institutional
or 'contentious' forms of politics as well.[1]

At the same time, an examination of these movements will put
us in a better position to see what, if anything, is distinctive about
contemporary social movements. The substantive features of a social
movement are those features that serve to define or identify it as

[1] The term 'contentious' politics is associated with the influential studies of
Charles Tilly, including *Social Movements, 1768–2004* (Boulder and London,
Paradigm Publishers, 2004).

well as to differentiate it from other movements. The various goals of abolishing slavery, improving the conditions of the working class and gaining equal citizenship for women serve to identify the anti-slavery, workers' and (first-wave) women's movements, respectively. These defining concerns are reflected in the kinds of people who are active in the movement as well as the interests and issues, goals, values, beliefs and ideology of the movement. Its substantive features also reflect in various ways its historical context: the kind of society in which it operates and that society's level of development, population and modes of economy; the state of religion and religious belief; levels of urbanization, education and communications, etc. To the extent that societies have undergone significant changes in the last century or so, we might expect contemporary social movements to be correspondingly different as well. Knowledge of the history of extra-political activism will allow us, more specifically, to assess a claim, popular in the 1970s and 1980s, that western societies are being challenged by a series of 'new social movements', which are significantly different from the 'old' social movements concerned with nation-state, religion and class that preceded them. Our brief historical survey will help us to see what, if anything, is new about these supposedly new movements.

Obviously, this is not the place for a detailed history of the origins of current institutional and extra-institutional forms of politics. What follows is a selective discussion of some key episodes, tracing some of their most important genealogical lines of descent. In the following section, we focus on the origins of nation-states in early modern Europe and the role of religious and nationalist movements. The religious wars and upheaval following the Reformation helped to provoke a new international regime of sovereign states supported by a nascent nationalism. The liberal and democratic institutions of most western states are traced (in section 2.3) to the middling or 'bourgeois' social movements which, as capitalist economic relations became more pervasive, challenged absolutist monarchies and aristocratic privileges of the 'old order' in Europe. The French Revolution, urbanization and industrial society set the scene for later social movements. The fourth section looks at some challenges to emerging liberal and democratic states during the nineteenth and twentieth centuries. The labouring or working classes were formed – and significantly also formed themselves as a distinct class and identity – during the early stages of the Industrial Revolution. Their often illegal and sometimes violent challenge to liberal capitalism gave rise to both social democratic and revolutionary strands of socialism. Their activism contributed to the institutions of representative democracy and the welfare state. The anti-slavery movement from the eighteenth century, and the 'first wave' of the women's movement from the nineteenth, eventually won universal suffrage and citizenship rights for all.

2.2 The Formation of the Modern Nation-State: Religious and Nationalist Movements

Contemporary institutional politics presupposes the modern system of nation-states, notwithstanding the fact that processes of globalization are currently modifying this system. This presupposition is reflected in the now usual division of the study of politics into the two disciplinary areas of Government or Political Science – which is concerned with the politics of particular nation-states – and International Relations – which considers the relations between nation-states.[2] But as the epithet 'modern' implies, the system of nation-states emerged during a particular period as a result of complex historical processes including the actions of extra-institutional agents and social movements. Historical explanation is, of course, always contentious. The emergence of modern nation-states in the West is in part the result of decisions taken by individual monarchs, priests and theologians. It is associated with new modes of political thought and ideas. In addition, the nation-state is a by-product of societal 'modernization' or 'development'. An expanding population and economy and changing economic relations, sometimes described as the rise of commercial society or capitalism, make an important contribution. However, extra-institutional political agents including religious and nationalist movements play an essential formative role as well.

At one level, the European nation-state can be seen as the work of conventional political actors including monarchs, rulers, government officials and, at a time when religion was central to the exercise of political authority, Christian theologians and clergy. One decisive event was the Protestant Reformation, signalled by Martin Luther's famous 'protest' (or *protestatio*) of 1517. Drawing on a longer tradition of dissident tendencies and sects including the Hussite followers of Jan Hus, Luther catalogued abuses and what he saw as heresies of the Roman Catholic Church. What ensued was a cascading series of events, which would eventually lead to the division or 'schism' of western Christendom into rival Protestant and Catholic confessions. In fact, there were many, often mutually hostile, Protestant sects as well. Because the Church and religion were then so central to the exercise of political power, the Reformation sparked a further series of political events. Religious differences inspired wars, which justified the further expansion of state power and military strength. The eventual outcome,

---

2   Although writing on the relation between states goes back at least to Thucydides, the academic sub-discipline or discipline of International Relations with its own distinctive concerns and methodology emerged only in the twentieth century. Until recently, political scientists and theorists often simply assumed that politics is what takes place *within* a nation-state.

formalized by the treaties known as the 1648 Peace of Westphalia, was a new national and international order of sovereign nation-states, each enforcing its own version of Catholic or Protestant Christian faith.[3]

The Protestant Reformation and the emergence of European nation-states both encouraged and were justified by developments in the not-yet-clearly-separated domains of theology and political thought. In fact, the clear demarcation between religious and secular thought and the corresponding separation of church and state were important outcomes of the protracted and hotly contested wars of religion. Eventually, the novel principle was established that the prince's authority included the right to impose on his subjects his own version of the 'true' faith. Emboldened by the example of Henry VIII of England, rulers could ignore the wishes of the Pope and impose their own interpretation of Christianity. Paradoxically, this assertion of religious authority ultimately led to the secular conception of politics as an order of human activities more or less distinct from religion.[4] John Locke's defence of religious toleration was, in part at least, a pragmatic attempt by a Protestant philosopher, landowner and investor in the slave trade to provide a *modus vivendi*, which would allow rival Protestant sects to co-exist. In place of endless and destructive wars which, after all, were bad for business, toleration offers the possibility of peaceful co-existence and trade. The separation of religion and politics left governments with a clearer focus on what western political thought now regards as their proper concern, with the public rather than private affairs of the state.[5]

Alongside these historical events and intellectual developments were longer-term social, economic and demographic factors. Urban centres grew and became more wealthy and powerful. Cities and towns were connected by better roads and more rapid and efficient means of transport. Better communications expanded both the possible scale and impact of war and trade. New forms of commerce and industry presented new challenges but also rapidly increasing sources of revenue for governments. The centralization of territorial and warlike states encouraged the development of organized bureaucracies, which could gather, distribute and administer state revenues more efficiently. The need to raise revenue also made rulers more dependent on parliaments, who demanded the right to approve or disapprove of new taxes. Rulers also sought finance from moneylenders and bankers, which increased the power of the rising classes of financiers, merchants and manufacturers. Powerful, unified states were able to conduct larger

---

[3] A classic study focusing on political thought is Q. Skinner, *The Foundations of Modern Political Thought* (Cambridge, Cambridge University Press, 1978), 2 vols.

[4] For this complicated story, see Skinner, *Foundations of Modern Political Thought*, Vol. II, *The Age of Reformation*.

[5] See Locke, *An Essay Concerning Toleration*.

and more protracted wars against their neighbours. States were also able to exert authority more closely over the lives of subjects within what was defined as their sovereign territory. Max Weber understood these broad social and economic developments as processes of rationalization distinctive of western societies. Increasingly, both economic activity and state decisions were systematically aligned to secular political goals of profit and power without deference to either tradition or religion.[6]

From another perspective, however, the modern nation-state can be seen as the work of extra-institutional political actors. The early years of the Reformation were accompanied by waves of extra-institutional activism, including mass religious revivals and peasant uprisings against religious and political authority. At times, these Peasant Wars appeared to threaten the prevailing social order along with its stark inequalities of wealth and land ownership. Peasant Wars contributed to the break-up of older patterns of governance and the emergence of modern nation-states, even though that was not necessarily the intention of participants. The peasant uprisings were limited from the start by a number of factors and were quickly crushed by the superior military might of rulers and their allies. Although rebellion against authority was often contagious, spreading quickly to neighbouring communities, it was still largely parochial in character. Communication between localities was slow and unreliable and, where it existed, mainly designed to serve the propertied classes. Religious factors played a crucial role in these uprisings as well, although the ideas inspiring rebellion varied from place to place. Illiterate peasants with little or no education were attracted to superstitious millenarian cults as much as to egalitarian ideals.[7]

Self-conscious nationalism and associated strands of extra-institutional politics in its support emerged later in response to the slowly crystallizing structures of the state. Nationalist movements assert nationality as the most important political identity and seek to align the state's sovereignty and territorial boundaries with a corresponding nation or national community. The concepts of nation and nationalism are, in fact, complex and problematic. 'Nation' derives from the Latin word *natus* meaning 'born'; the nation is supposedly a human population sharing common ancestry and, by implication, common beliefs, values and allegiance. Nationalism is a complex phenomenon involving both the actions of rulers and states and grassroots or 'bottom-up' support from extra-institutional agents. National identi-

---

[6] See M. Weber, *The Protestant Ethic and the Spirit of Capitalism* (Los Angeles, Roxbury, 2002), trans. S. Kalberg.

[7] The classic Marxist study is F. Engels, *The Peasant War in Germany* (1850) (London, Allen & Unwin, 1927).

ties were at first encouraged by the rulers of emerging states, who had a pressing need to encourage their subjects' loyalty and readiness for self-sacrifice, whether financially or in war. National identity promised to simplify the complex web of loyalties and personal allegiances associated with feudal society. It would unify the population in support of ruler and state, particularly at a time when the boundaries of a monarch's territories might be the result of dynastic relationship, royal marriage or conquest rather than any relationship with his subjects.

At the same time, the strategies of rulers were reinforced by extra-institutional political actors who acted in support of broadly nationalist goals. Like nationalism, nationalist movements can be hard to classify. For one thing, they vary significantly in their degree of self-consciousness. There is a slow transition from loyalty to a monarch, who may have been born in a different country and even speak a different language from most of his subjects, to loyalty to the nation. Chauvinist riots against Catholics and foreigners in Protestant countries were an unattractive reflection of the shift in allegiance. The 1780 Gordon Riots in England began as protest against a law removing some of the official discrimination against Catholics imposed during the Reformation. Later incarnations of nationalism could take advantage of Romantic ideas reinforcing the argument for nationhood. Herder and other German Romantics argued for the essential role of language in defining a distinct and incommensurable culture and way of life for each language-community. Although rulers and the decline of the Habsburg Empire were also involved, the reunification of Italy or *Risorgimento* was driven in considerable part by autonomous movements and extra-institutional actors including the *Carbonari* of southern Italy, Giuseppe Mazzini's *La Giovine Italia* (Young Italy) and the insurrectionary campaigns of Giuseppe Garibaldi.[8]

The importance of the extra-institutional dimension of nationalism, whether fully self-conscious or not, is reinforced by the constructed nature of national identity. In fact, national identity often bears at best a questionable relationship to historical facts of common ancestry. The nation is not, as nationalists often claim, some eternally existing essence that must be defended or realized, but more often something that is constructed or created. For this reason, Benedict Anderson has influentially described nations as 'imagined communities'.[9] Indeed, the intensity of nationalism sometimes seems to bear an inverse relationship to any substantive grounds. The partially or wholly constructed

---

[8] See F. M. Barnard, *Herder's Social and Political Thought: From Enlightenment to Nationalism* (Oxford, Clarendon Press, 1965), and N. Riall, *The Italian Risorgimento: State, Society and National Unification* (London and New York, Routledge, 1994).

[9] See B. Anderson, *Imagined Communities: Reflections on the Origins and Spread of Nationalism* (London, Verso, 1983).

nature of nations implies that nationalism is as much a cultural as a political phenomenon. Self-conscious nationalism both encourages and is encouraged by emerging national cultures and identities. Unified and standardized national languages such as English, French and Spanish became important markers of nationality and national allegiance. Whereas feudal princes or monarchs had often spoken a different language from their subjects, who may themselves have spoken a range of more or less closely related dialects, proficiency in the national language became critical. At the same time, writers, intellectuals and teachers, predominantly educated and middle-class, produced dictionaries and assembled national literatures as privileged sites for the nation's culture and history. Canonical works were selected in part because they expressed the national character and provided definitive narratives of the nation's founding myths, heroes and legends.

Although nationalist activism may begin either as a reflex to the decisions of princes or within the cultural and intellectual spheres, mature nationalist movements are essentially statist. Their ultimate aim is to align the boundaries of a sovereign state with a given national population. Within the state's territory, nationality is championed as the overriding and even exclusive identity of those deemed to belong to it. National identity is not just one identity amongst others. One reason that nationalism has been promoted by rulers and ruling classes is precisely in order to *obscure* and *displace* antipathies and conflicts deriving from other identities, other dimensions of social inequality or oppression such as social status or class and gender. Disraeli's 'one nation' politics and, more broadly, the jingoistic nationalism of nineteenth- and twentieth-century European imperialism was self-consciously promoted in order to divert attention from social inequalities and class hostilities.[10] Although nationalism is, in principle, compatible with any form of government or rule, the exclusiveness of national identity means that nationalist movements have an affinity with strong, centralized states rather than with pluralism and liberal democracy. Strong states are more able to impose the will and often the culture and language of the dominant nationality on the rest of the population. The territorial aims of nationalism often lead to wars with other states. The aggressive foreign policy associated with nationalist politics reinforces the need for centralized bureaucracy and military might. The high status of military leaders strengthens tendencies towards hierarchy, authoritarian rule and sometimes military dictatorship.

If extra-institutional activism plays a significant role in the emergence of modern nation-states, those states in turn provide an important

---

[10] Nationalism as a movement and ideology is also associated with former communist states of Eastern Europe and the Soviet Union as well as with China and Vietnam.

condition for further extra-institutional activism and social movements. Social movements henceforth increasingly assume a national character, even when they are not explicitly nationalist. From this time, centralized and hierarchical states could be challenged directly on a national rather than a merely local or parochial scale. Secular states are increasingly challenged in secular terms without the mediation of religious affiliation or doctrine. The result over the course of decades and centuries would be a gradual transition from modes of contention characteristic of peasant societies to something more like the contemporary politics of social movements. Social movements emerge as a mode of extra-institutional politics with their own distinctive repertoire of political tactics.[11] However, the emergence of the modern form of social movement was motivated by other changes occurring within society as a result of the increasingly rapid expansion of capitalism and industrial forms of production.

2.3 Liberalizing the State and Commerce: Bourgeois Social Movements

The rise of capitalism and bourgeois classes is part of the genealogy of liberal democracy in western states. Institutional features of contemporary western states such as parliamentary rule, freedoms of thought and religion, and free market economics can be traced to bourgeois social movements. Although these features of liberalism are now largely taken for granted, it is important to recall their origins in the actions of extra-institutional agents, who contended with illiberal and authoritarian institutions of the 'old order'. The contributions of extra-institutional politics were essential, precisely because it was never inevitable that capitalism would lead to liberalism or democracy. The possibility of authoritarian capitalism is confirmed – at least for the time being – by the example of China, which has achieved rapid economic development on a market-based model of capitalism 'with Chinese characteristics' making few concessions to liberal democracy. By the same token, there is no guarantee that liberal democratic institutions will not be eroded in the future, for example as a result of the West's responses to terrorist attacks or climate change. In all of these cases, social movement activism will play an essential role in deciding between authoritarian and liberal democratic outcomes.

Once again, a variety of explanations for the liberalization of western states can be proposed. According to the Whig interpretation of history, the spread of freedom and liberal institutions represents an

---

[11] See Tilly, *Social Movements, 1768–2004*, esp. chs 1–3.

inevitable tendency or direction of historical development.[12] On this view, freedom becomes institutionalized and spreads from one area of society to another and from one country to another as a result of broader social developments. For the predominantly rationalist and secular Enlightenment, the advance of rational philosophy and scientific knowledge inevitably lead to greater freedom as an aspect of more general 'improvement' or 'progress'. In Hegel's more nuanced philosophy, the increasing depth and extent of freedom are regarded as the essential goal of history's conflict-ridden or 'dialectical' advance: 'The History of the world is none other than the progress of the consciousness of Freedom. . . . The destiny of the spiritual World . . . we allege to be the *consciousness* of its own freedom on the part of Spirit, and *ipso facto*, the *reality* of that freedom.'[13]

Putting aside dubious metaphysical or religious assumptions that history has a fore-ordained goal, it is possible to point to sociological, demographic and technological factors that play a role in the extension of what liberals understand as freedom or liberty. Johannes Gutenberg's propagation of movable-type printing in fifteenth-century Europe facilitated the pursuit of knowledge, enquiry and intellectual debate.[14] The wide availability of the Bible, first in Latin and then in a variety of vernacular tongues, encouraged critical discussion and rival interpretations of Christianity's sacred text. The discovery of the Americas and exploitation of their resources helped to fund rapid economic expansion in Europe. Increasing population and technological developments (some imported from China and India) fostered economic expansion as well.[15] The growth of cities and slowly improving means of transport facilitated communication between people, particularly those of middling social status between peasantry and landowning gentry. Cities provided a setting for the rapid proliferation of capitalist economic relations and new forms of finance, trade and manufacture based on the investment of private capital in productive enterprises employing wage labour.

There were, in turn, complex interactions between the rise of capitalism and the Protestant Reformation. Capitalist economic forms developed most rapidly in Protestant countries and, within predominantly Catholic countries, in Protestant communities. Weber's *Protestant Ethic and the Spirit of Capitalism* argues that Protestant ideas

---

[12] H. Butterfield, *The Whig Interpretation of History* (London, George Bell, 1950).

[13] G. W. F. Hegel, *The Philosophy of History* (New York, Prometheus, 1991), trans. J. Sibree, p. 19.

[14] Printing by movable type was achieved at an earlier date in Korea and China.

[15] On the eastern origins of many technical innovations, see J. M. Hobson, *The Eastern Origins of Western Civilization* (Cambridge and New York, Cambridge University Press, 2004).

were particularly favourable to capitalist development. Calvinist theology preaches individual salvation through good works and allows worldly success to count as evidence of the latter. Traditional Christian suspicion of wealth is reinterpreted to imply condemnation of indulgent consumption and sensuality rather than wealth as such. Hard work, discipline and deferred gratification encourage the reinvestment of surplus wealth in further production, leading to the increasing income and further accumulation of capital. Later historians and social theorists have argued over competing 'idealist' and 'materialist' explanations of this relationship between theology and economics. Did Protestant ideas foster capitalist economic relations or did the spread of capitalism encourage wider acceptance of Protestant values? Marx and Marxism favour the materialist alternative; Weber emphasizes changes of culture and religion, law and philosophy, at what Marxists call the 'superstructural' level of 'ideology'. In fact, neither Weber nor Marx gives absolute priority to either factor, allowing for the reality of complex causal explanation. The debate between idealists and materialists points rather to the inextricability of ideal and material factors.

Whatever the ultimate outcome of the controversy between idealists and materialists, there is undoubtedly a close relationship between liberalism, capitalism and the actions of an increasingly numerous and powerful class of people. At a social level, the gradual but accelerating displacement of feudalism by capitalism contributed to the rise of a new stratum of middling or 'bourgeois' classes, who promoted and profited from new economic activities. Despite their contemporary image as conservative upholders of capitalism, these bourgeois classes were, at first, radicals who challenged the existing institutions of the 'old order' or *'ancien régime'*. The old order preserved the patterns of a feudal and landowning aristocratic society and so disadvantaged the emerging bourgeois interest in trade and manufacturing. That interest was represented at first through an emerging 'bourgeois public sphere', which rose to prominence in seventeenth- and eighteenth-century Europe. Enlightenment ideas may first have been formulated by a few *philosophes*, but they owed their widespread social impact to this public sphere. The urban 'burghers' (hence 'bourgeois') met in salons and coffee shops in order to identify their common interests – sometimes criticizing government policies unfavourable to their commercial activities and formulating more favourable alternatives.[16]

Undoubtedly the most explosive event associated with bourgeois activism was the French Revolution of 1789. Although the Revolution asserted universal rights of citizenship and drew in a wide range of

---

[16] See J. Habermas, *The Structural Transformation of the Public Sphere: An Inquiry into a Category of Bourgeois Society* (1962) (Cambridge, MA, MIT Press, 1989), trans. T. Burger.

actors including peasants and progressive members of the aristocracy, it was predominantly bourgeois in character and outcome. Certainly, in the early phases of the French Revolution, the 'social question' and the condition of the poor played a more prominent role than in the American Revolution, leading bourgeois radicals to enter at times into uneasy alliance with more radical, proletarian forces.[17] But as the Revolution proceeded, the rights of private property and wealth increasingly gained the upper hand. The ultimate outcome of what Marx and Engels saw as the archetypal 'bourgeois revolution' was, in essence, a compromise between the old landed interest and emerging mercantile, financial and industrial elites. The landless, the poor, the artisans and manual labourers were excluded from a political order whose commitment to 'liberty, equality and fraternity' implied only formal equality before the law. The revolution's commitment to private property was demonstrated over the issue of colonial slavery. Slaves were treated not as human beings deserving of universal citizenship rights, but rather as the private property of their colonial masters.[18] Under Napoleon, the radical democratic aims of early revolutionaries were quickly replaced by nationalist and imperialist ambitions and, after being abolished for a short time, slavery was reintroduced.

In England, movements of middle-class liberals and radicals fought against the privileges of aristocrats and landowners and for parliamentary control over government expenditure and taxation.[19] In response to new taxes and levies imposed by ambitious national rulers to fund their expensive wars, parliamentarians fought for the principle that there should be no taxation without parliamentary approval or, according to the phrase originating in the American Revolution, 'no taxation without representation'. These principles are now entrenched in the constitutions of parliamentary democracies, whose procedures typically pay particular attention to budgets and other fiscal measures. The anti-institutional activism of the middle classes contributed to the English Civil War of 1642–51. The Glorious Revolution of 1688 saw James II replaced by William of Orange on condition that he make significant concessions to constitutional government. In nineteenth-century England, the role of religious differences declined and bourgeois activism on behalf of liberal or *laissez-faire* economics took centre stage. The views of political economists like Adam Smith, David Ricardo and John Stuart Mill gave rise to classical liberal doctrine, which advocated

---

[17] For this contrast between American and French Revolutions, see Arendt, *On Revolution*, ch. 2.

[18] See C. L. R. James, *The Black Jacobins: Toussaint L'Ouverture and the San Domingo Revolution* (London, Allison and Busby, 1980).

[19] See É. Halévy, *The Growth of Philosophic Radicalism* (London, Faber, 1949), 2nd edn, trans. M. Morris.

the sanctity of private property, limited government interference in economic activities and free trade. Early struggles were fought for the freedom of corporations to engage in profitable activities without the need to obtain a special licence from the state, as had previously been the case.[20] Free trade was a central nostrum of the Manchester School of liberalism associated with Richard Cobden and John Bright. Formed in 1838, the Anti-Corn Law League agitated for the abolition of protective tariffs on corn and other foodstuffs, which protected the interests of landowners but raised the cost of workers' subsistence and, as a result, the wages that industrialists had to pay them.

Just as important as the institutional contributions of the bourgeois movements, which are still recognizable today, are their limitations and omissions.[21] Liberal doctrines offered little consolation to the poor and propertyless, who were often adversely affected by the disruption of traditional economic forms. Economic issues were treated as 'private' and unpolitical matters lying outside the proper sphere of state activities. This was essential from the point of view of bourgeois activists, who asserted their right to pursue profit without state interference or regulation of wages, workers' conditions and contracts. Economic freedom was understood as the *negative* freedom to become wealthy through one's own efforts. It did not imply *positive* economic rights or social justice in the sense of actual access to resources, income or welfare. Liberal ideas were, after all, advocated mainly by people who both had little need of economic assistance from the state and would bear much of the cost of social welfare measures. Liberal notions condemned efforts to help the poor and indigent as interference in the free market. The Great Irish Famine (1845–9) and the Indian famines of 1865–6 and 1877–89 are notorious cases of the British government's inaction on doctrinaire liberal grounds, leading to the loss of millions of lives from starvation.[22]

A further limitation of both the rising bourgeois classes and liberal doctrines was their ambivalent relationship to representative democracy. Liberals advocated limited government in order to protect

---

[20] See J. Micklethwait and A. Wooldridge, *The Company: A Short History of a Revolutionary Idea* (New York, Modern Library, 2003), and, for a more hostile account, J. Bakan, *The Corporation: The Pathological Pursuit of Profit and Power* (New York, Free Press, 2004).

[21] Classical liberal doctrines are revived with some alteration in contemporary neoliberalism and the Washington Consensus, and have been applied to the core institutions of corporate globalization. On the contrast with neoliberalism, see below, chapter 6, pp. 131–3.

[22] See C. Woodham Smith, *The Great Hunger: Ireland 1845–49* (London and New York, Penguin, 1992), or C. Kinealy, *A Death-Dealing Famine: The Great Hunger in Ireland* (London, Pluto Press, 1997), and H. S. Srivastava, *The History of Indian Famines and Development of Famine Policy, 1858–1918* (Agra, Sri Ram Mehra, 1968).

citizens, their religious beliefs and economic activities from undue state interference. Their concern to limit government spending and taxation led them to support the authority of parliaments. But they did not initially advocate democracy in the sense of the active participation of all citizens in government. Liberal advocacy of negative freedom from government interference did not imply *political* freedom, in the sense of the right of all citizens to govern themselves through democratic institutions.[23] In fact, classical liberals were at first hostile to democratic reforms delivering greater influence to the poor and uneducated, who were thought to have little appreciation of the benefits of capitalism and private property. Even John Stuart Mill, who advocated representative democracy as a way of limiting abuses of governmental authority, consistently warned of the dangers of a 'tyranny of the majority'. In order to avoid this danger, he advocated plural votes for propertied and educated citizens, so that they might outvote the greater numbers of the ignorant and impoverished masses.[24] Both limitations – the neglect of social justice and suspicion of democracy – were the target of other social movements emerging during the nineteenth century.

2.4 Movements for Equal Citizenship, Social Justice and Democracy

A further constellation of social movements and extra-institutional activism would eventually help to ensure that democratic institutions and some commitment to social justice were grafted on to liberal capitalist institutions. The extension of democratic rights to people of all social backgrounds and the gradual recognition of social rights and social justice were, in considerable part, the work of working-class and feminist activism. The distance from fully representative democracy was certainly great at the end of the eighteenth century in Britain. Not only were all women excluded from those entitled to suffrage or the vote, also left out was the overwhelming majority of the population who did not own sufficient property. Even after the Reform Act of 1832 only about a sixth of adult males were entitled to vote. In the USA before the abolition of slavery, slaves and former slaves were denied the vote. A vote for *all* men irrespective of class or property ownership was won only after a century of activism in both Europe and north America. Towards the end of the century, the 'first wave' of the women's movement began to fight for women's suffrage and other

---

[23] This distinction is clearly argued in F. A. von Hayek, *The Constitution of Liberty* (Routledge and Kegan Paul, London, 1976).
[24] J. S. Mill, *On Liberty, and Considerations On Representative Government* (Basil Blackwell, Oxford, 1946).

citizenship rights. Universal suffrage for both men and women was achieved in the United States in 1920 and in the United Kingdom in 1928. In the United States, however, African-Americans were not fully enfranchised until the 1965 Voting Rights Act.

Although workers shared their employers' interest in expanding production and profits, their interests were more often opposed to those of the capitalist class, whose profits could be maximized by making workers work as hard as possible for as little as possible. At the same time, the restrictive nature of the franchise meant that workers' interests were not directly represented in parliament. Combination Laws and other legislation prohibited trade unions and other working-class organizations. In fact, it was usually conservative members of parliament, who were closer to the landed and aristocratic interests than to business and industry, who supported some measures to protect workers from the excesses of industrial capitalism. These measures included laws prohibiting the most dangerous forms of children's and women's labour. Later acts progressively restricted the length of the working day. These measures were usually opposed by Whig and Liberal politicians, who defended the freedom of industrialists to conduct their 'private' business and make contracts with their workers without legal interference from the state.

Although the clash of interests between workers and employers is obvious in retrospect, a self-conscious movement emerged only when working-class people began to see themselves as a distinct social class. The increasingly large class of wage-labourers first had to become conscious of its common identity and interests. Class identity and solidarity was achieved in the face of longstanding distinctions of craft, skills and occupation, local attachments and, in some cases, ethnic and national prejudices. The working class as it emerged was an active and creative response to the Industrial Revolution. As E. P. Thompson classically argues in *The Making of the English Working Class* (1963), far from being the inevitable by-product of ascendant capitalism, the working class *made itself* through forms of extra-institutional activism that have much in common with more recent social movement activity. The birth of working-class self-consciousness required a cultural revolution, which challenged widespread assumptions that ordinary working people did not deserve and could never benefit from education, and which established the worth and dignity of physical labour. Thompson describes how, inspired by Jacobinism and the French Revolution, 'corresponding societies' (in effect radical discussion groups), clubs and educational associations began to transform cultural assumptions about working people, not least assumptions working people had about themselves. The self-making of a united working class was the product of a plurality of diverse groups and activities. The transformation of working-class self-consciousness and identity laid the basis for that web of emotional bonds and moral obligations that constitutes working-class solidarity.[25]

A working class united by bonds of identity and solidarity was eventually able to force its way into the institutional order that systematically excluded it. The range of groups and activities during the accelerating Industrial Revolution was immense. Groups of artisans tried to stop the Industrial Revolution in its tracks by destroying the increasingly sophisticated machines which, because they required less skilled labour, ruined their livelihoods. In Nottinghamshire, Luddites smashed mechanical looms in a campaign that was eventually suppressed by the British army.[26] Early socialists made an attempt – futile and utopian according to Marx and Engels – to halt the development of capitalism, arguing for a socialist order based on common ownership of the means of production rather than wage labour and exploitation. Inspired by such ideals, workers founded new communities based on socialist principles. In the first decades of the nineteenth century, the philanthropic industrialist Robert Owen founded communities in New Lanark in Lanarkshire, Harmony, Indiana, and Orbiston near Glasgow. He encouraged the formation of co-operative associations, which provided insurance and other assistance in the face of the vicissitudes of early capitalism.[27] Other workers, resigned to the inevitability of capitalism, sought to protect their interests *within* the emerging economic order. Owen was also active in the trade union movement, helping to found Britain's Grand National Consolidated Trades Union in 1834. Crucial to trade union activism was the right of workers to act collectively in defence of their economic interests at a time when laws prohibited such 'combinations'. Workers who defied these laws were punished with imprisonment and, in the case of the Tolpuddle Martyrs, transportation to the penal colonies of Australia.[28] Eventually, the fight for legal recognition of trade unions would be won in most of the developed world, even if it would be a partial and always contested victory.

Artisans and other workers were a major force in England's Chartist Movement, which fought for democratic reforms and extension of the suffrage to working people. The Chartist Movement was named after the People's Charter which, between 1838 and 1848, galvanized a widespread popular movement. The demands of the Charter included

---

[25] E. P. Thompson, *The Making of the English Working Class* (1963) (London, V. Gollancz, 1980).

[26] B. Bailey, *The Luddite Rebellion* (Gloucestershire, Sutton Publishing, 1998).

[27] Cf. J. F. C. Harrison, *Robert Owen and the Owenites in Britain and America: The Quest for the New Moral World* (London, Routledge and Kegan Paul, 1969).

[28] W. Z. Foster, *Outline History of the World Trade Union Movement* (New York, International Publishers, 1956).

universal male suffrage, abolition of the property qualification, and payment for members of parliament, which would allow people without independent wealth to stand for office. Secret ballots (rather than the open ballots usual at the time) would free elections from the taint of corruption and the undue influence of wealth and power. Equal electoral districts were designed to prevent 'gerrymandering', the practice of manipulating electoral boundaries to give one candidate an unfair chance of victory.[29] Chartists also advocated annual elections in order to prevent government complacency and other vices of incumbency. Although the Chartists' successes were limited at the time, their democratic agenda has (with the exception of annual elections) become something like the 'common sense' of representative democracy.[30]

Even the Chartist Movement only advocated votes for all males over twenty-one years of age. Suffrage for women was advocated by the 'first wave' of the women's movement from the 1860s in the USA and 1880s in England.[31] Many early suffragists engaged in other forms of extra-institutional activism, including the anti-slavery movement and campaigns for 'moral reform' in opposition to prostitution, alcoholism and male violence. They campaigned for women's access to the professions, and more equal property and inheritance rights. These early feminists were not only, of necessity, acting outside existing institutions but also in decidedly anti-institutional ways. The Suffragettes in England broke the law and were sometimes violent in pursuit of their goals. As a result of their activities, women were gradually recognized as equal citizens before the law. Women gained the right to own property in their own right rather than in their husband's name. Women won the right to vote in elections in France in 1844, the UK in 1928 and USA in 1920.[32]

A series of other movements challenged the legacy of European and US colonialism. The rapid industrial development of western countries was facilitated by the colonization and exploitation of vast new territories in the Americas, Africa and Southeast Asia. Colonialism imposed foreign rule, relegating colonized populations to the status of subjects

---

[29] The term derives from Governor Elbridge Gerry of Massachusetts, an early nineteenth-century pioneer in such activities, who was satirized in a cartoon depicting his electoral district in the shape of a sala*mander*.

[30] See O. Ashton, R. Fyson and S. Roberts, eds., *The Chartist Legacy* (Woodbridge, Suffolk, Merlin Press, 1999).

[31] For more on the women's movement and second-wave and subsequent feminisms, see below, chapter 4.

[32] On the early history of feminism, see R. J. Evans, *The Feminists: Women's Emancipation Movements in Europe, America, and Australasia: 1840–1920* (New York, Croom Helm, 1977); O. Banks, *Becoming a Feminist: The Social Origins of 'First Wave' Feminism* (Brighton, Wheatsheaf, 1986); and E. Sarah, ed., *Reassessments of 'First Wave' Feminism* (Oxford and New York, Pergamon, 1983).

with few, if any, civil and democratic rights. Some were enslaved, reduced to the status of chattels. Colonialism was justified by racist doctrines, which insisted on the inferiority of non-European ethnic groups and non-Caucasian physical types. Many factors played a role in the eventual emancipation of slaves, but the campaigning of the anti-slavery movement made an indispensable contribution. Activists in the anti-slavery movement were mainly educated middle-class individuals, who were inspired by their religious convictions and humanitarian concerns. But economic and self-interested motives played a role as well, as some employers found that they were able to make larger profits from free than from slave labour. William Wilberforce formed the Committee for the Abolition of the Slave in 1787. Abolition of slavery was achieved first throughout the British Empire in 1833 then, after the American Civil War in 1865, throughout the United States.[33]

Later in the nineteenth century, anti-colonial social movements in countries colonized by European countries and the USA sought to win national self-determination and sometimes democracy for their peoples. From the Dervish state of Somalia and the Mahdi Revolution in Sudan from 1885, European colonialism was challenged and eventually eliminated by a series of movements of national liberation. Most influential for subsequent social movement activism was the Indian movement for independence inspired by Mohandas K. Gandhi. Gandhi's pacifist philosophy combined the ideas of *satyagraha* or 'truth force' and *ahimsa* or 'non-violence'. His advocacy of a strategy of active rather than merely passive non-violence translated into a series of civil disobedience campaigns in South Africa and then India, culminating in India's gaining independence from the British Empire in 1947. Gandhi's philosophy was an important influence on the early activism of the African National Congress (ANC) in South Africa. His style of activism is echoed in many social movements of the 1960s and beyond.[34]

2.5 Social Movements Hidden from History?

Extra-institutional politics and social movements have, then, made an essential contribution to the formation of liberal democratic institu-

---

[33] See R. Blackburn, *The American Crucible: Slavery, Emancipation and Human Rights* (London and New York, Verso, 2011), and F. Klingberg, *The Anti-Slavery Movement in England: A Study in English Humanitarianism* (Hamden, CT, Archon, 1968).

[34] See M. Meredith, *Mandela: A Biography* (New York, St Martin's Press, 1998). On the broader influence of Gandhi, see S. Scalmer, *Gandhi in the West: The Mahatma and the Rise of Radical Protest* (Cambridge and New York, Cambridge University Press, 2011), and cf. below, pp. 66–7.

tions in western societies. Historical explanation and, in particular, the attribution of exact causal relationships is notoriously contentious. The developments outlined in this chapter can be presented as partly the outcome of the decisions of political, religious and commercial elites. The gradual expansion of productive activity, the slow accretion of technological advances and the rise of capitalist or commercial society played an important role. Urbanization and industrialization helped to produce the social infrastructure of modern politics, both institutional and extra-institutional. Social and political thought has both responded to, and helped to inspire, these actions and events, as well as informing ensuing institutional changes. However, the foregoing brief sketch of a series of social movements has shown that the emergence of contemporary political institutions cannot be understood without, in addition, taking account of the contribution of extra- and anti-institutional action. This raises the question of why this formative history of institutional politics has been neglected, devalued and sometimes largely forgotten. Once again, this is not a merely historical question, since many of the reasons explored in what follows continue to operate.

In the first place, history tends to be written from the perspective of a particular context, with its associated values and beliefs, which treats the past as a slow and difficult ascent towards the present position. The so-called 'Whig interpretation' of history finds everywhere signs of a slow and painful advance towards liberal democracy. Hegel sees history's goal as an increasing consciousness and realization of freedom. More recently, Francis Fukuyama announced the 'end of history' on the grounds that liberal democracy has become the ultimate institutional model for the world.[35] Tendencies to write history from the perspective of the present are reinforced by the fact that it is usually the victors who write history. From the standpoint of the victors, including those who owe their position to earlier extra- and anti-institutional struggles, the institutions we now have are regarded as either ideal or as good as they can practically be. Those who have benefited from earlier waves of anti-institutional activism – revolutionaries, bourgeois liberals or organized workers – may have little to gain and much to lose from *further* waves of anti-institutional action. Anti-institutional political action may have been necessary to reach the present 'legitimate' and 'just' political order but, precisely because this order is seen as legitimate and just, cannot be justified in the future. Extra-institutional action is at best unnecessary and at worst a threat to the benefits of the established order.

Some of the movements outlined in previous sections have, secondly, strategic or ideological reasons for obscuring and devaluing the

---

[35] On the Whig interpretation of history, see above, pp. 35–6. Cf. F. Fukuyama, *The End of History and the Last Man* (New York, Free Press, 1992).

role of social movements. The emergence of nation-states and associated nationalist movements and ideologies is distinguished by a strong
commitment to the state and state sovereignty. Nationalist movements
are, as a result, intrinsically ambivalent towards extra-institutional
activism. As movements, they are strongly anti-institutional, because
not only do they act outside existing institutions but their goals
are incompatible with already-existing state structures and territorial
boundaries: they aim either to form new states or to divide existing
ones. On the other hand, once the new state is formed, then nationalist
ideologies are unreservedly hostile to further challenge. A simple reverence for the authority and sovereignty of the state accounts for part
of this bias. From a conservative perspective, the Hobbesian insistence
on the overriding importance of the state's sovereignty as the only way
to prevent a destructive 'war of every man against every man' similarly
implies absolute loyalty to the existing political order. Conservatism, in
this form, involves a bias against change and, in particular, a dislike of
political action beyond the limits of prevailing institutions. But if that
order is challenged and replaced by a new regime, then loyalty to the
new regime is equally automatic and absolute. The overriding consideration is the avoidance of further instability and insurrection rather
than what could only be the very disruptive and perhaps futile attempt
to resurrect the old order. 'The King is dead, long live the King!' Even
in liberal democracies, extra-institutional social movement activity
has often been dismissed. What could justify extra-institutional action
when the political institutions are already pluralist, democratic and
accord full citizenship to all?

Initially more surprising is the fact that some influential strands of
social democracy and Marxism, which are associated with the emergence of extra-institutional working-class activism in the nineteenth
century, have served to divert attention from social movement activism as well – although it should be noted from the outset that the
following comments only apply to these influential strands.[36] In the
first place, socialist ideologies have encouraged a narrow view of extra-
institutional movements by emphasizing the primacy of economic
conflict and class struggle. Marxism regards the capitalist mode of production as the essential core, and the class struggle between workers
and capitalists as the central conflict, of contemporary society. Other

---

[36] There are some notable exceptions: for the tradition of autonomist Marxism,
see footnote 39 below; approaches associated with the 'Western Marxism' of
the Frankfurt School are considered in chapters 8 and 9 below; the New Left
of the 1960s and 1970s was also, in effect, an attempt to avoid the deterministic
and economistic tendencies of 'actually existing' socialism and communism: see
chapter 3, pp. 68–70 below. Compare the alternative reading of Marx's writings
by K. B. Anderson, *Marx at the Margins: On Nationalism, Ethnicity, and Non-
Western Societies* (Chicago, University of Chicago Press, 2010).

movements, along with the ideologies and modes of action associated with them, are accordingly relegated to a secondary status. Even social democratic and labour parties have assumed that class position and wealth are the decisive factors in party affiliation. As a result, until quite recently relatively little attention was paid to movements concerned with other issues, such as the first wave of the women's movements, the campaign against slavery, and anti-colonial struggles in the 'Third World' (discussed in the previous section). Even manifestations of working-class activism have been neglected, when they fail to follow either revolutionary or parliamentary paths to socialism. Those like the Luddites, who sought to prevent the mechanization of production spurred by capitalist competition, were dismissed as misguided, destructive and counter-productive agitators. The 'utopian socialists' castigated by Marx and Engels were regarded as well-meaning but naïve predecessors of scientific socialism, whose futile protests against the evils of capitalism did little to advance the socialist cause.[37]

From the perspective of Marxism and social democracy, even the working-class movement tends to be neglected *qua* social movement, even though the working class is obviously at the centre of their world-view. In part, this is because the emergence of the working class as the 'gravedigger' of capitalism and agent of socialist revolution is portrayed as inevitable. By pointing to the various ways in which the further development of capitalism prepares the ground for socialist revolution, Marx and Engels divert attention from the need for the working class to engage in deliberate political action. At the same time, both variants of socialism emphasize the decisive role of organizations. In the case of the Leninist tradition, the key role falls to the militant revolutionary party, which is destined to seize state power and impose a 'dictatorship of the proletariat'. To that end, organizational unity is the overriding goal and, paradoxically, endless sectarianism is the practical result. Lenin's working-out of the Marxist tradition in the context of pre-revolutionary Russia reduces the working-class social movement to the role of an 'elemental force' to be guided by the militant party.[38] The aims of the working-class movement, its decisions and its agency are transferred to the party leadership, supposedly informed and justified by scientific Marxist theory. In the social democratic tradition, trade unions, parliamentary labour parties and state bureaucracies are regarded as the primary agents of social transformation, and there is similar ambivalence as a result towards less organized and extra-institutional modes of politics. In a way analogous to the

---

[37] F. Engels, *Socialism: Utopian and Scientific* (London, Allan & Unwin, 1920), trans. E. Aveling.
[38] V. I. Lenin, *What Is To Be Done?* (Harmondsworth, Penguin, 1988), ed. R. Service.

Whig interpretation of history as the difficult ascent to freedom, the Marxist and 'Labourist' versions of history have portrayed the working-class social movement as the gradual discovery of approaches to politics corresponding to their own. Mainstream traditions of both Marxism and social democracy have underestimated the extent to which working-class politics should be understood as an active and creative response to the changing conditions of industrial capitalism. It should be remembered, though, that there was an intense debate involving Lenin and Rosa Luxemburg over the role of 'spontaneity' in the early revolutionary movement, and other Marxist currents such as autonomist Marxism also offer greater recognition of the working class as an active agent.[39]

It is, however, with the activities of more recent and contemporary movements from the 1960s that attitudes to social movements, both historical and contemporary, have been more broadly transformed. Even then, the new movements were at first often treated on the left as mere diversions from the ultimately decisive class conflict or victory at the next election. This is because radical politics was still dominated by models of politics and social transformation inherited from the socialist tradition, which saw states as the essential vehicles of change, and centralized party organizations (whether revolutionary or reformist) as the necessary means to capture them. By the same token, the rejection of Marxist, Leninist and social democratic models of political change was a crucial source of the conviction that something about the new waves of social movement activism was actually new. With a series of waves of radical activism from the 1950s and the emergence of new social movements – including women's, lesbian and gay, anti-racist, peace and environmental movements – from the 1970s has come a fresh appreciation of the formative contribution, historical importance and democratic value of extra-institutional social movements.

---

[39] V. I. Lenin attacks reliance on the spontaneity of the masses in *What Is To Be Done?*, ch. 2. Rosa Luxemburg argues that spontaneity and organization interact dialectically: cf. R . Luxemburg, *Selected Political Writings* (London, Cape, 1972), ed. R. Looker. The tradition of *autonomia* or autonomist Marxism is associated mainly with thinkers such as Mario Tronti, Antonio Negri and Mariarosa Dalla Costa in Italy, but also has connections to the ideas and activism of C. L. R. James, Raya Dunayevskay, John Holloway and Harry Cleaver. At its heart is recognition of the persistent activism and agency of the working class beyond the confines of party (whether revolutionary or electoral), trade unions and the state. For a recent guide to both ideas and sources, see D. Eden, *Autonomy: Capitalism, Class and Politics* (Farnham and Burlington, VT, Ashgate, 2012), and S. Lotringer and C. Marazzi, eds., *Autonomia: Post-Political Politics* (New York, Semiotext(e), 2007), 2nd edn.

Further Reading

The emergence of the modern nation-state and the role of social movements is charted by Charles Tilly in *Contention and Democracy in Europe: 1650–2000* and *Social Movements, 1768–2004*, amongst numerous other works. Benedict Anderson's classic book on nationalism is *Imagined Communities: Reflections on the Origins and Spread of Nationalism*. A succinct survey of nationalism is provided in Andrew Vincent, *Modern Political Ideologies*, ch. 9. E. P. Thompson's *The Making of the English Working Class* is a classic account of the active self-formation of the working class. For discussion of three contemporary exponents of autonomist Marxism, which also emphasizes the active role of the working class, see Sylvere Lotringer and Christian Marazzi's edited collection, *Autonomia: Post-Political Politics*, and David Eden, *Autonomy: Capitalism, Class and Politics*. On the history of the anti-slavery movement, see Robin Blackburn, *The American Crucible: Slavery, Emancipation and Human Rights*, and Frank Klingberg, *The Anti-Slavery Movement in England: A Study in English Humanitarianism*. The 'first wave' of the women's movement is discussed by Olive Banks in *Becoming a Feminist: The Social Origins of 'First Wave' Feminism*, and R. J. Evans, *The Feminists: Women's Emancipation Movements in Europe, America, and Australasia: 1840–1920*.

Part II

Social Movements in Contemporary Politics

3

Illusions of Stability: The Surprising Emergence of New Social Movements

Outline

Contemporary politics has been shaped by the activities of a series of 'new social movements' concerned with (amongst other issues) gender, sexuality, racism, peace and the environment. These movements have been described as new in part, at least, because they represented a surprising challenge to the institutions of affluent and seemingly stable western states. These institutions are not only liberal and democratic, they also recognize the rights of workers and trade unions and provide a wide range of welfare and social security benefits. In fact, the new movements followed, and were able to benefit from the experience of, earlier waves of activism including Gandhian civil disobedience during the early twentieth-century movement for India's independence and, from the 1950s, the African-American Civil Rights Movement and campaigns for nuclear disarmament. The more immediate origins of the new movements can be found in social changes of the 1960s, sexual permissiveness and the 'counter-culture', student radicalism, the New Left and opposition to the Vietnam War. Important as a symbolic and theoretical threshold in the emergence of these movements are the so-called 'May Events' of 1968 in France and a series of other protests and conflicts during that year.

3.1 Introduction: A New Politics?

The institutional politics of contemporary western societies owes many important features, indeed many of its *best* features, either wholly or in part to the extra- and anti-institutional politics of previous social movements. Yet, for a variety of reasons this contribution has tended, until recently, to be either neglected, denied or altogether forgotten.[1] The present chapter considers the upsurge of social movements and extra-parliamentary protest that took place in western societies after the Second World War and particularly from the 1960s. New waves of social movement activism have challenged the institutions of liberal democratic and welfare state societies in significant and unexpected ways. These 'new social movements' include the second wave of the women's movement, gay, lesbian and queer politics, environmental and peace movements, anti-racist and indigenous politics.

In a number of ways, the new movements set the scene for contemporary politics, both institutional and extra-institutional. In the first place, they politicize previously neglected but now unavoidable issues, including gender, sexuality, ethnicity or 'race', environment and nature. They also contribute substantially, secondly, to the distinctive mood and style, strategies and tactics of contemporary political activism. At the same time, thirdly, the appearance and successes of these movements have encouraged theorists and commentators to reassess the importance and value of extra-institutional activism. These movements have transformed theories of the nature of politics by encouraging a revised view of the role and impact of social movements, which are increasingly recognized as crucial factors in the formation and reformation of political institutions. Accompanying this theoretical shift is a normative shift towards greater recognition of extra-institutional politics as a legitimate mode of political action and, indeed, as an essential condition of a fully adequate democracy.

At this stage, the movements discussed here as *new* social movements are assigned to this category in a provisional way. In fact, it is not easy to define with any precision what, if anything, is exclusive to or new about these movements.[2] A more adequate answer to this question will emerge over the course of the following chapters. But at least part of the explanation of the seeming novelty of new social movements is the fact that their arrival on the political scene was surprising and, indeed, surprising on a number of levels. In one sense, extra-institutional movements are always surprising. By definition, being extra- and often anti-institutional, social movements do not follow the accepted practices and norms of institutionalized politics. The historical movements considered in the previous chapter were, in that sense, unexpected as well. Even if it might have been anticipated that, for example, people would eventually fight to throw off the shackles of slavery or that women would seek equal citizenship rights, the timing, nature and eventual success of the corresponding movements

---

[1] See section 2.5.
[2] There has been a long and involved debate in the academic literature over precisely this question: see below, chapter 8.

were not anticipated and could not have been predicted. Indeed, an important general reason to be concerned with social movements stems from their very unpredictability. What is more, because institutional politics is always liable to be challenged and sometimes transformed by extra-institutional movements, institutional politics is ultimately unpredictable as well. The political system's apparent stability may always turn out to have been illusory.

However, the new social movements were surprising in a stronger sense as well, because they occurred within societies that prized themselves (somewhat complacently, as it turns out) on their prosperity, technical sophistication, economic development and, above all, their liberal freedoms, democratic rights and social justice. The USA, Western Europe, Japan and similar developed societies belonged to the 'free world' of liberal democracies. They contrasted sharply with poor, developing countries, often with dictatorial regimes. They were ideologically and militarily opposed to the authoritarian communist one-party states of Eastern Europe, the Soviet Union and China. Liberal democratic institutions allow legitimate democratic challenges protected by freedoms of thought and association. Most citizens within these societies must surely be, if not happy, then at least sufficiently contented to make the likelihood of extra-institutional challenges only slight at best. What possible cause and, equally importantly, what possible justification could there be for extra- or anti-institutional challenges to the institutional order of these societies? To most observers, the new movements represented a surprising disruption of an apparently well-founded stability.

The new movements were surprising, finally, because they addressed issues substantially different from the mainly material or economic conflicts over taxation, welfare and trade union rights which dominated the agenda of institutional politics after the Second World War. Instead, these movements addressed issues like gender, sexuality, ethnicity and race. Environmental and green movements even advocated policies that implied a reduction in production and consumption, contradicting the commitments to growth and ever-increasing living standards shared by both left and right of the established political spectrum.

3.2 The Deceptive Stability of Western Liberal Democracy

To understand why the emergence of so-called 'new social movements' was so surprising, we need to consider in more detail why western societies were regarded as stable. They appeared stable, in the first place, in comparison with the preceding century or so of conflicts and wars. During the nineteenth century, there were deep-seated class tensions sparked by the upheavals of the Industrial Revolution, the movement against slavery, women's activism for moral reform and women's suffrage, and anti-colonial rebellions and massacres. These conflicts were often violent and, in the case of European countries, sometimes led to the overthrow of established regimes. The first half of the twentieth century had been even more cataclysmic. The Great Depression of the 1930s devastated the world's economy and intensified social conflict. Partly in response to economic dislocations, fascist regimes in Italy, Germany and Spain imposed brutal dictatorships. The expansionism of Germany's National Socialist state started the Second World War. Hitler's regime perpetrated a horrifying holocaust of Jews, communists and homosexuals. There were successful communist revolutions in Russia (1917), China (1949) and Cuba (1959). Anti-colonial movements of liberation challenged European rule across Africa and Asia, all but ending the 'age of empire'.[3]

Against the calamitous backdrop of preceding decades, the apparent calm and affluence of the period after the Second World War in the West comes into sharper relief as a period of calm and stability. These were years of continuous growth and ever-increasing economic prosperity, the 'long boom' of rapid economic expansion between 1945 and 1973. The German and Japanese 'economic miracles' were only the most dramatic examples of widespread recovery, funded in considerable part by the US Marshall Plan. Levels of economic production and share values returned at last to the levels reached in 1929 before the onset of the Great Depression. Unemployment fell to all-time lows, levels which have only rarely been approached since then. Far fewer people were condemned to the daily struggle for mere existence, as more and more people gained access to what were previously regarded as luxuries of the rich. Consumer goods like radios, automobiles, televisions and refrigerators became available on a mass scale for the first time in the USA and Europe during the 1940s and 1950s. Significantly, the spread of affluence helped to generate a distinctive youth culture through markets in music, clothing, film and other forms of entertainment. These markets provided a foothold for the 'counter-culture' of the 1960s, which was in turn reflected in the styles and symbolism of the new movements.[4]

There were, however, more strictly political reasons for thinking that western societies had entered a new period of stability. After the defeat of fascism and in the face of communism, liberal democracy

---

[3] For a succinct account of the 'end of empire', see N. Ferguson, *Empire: How Britain Made the Modern World* (London, Allen Lane, 2003), esp. ch. 6.

[4] See T. Judt, *Postwar: A History of Europe since 1945* (London, Pimlico, 2007), and D. W. Urwin, *A Political History of Western Europe since 1945* (London, Longman, 1997), 5th edn. On the counter-culture, see below, pp. 67–8.

came to be taken for granted as the essential condition of peaceful and harmonious co-existence. Representative democracy with universal suffrage was now the norm. In contrast to the 'people's democracies' of the communist world, free electoral competition between several major parties gave electorates a choice between usually two or three major parties representing, broadly, the interests of business, property or 'capital' on one side and working people and welfare recipients on the other. Democratic institutions were reinforced by liberal freedoms of the press and media, and freedoms of assembly and association. What is more, outside of the parliamentary context were organizations representing a plurality of cross-cutting interest groups and pressure groups. Theorists of democratic pluralism argued that negotiation and compromise between diverse interest groups and the state would defuse any tensions that might otherwise arise.[5]

The dissipation of social conflict through pluralist and representative democracy was reinforced by a seemingly permanent division of the world into mutually hostile capitalist and communist blocs, which helped to divert attention from domestic conflicts. The First World of western liberal democracies faced the Second World of communist states. Those parts of the world not included in these antagonistic blocs were relegated to the residual category of 'developing' or Third World.[6] The rivalry between capitalism and communism resulted not in war but in Cold War, because the Mutually Assured Destruction (MAD) guaranteed by thermonuclear ballistic arsenals made direct mutual aggression too costly. Beyond the frozen antagonism of two hostile blocs, however, raged a number of 'proxy wars' between Third World countries allied to one or other of them – wars supplied and sometimes instigated by them as well – notably in Korea, Vietnam, the Middle East and Latin America. The Cold War reinforced a broad consensus about foreign policy in Britain, Japan, Australia and, to a lesser extent, Western Europe. In the USA, the central foreign policy commitment was to the 'containment' and, if possible, rollback of communism.[7] Other western states were tied to the USA by a series of treaties and financial relations in a global anti-communist alliance: European countries in the North Atlantic Treaty Organization (NATO) formed in 1949, Pacific rim countries in the Southeast Asia Treaty Organization (SEATO) from 1955,

---

[5] See R. A. Dahl, *Who Governs? Democracy and Power in an American City* (New Haven, Yale University Press, 1961). For a critical account, see C. B. Macpherson, *The Life and Times of Liberal Democracy* (Oxford and New York, Oxford University Press, 1977), esp. ch. 4.

[6] The term 'Third World' was first used by French social scientist Alfred Sauvy in 1952.

[7] The policy of containment was first formulated by US diplomat George F. Kennan in 1946. The rollback of communism was advocated by James Burnham: see J. Burnham, *The Coming Defeat of Communism* (London, Cape, 1950).

and similar international organizations elsewhere. Under the umbrella of these treaties, nuclear missiles were deployed and military bases set up around the globe. France and the United Kingdom developed their own nuclear weapons within this framework. American military personnel were stationed on bases within the territory of many US allies, including Britain, Germany, Italy, Israel, Japan, South Korea, Australia and Turkey. The western alliance exerted strong pressure on a number of countries to participate in US military campaigns in the Korean War (1950–3) and Vietnam (1955–75).[8]

The Cold War was an important factor in consolidating consensus on domestic matters within western states as well. Major political parties could agree on the need to fight the 'red menace', which was a threat both externally and as a 'fifth column' within. This made it easier, in fact almost obligatory, for established politicians to vilify communism both at home and abroad. In the USA, support for 'liberal' (in the European context, social democratic or welfare) policies was suspiciously 'red' or 'pink'. In the 1950s, Senator Joseph McCarthy was the chair of a Senate committee investigating alleged communists and leftists in the army, public service and the arts. McCarthy's 'witch-hunts' drove even quite moderate supporters of liberal social policies from public life – from the theatre, cinema and publishing as well as from more strategically sensitive positions in defence and intelligence. In a similar atmosphere, the attempt by Australia's longest-serving Prime Minister, Robert Menzies, to proscribe the Australian Communist Party was only narrowly defeated (1951). Even when overt persecution of communists was avoided, the excesses of Stalinist show trials, purges and overt repression (such as the invasion of Hungary in 1956) combined with the drabness and authoritarianism of Soviet life to discredit the socialist alternative to capitalism. Both of the 'totalitarian' alternatives to capitalism – fascism and Stalinism – were evidently unappealing. Fundamental ideological conflict, whether between liberalism and fascism or communism and capitalist democracy, came to be seen as obsolete. The basic contours, if not the finer details, of the best of all possible societies were now clear. Triumphalist western intellectuals pronounced the 'end of ideology' (just as, after the end of the Cold War, they would announce the 'end of history').[9]

---

[8] This pressure was occasionally resisted, for example by Harold Wilson's Labour Government which refused to send British troops to Vietnam even though Wilson consistently supported US policy. Australia has participated in every major US engagement since 1945.

[9] See D. Bell, *The End of Ideology: On the Exhaustion of Political Ideas in the Fifties* (Glencoe, IL, Free Press, 1960). Cf. Fukuyama, *The End of History*.

3.3 Welfare State Capitalism: Farewell to the Working Class?

The impression that all major political issues had been resolved, in theory if not yet quite in practice, was reinforced by a broad consensus of the major political parties concerning domestic affairs. The upheavals of the Great Depression and the sacrifices of the Second World War contributed to a new political settlement. This 'social democratic' consensus was grounded in a basic compromise between capital and labour and manifested in the institutions of welfare state capitalism. Economic boom and uninterrupted growth thus took place in the context of a transformed social and economic order. The New Deal in America and elements of a welfare state in Britain, Australia and Western Europe contributed to a class compromise between the interests of capital and labour. Major electoral adversaries came to share a core of social principles and policies. Whilst conservative parties and representatives of business made significant concessions to trade unions and working people, social democratic parties effectively abandoned the commitment to 'socialize the means of production'.

The concessions made by both capital and labour formed the basis of the post-war social democratic consensus around the institutions of what has been called welfare state capitalism.[10] In fact, the institutions of the welfare state were often supported by socially minded liberals and 'new conservatives' as well. Initially committed to the defining socialist aim of socializing the means of production, social democrats had abandoned revolutionary means for the sake of a gradual, evolutionary path to socialism. Once the working-class social movement had achieved both universal male suffrage and legal recognition of trade unions and strike action, workers' parties and social democrats set out to reform capitalism through the agency of parliamentary democracy.[11] These efforts were labelled 'reformist' by would-be revolutionary socialists, who argued that social reforms that left capitalist relations of production in place could not bring the working class any nearer to socialism. At the heart of the social democratic agenda were policies to socialize or 'nationalize' more and more areas of the privately owned capitalist economy. Socialization of the strategic sectors or 'commanding heights' of the economy would both effect greater government control of economic activity immediately and, in theory, prepare for the eventual socialization of production as a whole. These policies

---

[10] See G. Esping-Andersen, *The Three Worlds of Welfare Capitalism* (Princeton, NJ, Princeton University Press, 1990).

[11] See M. B. Steger, *The Quest for Evolutionary Socialism: Eduard Bernstein and Social Democracy* (Cambridge and New York, Cambridge University Press, 1997). On the working-class social movement, see above, chapter 2, pp. 41–3.

continued in the name of 'mixed economy', even after the commitment to 'socialize the means of production' was effectively abandoned.[12]

Under the influence of labour parties, states even accorded official, institutional recognition not only to representatives of business or capital but also to labour and trade unions. Descriptions of the new order as a form of neo-corporatism reflected this institutional recognition of labour organizations and interests. Labour had gained a significant, if still subordinate, place within the institutional structures of the state. The social democratic consensus also favoured progressive taxation and other measures to promote social equality. Conflicts over the distribution of wealth were more easily defused, because levels of material affluence were continually increasing. As theorists on all sides recognized, it was much easier to divide an expanding economic 'cake', since everyone's share could increase at the same time, even if the shares of a few were increasing at a faster rate.

From the beginning of the twentieth century, social security, sickness and unemployment benefits had been introduced in order to protect poor and working people from the insecurities of life in capitalist society – often with the support of socially minded or 'social' liberals as well. Additional measures in Britain and Europe after the Second World War expanded these limited protections into something more like an inclusive welfare state. Free or subsidized health care was provided through compulsory insurance schemes and Britain's National Health Service. State provision of education was expanded to include secondary schooling and then tertiary-level college and university studies. Welfare measures were financed by progressive taxation, reinforcing other measures of economic redistribution. Any surpluses generated by nationalized industries helped to fund social assistance programmes. The combination of welfare measures and redistribution reduced the number of people living in poverty and helped to ameliorate social and economic inequalities. Both absolute and relative poverty were reduced to levels not seen before or, indeed, since. In the words of Harold Macmillan, the workers had 'never had it so good'.[13]

The social democratic consensus was underpinned at the level of economic theory by a shared commitment to the economic doctrines of John Maynard Keynes (1883–1946). Rejecting the absolute commitment of neo-classical economists to *laissez-faire* and the unfettered

---

[12] In some countries, like Britain, however, the commitment to socialism remained official party policy for many years. Clause IV of the Labour Party's Constitution was abandoned only in 1995.

[13] On the history of European welfare states, see D. Gladstone, *The Twentieth-Century Welfare State* (New York, St Martin's Press, 1999), and B. S. Jansson, *The Reluctant Welfare State: A History of American Social Welfare Policies* (Belmont, CA, Wadsworth, 1988).

free market, Keynes argued that during cyclical economic recessions, governments should increase public expenditure in order to stimulate demand and reduce unemployment. During recessions governments should borrow or even print money – what is now more reassuringly referred to as 'quantitative easing' – in order to finance public works such as large infrastructure projects (building highways, hydroelectric schemes, railways, etc.), which would improve the long-term productivity of the economy. The workers employed by these schemes would then create further demand as they spent their wages, leading to a virtuous cycle or 'multiplier effect'. Government 'demand management' not only aimed to provide full employment for workers, but evidently also promised benefits to employers as well. Unnecessary bankruptcies could be avoided; the economy would quickly return to profitable growth. Keynesian economic theory implied – and the long boom appeared to confirm – that governments could now prevent the capitalist crises that Marxists had optimistically seen as precursors of socialist revolution.[14]

At the same time, of course, even during this period of broad consensus, there was still significant disagreement between the major parties. The redistributive role of progressive taxation was largely accepted, but arguments persisted over the appropriate *degree* of redistribution. There was broad commitment to the welfare state, but there was disagreement about how much money should be spent on welfare and social security, education and health care. Trade unions were recognized and incorporated into the institutions of the state, but the extent of trade union rights and influence was subject to argument. The size of the public versus private sectors was similarly controversial. In Britain, some industries like steel were nationalized, reprivatized and even taken into public ownership once more. But the mixed economy, part private and part state enterprise, was a shared commitment. The differences between left and right of the political spectrum within some countries are matched by considerable variation between countries. Welfare states were more or less generous, more or less paternalistic and intrusive, more or less universal in different countries. The extensive welfare states of Sweden, Denmark, Norway and (to a lesser extent) Germany, France and Britain contrasted with weaker and more conditional systems in Australia, Japan and the USA.[15]

It seemed that workers no longer had much reason to engage in radical extra-institutional activity, let alone to support socialist revolution. The apparent incorporation and pacification of the working class was acknowledged on both left and right, though revolutionary

---

[14] See P. Clarke, *The Keynesian Revolution and its Economic Consequences: Selected Essays* (Cheltenham, Edward Elgar, 1998).

[15] See Esping-Andersen, *Three Worlds of Welfare Capitalism*.

Marxists continued to advocate socialist revolution. Herbert Marcuse, a thinker associated with the 'critical theory' of the Frankfurt School, described western societies as 'one-dimensional', because there was no longer any essential conflict between capital and labour. With fewer regrets and understandably less nostalgia for class struggle, conservative and centrist thinkers announced the 'end of ideology'.[16] If the prospects of revolutionary socialism were slight, then welfare state capitalism did at least appear to provide grounds for optimism concerning the social democratic project itself. The broad consensus between major electoral parties suggested that the welfare state would be an enduring achievement. Just as representative democracy, liberal rights and women's enfranchisement were now taken for granted, the mixed economy, welfare provision and progressive taxes were permanent advances towards, if not socialism, then at least a socially just society. What is more, there were even grounds to expect further advances in the direction of social justice and equality. The experience of a partially socialized economy would surely diminish exaggerated fears about state ownership and planning. The welfare state demonstrated the benefits for the whole of society from providing essential goods like education and health care on the basis of need rather than wealth. Industry (like the army) requires healthy and well-educated personnel. Improved education would also encourage workers to see through the ideological excesses of both capitalism and communism. Relieved of material insecurities and class hatreds, working people would be able to transcend the limited perspective of their immediate interests and join in the political task of creating a more productive and more humane society for all.[17]

In retrospect, however, it is clear that 1960s' welfare state capitalism was really the high point of social democracy. The 'forward march' of labour has since been halted.[18] The economic 'stagflation' experienced after the oil crisis of 1973 caused by OPEC's decision to raise oil prices and again in 1979 as a result of the Iranian Revolution combined with perceptions of excessive union power and wage-driven inflation to provide fertile ground for the opponents of social democracy. Classical liberal and libertarian ideas were restored by the likes of Friedrich Hayek, Milton Friedman and Robert Nozick, reviving ideals of *laissez-faire* capitalism, free markets and small government. In the 1980s and 1990s, these ideas were taken up with enthusiasm by Conservative

---

[16] H. Marcuse, *One-Dimensional Man: Studies in the Ideology of Advanced Industrial Society* (London, Routledge and Kegan Paul, 1964). On the end of ideology thesis, see above, footnote 9.

[17] See above, footnote 11.

[18] M. Jacques and F. Mulhern, *The Forward March of Labour Halted?* (London, NLB, 1981).

and Republican politicians like Margaret Thatcher in Britain, Ronald Reagan in the USA, and John Howard in Australia. Even labour and social democratic leaders accepted many of the orthodoxies of neo-liberal political economy. Later, in the USA, Democrat President Bill Clinton charted a middle course. Labour politicians Robert Hawke and Paul Keating introduced 'economic rationalism' to Australia.[19] Labour Finance Minister Roger Douglas introduced a similar programme of 'Rogernomics' in New Zealand in 1984. Even when not fully embracing the new right agenda, parties of the left found no way of reviving the social democratic project. It would be wrong, however, to regard this failure as a straightforward betrayal of the working class. When not driven by their own economically rationalist convictions, social democratic leaders were moved by electoral considerations. Multiple electoral defeats led to the inescapable realization that much of the traditional working class had already deserted the cause. A more secure, healthier, wealthier and more educated working class had, paradoxically, proved *less* rather than more enthusiastic about social democratic reforms. For the majority of working people, individual advancement and consumerism had displaced class solidarity and labour activism. The institutional achievements of labour and social democratic organizations in the twentieth century led not to the flourishing, but to the dissolution of the working-class movement.

As a result, the welfare state has lost much ground to those who have found new ways to assert the interests of wealth and property. But the welfare state was, even at its most developed and successful, a less than ideal form of polity. Since the 1970s, the institutions of welfare states have been challenged not only by the interests of wealth and capital, but by other more radical interests as well, including new and emerging constituencies of women, gays and lesbians, ethnic and cultural minorities, environmentalists and campaigners for peace. The character, activists and goals of these new forces react against, but also echo, some of the main features of welfare state society.[20] However, the new movements were also able to draw not only on a long history of extra-institutional activism but also on a number of significant social movements that flourished amidst the seeming calm of capitalist liberal democracy.

---

[19] See M. Pusey, *Economic Rationalism in Canberra: A Nation-building State Changes its Mind* (Cambridge and New York, Cambridge University Press, 1991). The term 'neoliberal' is now used mainly in a pejorative sense by those opposed to the revival of classical liberal ideas. It was originally used more positively by the German sociologist and economist Alexander Rüstow in 1938.

[20] A number of *theories* of new social movements refer to central features of this form of society: see below, chapter 8.

3.4 Cracks in the Image: Extra-institutional Politics of the 1960s

Even before the arrival of new social movements, a number of extra-institutional social movements caused some significant cracks in the West's complacent self-image. What is more, they proved to be far more than merely transitory and inconsequential events. They were rather harbingers of other wide-ranging challenges to the institutions of liberal democracy, part of what Sydney Tarrow describes as a new 'cycle of protest'.[21] The conflicts of the 1950s and 1960s revived and sometimes pioneered styles of political action that were taken up with enthusiasm by other movements and activists.

The African-American Civil Rights Movement in the United States was an early and influential movement highlighting fundamental gaps in the supposedly universal rights and freedoms of liberal democracy. Major western states had reached their position of affluence and apparent stability only thanks to their colonial past, whose legacy was a series of deep ethnic and 'racial' fault-lines. Systematic inequalities based on ethnicity and race reflected and reinforced deeply ingrained racial prejudices. Ethnic and racial cleavages overlapped with, and complicated, divisions of class and wealth. In the case of the USA, the racial divide assumed a particularly virulent form as a result of the long history of slavery. Although slaves had been legally emancipated in the aftermath of the Civil War of 1861–5, the position of African-Americans remained one of systematic exclusion, discrimination and disadvantage. Social and economic inequalities were entrenched by measures denying them full and effective civil and political rights. They were excluded from the electoral process by arbitrary obstacles to enrolling and voting in elections. Segregation was officially sanctioned in schools, hotels and public transport. Any challenge to these racist institutions was met with violence, usually tolerated if not officially sanctioned by police and government officials. Secret societies like the Ku Klux Klan organized beatings, murders and lynchings with relative impunity well into the twentieth century.[22]

In this hostile environment, the Civil Rights Movement campaigned against segregation in education and housing and for equal rights in voting. The Supreme Court's 1954 *Brown* v. *Board of Education* decision on school desegregation and the 1955 Montgomery bus boycott campaign, initiated by Rosa Parks and organized by the Montgomery Improvement Association, were important early catalysts of the move-

---

[21] See S. Tarrow, *Power in Movement: Collective Action, Social Movements and Politics* (Cambridge and New York, Cambridge University Press, 1998).

[22] See J. Hope Franklin and A. Moss, *From Slavery to Freedom: A History of African Americans* (New York, Knopf, 2000), 8th edn.

ment. The movement drew on a variety of ideas and tactics. Martin Luther King and James Morris Lawson Jr advocated the Gandhian philosophy of *satyagraha* or 'truth force' and non-violence (*ahimsa*) and his strategy of peaceful civil disobedience. The movement, which also drew support from white student radicals and liberal politicians, conducted boycotts, sit-ins at lunch counters, demonstrations and marches (including the 1963 March on Washington). Freedom rides were organized by the Student Nonviolent Coordinating Committee (SNCC) in 1960. Voter registration campaigns in the American south were met with violence and abuse. The movement achieved significant victories with the Civil Rights Act (1964), which prohibited segregation and other forms of overt racial discrimination in public transport, housing and public facilities such as libraries and restaurants. The 1965 Voting Rights Act protected the voting rights of African-Americans in southern states. However, after the assassination of Martin Luther King in 1968, the movement broke into disparate strands and currents.[23]

Associated with the broader movement were important innovations in tactics and ideology, which have made a seminal contribution to later movements. 'Black Power' and Malcolm X's Nation of Islam developed a more confrontational and aggressive approach than Martin Luther King's pacifist direct action. The Black Power movement also excluded white participation. The demand for Black Power referred beyond legally sanctioned discrimination and economic disadvantage to the cultural, social and psychological roots of oppression in a racist society. Racism is undoubtedly more than socially sanctioned prejudice: racism exists where one racial or ethnic group is able to exploit its position of power over other groups. But the culture of racism is also intrinsically oppressive, in that it inflicts a particular kind of suffering in addition to the exclusion and discrimination it justifies. Oppression disempowers its victims, making them less hopeful and confident and, as a result, less likely to act to overcome their subordinate position. By the same token, the emphasis on Black Power and Pride is designed to encourage the oppressed to liberate themselves from their oppression and to empower them to undertake this task. The associated politics of identity and consciousness was adopted by later movements, in particular second-wave feminism and gay and lesbian liberation movements. The movement's ideology and strategy also encouraged international resistance to South Africa's *apartheid* regime and contributed to a more assertive phase of indigenous politics in Australia and elsewhere.[24]

---

[23] See D. McAdam, *Freedom Summer* (Oxford and New York, Oxford University Press, 1988); K. Verney, *Black Civil Rights in America* (London and New York, Routledge, 2000).

[24] See P. E. Joseph, ed., *The Black Power Movement: Rethinking the Civil Rights – Black*

Less happily, the example of Black Power also encouraged separatism or, in other words, the exclusion from the movement of all those who could not claim to belong to the oppressed group.

Another influential social movement of the 1950s and 1960s was the peace movement, which responded to the Cold War's precarious balance of terror and associated fears of nuclear holocaust. The Campaign for Nuclear Disarmament (CND) in Britain and elsewhere revived pacifist ideals, which had thrived previously only in times of war, notably during the First World War. The CND was founded in 1957 at a time of nominal peace and included figures like Bertrand Russell, the well-known Cambridge philosopher who had been imprisoned for opposing the First World War, and socialist historian E. P. Thompson. The pacifist commitments to end violence and abolish the threat of nuclear annihilation were central goals of the movement, but there was also an emphasis on social justice. Resources wasted on armaments designed to kill should be diverted to the world's poor, fulfilling the Biblical prophecy that 'they will beat their swords into ploughshares'.[25] The peace movement also shared with the Civil Rights Movement (at least in its earlier phases) the inspiration of Gandhi's philosophy of 'truth force' and active non-violence. The campaigns for nuclear disarmament mobilized a largely middle-class and often religious constituency, leading Frank Parkin to analyse the movement as an instance of 'middle class radicalism'.[26] From the perspective of institutional politics and even for the radical left, the peace movement was an anomaly. The fact that the movement appeared to be motivated mainly by religious, idealistic and ethical motives (although an understandable concern for survival surely motivated some participants as well) did not fit with the conventional view of politics as mostly materialistic and self-interested. For some sectors of the organized left, the peace movement was a middle-class indulgence, which diverted resources and attention from the strategically decisive issue of class. In retrospect (and more positively), the peace movement was an early example of a *prefigurative* approach to politics. Prefigurative politics insists that the means employed in campaigns should embody the values and goals of the movement. This emphasis can also be understood as an example of symbolic politics, since

Power Era (New York and London, Routledge, 2006), and cf. below, chapter 4, esp. pp. 81–3.

[25] See A. Carter, *Peace Movements: International Protest and World Politics since 1945* (London and New York, Longman, 1992), and R. K. S. Taylor, *Against the Bomb: The British Peace Movement 1958–65* (Oxford, Clarendon Press; New York, Oxford University Press, 1988). The prophecy is from the Book of Isaiah, chapter 2, verse 4.

[26] F. Parkin, *Middle Class Radicalism: The Social Bases of the British Campaign for Nuclear Disarmament* (Manchester, Manchester University Press, 1968).

non-violent demonstrations were designed above all to *express* the central values and goals of the movement rather than to manifest an intimidating show of force. CND organized annual Easter marches to the Atomic Weapons Research Establishment at Aldermaston, calling for unilateral and universal nuclear disarmament.

Less explicitly political (if explicit in other ways) was a series of cultural challenges from the so-called 'counter-culture'. The unprecedented affluence, stability and security of post-war welfare states did not, as might have been expected, induce a state of near-universal contentment. Instead, a substantial minority of citizens, particularly young people and students, Hippies and 'dropouts', turned their backs on material values and rewards in pursuit of alternative lifestyles. The counter-culture both reflected and contributed to a broader questioning of traditional values and standards. The legal prohibition of abortion became a prime target of second-wave feminism, which asserted women's right to control their own bodies. Censorship of plays and other literature was relaxed. The criminal prosecution of D. H. Lawrence's *Lady Chatterley's Lover* and James Joyce's *Ulysses* failed, encouraging even bolder works and more open discussion of sex and sexuality. The contraceptive pill, which was increasingly available in the USA and Europe from 1960, made it possible to avoid the reproductive consequences of extra- and pre-marital sex. Antibiotic treatments for sexually transmitted diseases virtually eliminated the remaining risks from promiscuous sex, at least until the arrival of HIV and AIDS in the 1980s.[27]

In the era of 'permissiveness', sexual pleasure could be enjoyed for its own sake rather than needing to be justified according to the norms of religious sexual morality – as reproductive acts between monogamous partners within a marriage sanctified by the Church. As divorce and illegitimacy became more acceptable, legal reforms made divorce more readily available. Permissiveness and counter-cultural attitudes thrived in alternative communities and 'communes' dedicated to communal values, self-sufficiency, 'free sex' and hallucinogenic drugs.[28] Rock festivals at Woodstock in the USA, Nimbin in Australia and Glastonbury in England advertised this way of life to a broader public. Rebellious youth culture went hand-in-hand with affluence and full employment. A combination of counter-cultural values and widespread dissatisfaction with the conformist consumer society of the 1950s found expression through commercial media and emerging youth markets in fashion and popular music. Similarly paradoxical was the fact that many of the Hippies and dropouts, who rejected the careers and lifestyles on offer from conventional society, belonged to

---

[27] See T. Roszak, *The Making of a Counter-culture: Reflections on the Technocratic Society and its Youthful Opposition* (London, Faber, 1970).

[28] Urwin, *A Political History of Western Europe since 1945*, p. 230.

the recently enlarged and state-funded ranks of university students, who came from better-off sectors of society.[29] In other words, those who benefited most from post-war affluence were most likely to reject (if only temporarily) its accompanying values and lifestyles.

The explosive social and political mixture of the 1960s was given major impetus by opposition to US involvement in the Vietnam War. In the dying days of the French Empire in Southeast Asia, America, as the dominant world-power after the Second World War, was drawn into the post-colonial morass. US involvement began modestly in the 1950s with the deployment of 'advisers', expanding gradually to become by 1968 a full-scale deployment of more than half a million American military personnel. The war resulted in some 2–3 million Vietnamese and almost 60,000 US deaths, with many more injured and disabled.[30] Opposition to the war grew in response to the escalating US involvement and daily reporting of casualties on the new medium of television. The introduction of conscription, which targeted men of university age, helped to provoke student activism. The combination of student radicalism and anti-war activism led to some of the most dramatic protests. A prominent organization throughout the sixties was Students for a Democratic Society (SDS) at Berkeley. Prominent events included the Vietnam Moratorium of 1968 and widespread sit-ins and demonstrations, culminating tragically in fatal shootings by the Ohio National Guard at Kent State University in 1970.

As with the peace and Civil Rights movements, student radicalism was criticized not only by conservative commentators, who were predictably hostile, but also by Marxists who regarded the students as a privileged and immature constituency. The student movement provided a new and appreciative audience for – and in turn received a more sympathetic response from – thinkers of the New Left. These included E. P. Thompson, who was active in the peace movement, Ralph Miliband in Britain, Herbert Marcuse and C. Wright Mills in the USA, Rudi Dutschke and 'Situationists' Guy Debord and Raoul Vaneigem in Europe. After the failure of official communist parties and their supporters to criticize the 1956 Soviet invasion of Hungary, New Left theorists sought to rescue the living kernel of Marxist thought. It was apparent to all but the most determinedly orthodox that the Soviet Union and Eastern European communist states could not be seen as stages on the way to socialism.[31] The New Left was more open to a

---

[29]   Indeed, many, like Richard Branson and Steve Jobs, would go on to successful careers in business and the professions.

[30]   On the Vietnam War, see D. L. Anderson, ed., *The Columbia History of the Vietnam War* (New York, Columbia University Press, 2011).

[31]   Some New Left thinkers were still attracted to Maoism and the cultural revolution in China; disillusionment with Maoism came later.

broad spectrum of issues, placing less exclusive emphasis on industrial conflict and labour organizations.[32] Marcuse and other thinkers interpreted alienation in much broader terms, extending the notion far beyond the sphere of production to encompass sexual repression, gender inequality and the exploitation of nature.[33] New Left thinkers were suspicious of bureaucratic hierarchies and the authority of the 'vanguard party' claiming scientific expertise in social transformation. The Stalinist doctrine of 'democratic centralism' was evidently little more than an excuse for autocratic rule. Their hostility to hierarchy and authority was confirmed by a commitment to prefigurative politics. The movement should *demonstrate* the values of freedom, equality and democracy that it aimed to bring about. A prefigurative politics should even be pleasurable. Indeed, only a pleasurable politics might avoid the authoritarian fate of so many revolutions, led by disciplined and ascetic militants who find satisfaction only in power.[34]

Both the New Left and much social movement activism emphasized the importance of grassroots or participatory democracy. Others, like Murray Bookchin, were drawn to anarchist ideas and styles of activism as well as a deep concern for ecology.[35] The anti-authoritarianism of the New Left made it more open to issues other than class. It was easier, as a result, for later theorists and activists to connect with the divergent issues of new social movements such as gender, racism, sexuality and ecology. E. P. Thompson and others looked back to the pre-Marxist past of the working-class social movement: to the formative years of the English working class when cultural activism, self-education and self-help were still prominent concerns.[36] These researches made it possible for later activists to connect with ideas, strategies and tactics that had been buried by the socialist tradition's overriding emphasis on class, party organization and state power. The counter-culture encouraged scepticism about the materialist emphasis on production and consumption shared by both defenders and Marxist critics of capitalism. Romantic philosophers and poets like William Blake could be acknowledged for their penetrating (if idiosyncratic)

---

[32] For example, The Student League for Industrial Democracy became Students for a Democratic Society in 1960.

[33] See Marcuse, *One-Dimensional Man* and *Five Lectures*.

[34] On the New Left, see V. Gosse, *Rethinking the New Left: An Interpretative History* (New York, Palgrave Macmillan, 2005), and K. Alexander and E. P. Thompson, eds., *Out of Apathy* (London, Stevens, 1960).

[35] See, for example, C. Pateman, *Participation and Democratic Theory* (Cambridge, Cambridge University Press, 1970); M. Bookchin, *Post-Scarcity Anarchism* (Palo Alto, CA, Ramparts Press, 1971); and Macpherson, *Life and Times of Liberal Democracy*, ch. 5.

[36] Thompson, *Making of the English Working Class*, and cf. above, chapter 2, pp. 41–2.

insights into the aesthetic and emotional deficits of industrial society. The ground was prepared for emerging concerns about nature and the environment.

3.5 From the Events of 1968 to New Social Movements

If the 1960s are widely known as a time of social upheaval and activism, the year 1968 stands out as a symbolic threshold to later social movements. It is dubious, of course, to claim particular significance for a single year or event, however noteworthy. That said, 1968 was an unusually eventful year. It was the year of the Viet Cong's Tet offensive, when the surprising vulnerability and shocking losses of US forces in South Vietnam spurred domestic opposition to the war. Martin Luther King and Robert F. Kennedy were assassinated. There were student sit-ins at Columbia University in New York, the London School of Economics, Cambridge University and many campuses in Europe, North America and Japan. It was also the year that student protests were suppressed in communist Poland. The Prague Spring led by Alexander Dubcek was cut short by the Warsaw Pact invasion of Czechoslovakia. Even more spectacular and symbolically potent were the Paris *Événements* or May Events of 1968.

The events themselves are well known and well rehearsed. Students protested against restrictions on visitors of the opposite sex to student accommodation at the University of Paris, Nanterre. Student demonstrations rapidly escalated in response to heavy-handed police actions. Workers stopped work in support of the students. When President Charles de Gaulle left France for a place of safety with French armed forces in Germany, it seemed that the government was close to collapse. Radical observers sensed the possibility of revolution. But if a revolutionary situation ever existed, it quickly disappeared. A general election was held and de Gaulle's conservative party was re-elected with a landslide majority. Although the government subsequently enacted some liberal reforms, it cannot be denied that the May Events had failed. However, what the events achieved in the short term should not detract from what they signified and the changes they provoked. These changes occurred on two levels: at the level of theory and ideology; and at the practical level of social movements and political events. In fact, as we shall see, both levels interact and cannot ultimately be separated.[37]

[37] For accounts of the political events of 1968, see A. Feenberg, *When Poetry Ruled the Streets: The French May Events of 1968* (Albany, NY, State University of New York Press, 2001), and A. Touraine, *The May Movement: Revolt and Reform* (New York, Random House, 1971), trans. L. F. X. Mayhew.

At the level of *theory and ideology*, the dramatic events of 1968 encouraged a further series of shifts on the left, increasing disillusionment with 'actually existing socialism' and the orthodox Marxist parties of the Old Left. The Soviet occupation of Czechoslovakia in 1968 was, like the invasion of Hungary in 1956, a severe blow. Closer to home, the May Events' challenge to the French state had not come about as a result of decisive leadership and disciplined organization by the French Communist Party (PCF) or the main trade union organization, the Confédération Générale du Travail (CGT). Their opportunistic attempts to regain control of the movement failed miserably and further alienated support. But even New Left thinking, which was more directly influential in the new activism, was for that very reason profoundly affected as well. Ironically, the ultimate failure of the uprisings also led to further distancing from socialist and Marxist assumptions of the centrality of class conflict. Although the New Left had been critical of bureaucratic socialism, they still assumed that the working class would be at the heart of any emancipatory movement. Gramsci's influential notion of 'moral and intellectual hegemony' accepted the need to assemble a broader coalition of constituencies and issues in support of socialism, but counter-hegemonic politics was still centred on the working class. After 1968, fewer radical thinkers and activists assumed that the working class would be the primary agent of change. The key role played by university students and teachers focused attention on broader transformations of culture, society and economy, which helped to explain the declining significance of class.[38] A related shift in New Left thinking was increasing distance from the faith of Marxism, social democracy and the labour movement in disciplined organization and state power. The many and varied events of 1968 were a potent reminder of the importance of the extra-institutional politics of social movements. The crisis of the French state had arisen from a diffuse and largely unorganized movement of school and university students and unorganized workers. Anarchist ideas and the unorthodox Marxism of the Situationist International had played a greater role than organizations inspired by Lenin and Trotsky. Murray Bookchin described the loose and fluid politics of 'affinity groups'.[39]

At the *practical level of movements and events*, the Events of 1968 were succeeded by a flourishing of new social movements. Second-wave feminism and women's liberation gained impetus from the beginning of the 1970s. One contributing factor was women's disillusionment with New Left activists who, despite their emancipatory ideology, still excluded women from important decisions and left them with menial

---

[38] See Touraine, *May Movement*, and cf. below, chapter 8, section 8.4.
[39] On 'affinity groups', see Bookchin, *Post-Scarcity Anarchism*, pp. 221–2. Compare the debate on 'spontaneism', above, chapter 2, footnote 39.

supporting roles. Women experienced sexual permissiveness and 'free love' as the freedom *of men* to enjoy women's bodies and sexuality. Second-wave feminists responded by radicalizing liberal feminist arguments for equal rights and citizenship. Socialist feminists pointed to the economic disadvantage of women and their 'double exploitation' by both capitalism and patriarchy. Radical feminists identified patriarchy as an overarching social order, which subordinated women to men in every area of life, from art, literature, philosophy and science to domestic life and sexuality.[40] Sexual liberation movements also emerged as significant social movements at this time. Sexual permissiveness in the sixties was not only patriarchal but largely heterosexual as well, treating homosexuality and other sexual variations as perversions. The riots at the Stonewall Inn in New York in 1969 sparked the US gay liberation movement, which inspired similar movements in the UK, Australia and other western countries after that. A separate lesbian movement emerged some years later in response to male dominance in gay liberation. Gay liberation did more than revive the apologetic humanitarianism of earlier proponents of reform. Arguments for the legalization of homosexuality and tolerance of diverse sexualities were embedded in a radical ideology of sexual liberation, which was influenced by Black Power and Pride. Gay and lesbian radicals sought to make connections with socialist and Marxist ideas, with feminism and psychoanalysis.[41]

Anti-racist campaigns also arose from the ashes of the New Left. Racial and ethnic discrimination were recognized as problems that could not be deferred until 'after the revolution'. The Anti-Apartheid Campaign was active internationally in support of Nelson Mandela and the African National Congress. The Aboriginal Tent Embassy, which began in 1972, was an important watershed in the emergence of an autonomous and assertive indigenous movement in Australia. In European countries, the children of migrants from the Caribbean, Africa and Southeast and South Asia fought against racial discrimination. Once again, there were complex relationships of support, tension and sometimes conflict between these movements and the organized left.[42] Green and environmental politics experienced similarly rapid

---

[40] On the origins of 'second-wave' feminism, see J. Freeman, 'Origins of the Women's Liberation Movement', *American Journal of Sociology*, 78:4, 1973, pp. 792–811, and cf. below, chapter 4, pp. 80ff.

[41] On the origins of gay and lesbian liberation, see A. Jagose, *Queer Theory* (Melbourne, Melbourne University Press, 1996), and cf. below, chapter 4, pp. 81ff.

[42] On the Aboriginal movement in Australia, see S. B. McGuiness, 'Black Power in Australia' in *Racism: The Australian Experience*, ed. F. S. Stevens (Sydney, Australia and New Zealand Book Company, 1977), 2nd edn, Vol. II, and cf. below, chapter 4, p. 97.

growth around the same time. A number of publications, including Rachel Carson's *Silent Spring* (1962), contributed to the growing awareness of the ecological costs of industrialization. Ecological activists openly challenged the left's longstanding claim to lead all the forces of opposition to 'the system'. Feminists, gays and lesbians, and anti-racist activists saw their own campaigns as autonomous, and by no means secondary (although perhaps related in complex ways) to class struggle. Some greens and environmentalists saw nature as a potential source of united opposition to the system, as the possible focus of an alternative 'counter-hegemonic bloc' to one centred on the working class, claiming to be 'neither left nor right but in front'.[43]

The new social movements would go on to produce significant and lasting changes to western societies. How much these movements were actually new has been much debated and is still contentious. Even from the perspective of the diminishing forces of the radical left – from the perspective of socialist and Marxist theorists and activists seeking the overthrow of capitalism – new social movements were puzzling. The new movements evidently bore little resemblance to the hoped-for working-class or 'proletarian' revolutions anticipated by Marx and Engels. In fact, some Marxists and mainstream social democrats were initially hostile to movements that they saw as diverting attention and energies from the defining struggle between labour and capital. Others on the left retained their belief in the industrial proletariat as the eventual 'gravedigger' of capitalism but strove for a more constructive engagement with the new movements as alternative sources of radical activists in support of a still essentially socialist agenda. The strongest advocates of the novelty of new social movements were those who finally broke from the class-centred analysis of Marxism and social democracy. These thinkers welcomed the new movements as possible successors to an increasingly quiescent working class, as a possible escape from the apparent stalemate of socialist politics. From this perspective, the new social movements were the diverse manifestation of a new proletariat made up of new and intrinsically plural agents of social transformation.[44]

The new social movements can be regarded as by-products of the decay of the New Left and associated student and left activism of the

---

[43] On the early stages of environmental and green movements, see A. Bramwell, *Ecology in the Twentieth Century: A History* (New Haven, Yale University Press, 1989), and cf. below, chapter 5, pp. 105–6.

[44] See below, chapters 7–9, for a more detailed exploration of theories of new social movements. Cf. D. West, 'New Social Movements' in G. F. Gaus and C. Kukathas, eds., *Handbook of Political Theory* (London & Thousand Oaks, CA, Sage, 2004), ch. 20, pp. 265–76.

1960s. But as by-products, it is difficult if not impossible to separate the levels of theory and ideology and of movements and events. Certainly, the new social movements display some novel features and, where their features are not entirely new, display them to a novel degree.[45] Where institutionalized politics was preoccupied with economic management, taxes, welfare and the distribution of wealth, the new social movements raise issues of gender and sexuality, the nature of the family and reproduction, peace, animal welfare and the environment. In contrast to the reigning assumption that politics in modern western societies is motivated by material self-interest, the new activists argued for non-material goods like pride, quality of life and autonomy. Sometimes they advocate *reductions* in consumption and *limits* to growth. Related to these differences in issues and values are innovative strategies and tactics. The new movements are less organized, less hierarchical and less bureaucratic. New Left and anarchist ideas of grassroots democracy and empowerment are taken up with enthusiasm. Tactics include personal politics and consciousness raising and the promotion of radical identities and pride, or so-called 'identity politics'.[46]

Neither agents and issues, nor forms of political action and organization are, of course, completely new. In fact, the new movements have encouraged academic research on the previously forgotten or 'hidden' histories of women, homosexuals, slaves, indigenous peoples and other constituencies. These studies remind us of the feminist proclamations of Mary Wollstonecraft and Abigail Adams in the eighteenth century and, in the nineteenth century, women campaigners against slavery, alcoholism and immorality and for women's suffrage.[47] Building on the achievements of nineteenth-century pioneers like John Addington Symonds and Karl Heinrich Ulrichs, Magnus Hirschfeld founded an energetic homosexual rights movement in Germany in 1897.[48] The wish to protect nature from industrial civilization is expressed in the poetry of William Blake and Romantics of the early nineteenth century, and

---

[45] These features will be examined in more detail in chapters 4 and 5.

[46] On the newness or otherwise of new social movements, see A. Melucci, 'A Strange Kind of Newness: What's "New" in the New Social Movements' in *New Social Movements*, ed. E. Larana, H. Johnston and J. R. Gusfield (Philadelphia, Temple University Press, 1994), and cf. below, chapter 8. For the politics of culture and identity, see below, chapter 4. Chapter 5 addresses the politics of nature, environment and ecology.

[47] See, for example, Evans, *The Feminists: Women's Emancipation Movements in Europe, America, and Australasia: 1840–1920*, and Banks, *Becoming a Feminist*.

[48] See J. D. Steakley, *The Homosexual Emancipation Movement in Germany* (Salem, NH, Ayer, 1993); Jagose, *Queer Theory*; and J. D'Emilio and E. B. Freedman, *Intimate Matters: A History of Sexuality in America* (New York, Harper & Row, 1988).

reverence for nature can, of course, be traced much earlier.[49] Forgotten and neglected traditions of socialism and working-class activism show that repertoires of political action were at first much broader than those favoured by Marxism and social democracy. Nineteenth-century anarchists and some early socialists (criticized by Marx and Engels as 'utopian') had already warned of the dangers of bureaucratic state socialism whilst advocating and sometimes practising tactics revived by 1960s movements, such as direct democracy, rotation of offices and the recall of delegates. Individual moral renewal and even 'free love' within alternative communities anticipated or 'prefigured' a more ideal society.[50] The 'making' of the English working class during the Industrial Revolution was less a matter of economic determination than a *self-making* through moral and cultural creativity, which has much in common with the identity and cultural politics of the new movements.[51]

The scale of the new movements and the prominence of their distinctive traits nevertheless provides qualified evidence of their historical novelty at the level of both theory and practice. In an age of human-induced climate change, nuclear weapons and unprecedented global ecological burden, the peace and ecological movements undoubtedly respond to a new historical situation. At the same time, the new movements reflect the distinctive theoretical and ideological context of their emergence. The theoretical shifts provoked by the failure of the New Left provided a novel lens for the interpretation of the new activism. From one perspective, the new movements may have been little more than a new cycle of protest, a new wave of challengers to established political institutions, who are destined to become incorporated within reformed political institutions.[52] But the new movements are also inspired by new ideas. The cultural and identity politics of the new movements is more self-conscious and durable than was the case for earlier movements. There has been an unprecedented flourishing of related critical theories in feminism, gay and lesbian liberation and queer theory, anti-racism and post-colonial studies. The concern with nature is more systematic and more scientifically informed. In green political thought, nature and the moral worth of non-human species occupy for the first time a central position. More generally, there is a new openness to the importance – both formative and enduring – of the extra-institutional dimension of politics.

---

[49] See K. Eder, 'The Rise of Counter-culture Movements against Modernity: Nature as a New Field of Class Struggle', *Theory, Culture and Society*, 7:4, 1990, pp. 28–32.

[50] On the history of socialism, see above, chapter 2, pp. 41–3; on prefigurative politics, see above, pp. 66–7.

[51] Cf. Thompson, *Making of the English Working Class*.

[52] See above, footnote 21.

Further Reading

For a historical survey and general background to the period, consult Tony Judt, *Postwar: A History of Europe since 1945*, and Derek W. Urwin, *A Political History of Western Europe since 1945*. For the May Events of 1968, see Andrew Feenberg, *When Poetry Ruled the Streets: The French May Events of 1968*. An account of the welfare state is provided by David Gladstone's *The Twentieth-Century Welfare State*. There are numerous accounts of individual movements: some examples are Kevern Verney on *Black Civil Rights in America* and Peniel E. Joseph on *The Black Power Movement: Rethinking the Civil Rights – Black Power Era*; April Carter on *Peace Movements: International Protest and World Politics since 1945*; on the history of ecology, see Anna Bramwell, *Ecology in the Twentieth Century: A History*. Van Gosse discusses the New Left in *Rethinking the New Left: An Interpretative History*. Annamarie Jagose's *Queer Theory* is a succinct account of the various phases of what became the gay, lesbian and queer movements. Rosemarie Tong's *Feminist Thought: A More Comprehensive Introduction* is just that.

4

Politics of Culture and Identity

Outline

The politics of new social movements emphasizes the role of culture and identity. Both in practice and in theory, anti-racist, feminist and sexual liberation movements combat cultural stereotypes, prejudices and oppression as part of their campaigns for recognition, political rights and equality. The focus on identity in this specifically political sense is associated with a range of distinctive strategies and tactics designed to transform the consciousness of both oppressed and oppressor and so to empower the movement's constituency. It is important to note that identity politics supplements and enriches but does not replace other politico-legal and economic dimensions of struggle. Once recognized, identity politics is readily found in other movements including those concerned with class. Whether based on chosen or unchosen characteristics, identity is always at stake as the subjective pole of the politicization of a particular group or constituency. At the same time, identity and culture figure differently within movements according to the size of their constituency and the nature of its relationship with the oppressor – whether that relationship amounts to exploitation, subordination, exclusion, stigmatization or mutual dependence. As critics of the 'essentialism of identity' make clear, identity is strategic and transitory rather than fixed, in the sense that movements aim precisely for the abolition of their identity *as political* or, in other words, as associated with some form of oppression.

4.1 Introduction: Features of the 'New Politics'

The 'newness' of new social movements results from an inextricable combination of facts and ideas. As Alberto Melucci comments regarding the 'symbolic thrust' of contemporary movements, 'we have been today awakened to take a better notice of the symbolic thrust of collective action through our encounter in actual society with phenomena in which this particular level [has] become more dramatically salient'.[1] New social movements emerged phoenix-like from the ashes of the 1960s' New Left, student radicalism and the counter-culture. These movements politicized new issues of gender, sexuality, race and ethnicity, animal rights and nature. Related shifts at the level of theory and ideology, as well as the perception that these extra-institutional challenges to affluent liberal democratic welfare states were surprising, encouraged the interpretation of these movements as *new* movements.[2] In this and the next two chapters, we will look in more detail at the transformation of both facts and ideas associated with these contemporary movements. The present chapter will focus on the role of identity, oppression and culture in contemporary social movements, or what is sometimes referred to as the politics of identity.

The politics of identity has become prominent in recent years as a result of the emergence of movements associated with newly salient political identities and conflicts and with the politicization of corresponding constituencies of women, gays and lesbians, ethnic and 'racial' and, more recently, religious groups. The women's movement politicizes differences and inequalities of gender between men and women. 'Racial' and ethnic divisions are addressed by anti-racist and ethnic movements. Gay, lesbian and queer politics are concerned with differences between people who identify as heterosexual or straight and those who identify as gay, lesbian, bisexual, transsexual, transgender, queer and so on. These issues and conflicts at first struck many observers as new, because they did not fit easily into the mainly socio-economic divisions between left and right, which had dominated institutional politics.

Attempts have nevertheless been made to understand the new conflicts in the terms of divisions between left and right, between progressive, conservative and radical. But although there is undoubtedly some association between the political left and new social movements, none of the new divisions is *essentially* about socio-economic differences. Gender, racial and sexual differences do not result from a person's socio-economic status or class position as conventionally understood:

---

[1] A. Melucci, *Challenging Codes: Collective Action in the Information Age* (Cambridge and New York, Cambridge University Press, 1996), p. 177.
[2] See above, pp. 71–5.

as wealthy or poor, as worker, manager or capitalist. These differences are, of course, frequently associated with socio-economic inequalities. Women have been (and still are) economically disadvantaged in comparison to men: they have been conventionally assigned to unpaid domestic roles within the family; they earn less income and own less property than men. Ethnic minorities similarly suffer discrimination at the hands of dominant ethnic groups in housing, health, education, employment and so on. The relationship between discrimination on the basis of sexuality and economic differences is less obvious: gay couples without children may be better off than the average. The important point, however, is that the new cleavages certainly cannot be reduced to such inequalities and they do not derive from them. The divergence between the 'new issues' and socio-economic factors has encouraged new ways of understanding social division, which involve recognizing cultural factors and identity as constituting an independent dimension of subordination or oppression.

4.2 The Politics of Identity

The concept of identity at the heart of identity politics refers to the manifold ways in which people identify themselves as members of a particular group, category or class. People obviously have many (perhaps even an infinite number of) characteristics, but they do not identify themselves in terms of most of them. The ways in which people identify themselves – their social identities – depend on what their society regards as salient or important. People identify themselves as men or women within certain family relationships, as free or slave, as farmer, merchant or warrior. In diverse societies, people are typically aware of other identities, reflecting their membership of particular religious or ethnic or racial communities. A social identity becomes *political* when it is recognized as the basis for political allegiances and action on behalf of the group in question. Political identities typically reflect relationships of power between dominant and subordinate groups. If these relationships are unquestioned, for example because slaves and their masters regard slavery as a natural institution, then the corresponding identities are not political. They only become political when the relationship is contested – in this example, when slaves contest their subordinate position. The emergence of new political identities thus corresponds to processes of *politicization*, so that previously unquestioned relationships or status become political issues.

The concern with identity and politicization adds complexity to liberal pluralist views of interest representation in two ways. First, from the perspective of liberal pluralism, different interests are the basis of collective actions (often through interest and pressure groups) to further those interests by political means. But liberal pluralism neglects the formative contribution of social movements and the cultural creativity involved in politicizing a previously non-political identity and, in that sense, forming a new political identity. A new identity must first define the interest of a particular group as a *political* interest. In addition, secondly, to the extent that social movements invoke notions of consciousness, identity and oppression, they further enrich the concept of self-interest by recognizing a dimension of subordination neglected by liberal and socialist traditions. Liberalism emphasizes civil rights and liberties, equality under the rule of law and, in its more democratic incarnation, equal political rights and representative democracy. Social liberalism and social democracy demand social rights to welfare, measures of economic redistribution and regulation of work and industry. Socialism sees capitalist economic relations as a form of exploitation. Beyond these legal-institutional and economic dimensions, the politics of identity emphasizes the cultural and psychological dimensions of subordination as *oppression*.

The notion of oppression refers to forms of subordination that are embodied in, and exercised through, social attitudes, norms and beliefs. Simone de Beauvoir provides an acute analysis of oppression in *The Second Sex* (1949), which adds a social and political dimension to Sartre's version of existentialism. Sartre sees freedom as a metaphysical absolute unaffected by social and political conditions, so that even a prisoner in chains can be said to be free. Beauvoir argues instead that individual freedom depends on the mutual recognition of subjects and, as a consequence, on social and political conditions. As Beauvoir puts it, 'Only man can be an enemy for man; only he can rob him of the meaning of his acts and his life because it also belongs only to him alone to confirm it in its existence, to recognize it in actual fact as a freedom. . . . It is this interdependence which explains why oppression is possible and why it is hateful.'

Oppression denies the subject's transcendence, assigning to an active self the status of a mere thing. For a person reduced to the status of a thing, genuine existence is no longer possible: 'living is only not dying'.[3] The result of systematically denying recognition to particular groups in society is oppression. Women as the 'second sex' are, of course, the primary focus of Beauvoir's account, but she applies the same notion of oppression to workers in a capitalist society and to victims of racism in a racist society.[4] In the absence of mutual recognition, oppressed individuals lack genuine freedom; they are constrained

---

[3] S. de Beauvoir, *The Ethics of Ambiguity* (Secaucus, NJ, Citadel Press, 1972), trans. B. Frechtman, pp. 82–3.

[4] S. de Beauvoir, *The Second Sex* (New York, Knopf, 2010), trans. C. Borde and S. Malovany-Chevallier.

and limited by their social condition. This is perhaps most obvious in the case of oppression on the basis of sexuality. It is intuitively clear that even if all legal obstacles and economic discrimination were to be removed, homophobia would still oppress gay, lesbian and transgender people in potentially devastating ways, a claim that is supported by, for example, statistics on youth suicides.[5]

The oppressed lack freedom, crucially, even when corresponding legal, economic and physical constraints do not exist or have been removed. This becomes clear if we consider a more extended example. The notion of oppression gained prominence through its role in the anti-racist politics of the African-American Civil Rights Movement and Black Power in the USA. Although claims of deep and essential differences between distinct 'races' have been shown to be illusory, racist attitudes and assumptions persist and have substantial detrimental effects on the victims of racism. Black Power activists and writers attest to the psychological and emotional suffering imposed on African-Americans by racism.[6] Consistently with Beauvoir's analysis, Black Power targets the subjective and cultural aspects of racist oppression as an independent dimension of racial subordination, which supplements and reinforces legal, institutional and economic dimensions. This means that, in addition to the material and institutional aspects of racism – denial of civil and political rights, inequalities of wealth and income, discrimination in housing and employment, segregation and apartheid – anti-racist movements must also directly target attitudes and beliefs.

Overcoming oppression involves redefining the interests and identities of those subjected to it. Furthering the interests of women, gays, lesbians or members of ethnic minorities involves challenging oppressive cultural attitudes and beliefs, which impose a limiting or constricting social identity. An oppressive social identity limits how the interests of the groups can be understood. By the same token, a movement of liberation both politicizes this social identity and proposes a more liberating understanding of the group in question. For the Black Power movement, this involved promoting positive views of black people with slogans such as 'Black is beautiful' and 'Black pride'. The women's movement has challenged the view of women as

---

[5] See, for example, A. P. Haas et al., 'Suicide and Suicide Risk in Lesbian, Gay, Bisexual, and Transgender Populations: Review and Recommendations', *Journal of Homosexuality*, 58:1, 2011, pp. 10–51, and M. Hatzenbuehler, 'The Social Environment and Suicide Attempts in Lesbian, Gay, and Bisexual Youth', *Pediatrics*, 127:5, 2011, pp. 896–903.

[6] On Black Power, see Joseph, *The Black Power Movement*, and F. B. Barbour, ed., *The Black Power Revolt: A Collection of Essays* (Boston, MA, Sargent, 1968). Steve Biko's Black Consciousness movement in South Africa was based on similar principles: see Meredith, *Mandela*, pp. 324–5.

irrational and unstable, as suited only to a domestic role. The gay and lesbian liberation movements have challenged the assumption that homosexuality is pathological by 'coming out', being 'out and proud'.[7] Transforming identity also involves the transformation of personal and even intimate aspects of people's lives, which helps to explain the popularity of the feminist slogan that 'the personal is political'.

However, oppression is not only a dimension of subordination that must be addressed in its own right, it is also something that must be overcome as a means to eliminate other dimensions. One reason for this is that oppression entrenches other forms of subordination: it is difficult to abolish forms of discrimination that are widely regarded as justified, natural or simply inevitable. Culturally grounded judgements that a particular group is inferior, less able or less moral serve to justify and so entrench legal, institutional and economic inequalities. In the ancient world, slavery was widely regarded as a natural and unalterable condition. Judging people to be inferior on the grounds of race reinforces their exclusion from citizenship and property rights. In apartheid South Africa, legal, employment and residential rights were allocated according to a racial hierarchy made up of Africans, Indians, Coloureds and Whites.

A related reason to be concerned with cultural oppression is the fact that it provides an always available basis for the reproduction of new forms of discrimination. If an oppressed group is able to achieve a degree of legal, institutional and economic equality even whilst oppressive attitudes persist, it is likely that new forms of discrimination will emerge in their place. After the abolition of slavery in 1865, African-Americans were the targets of a White Supremacist movement, Jim Crow laws (which enforced racial segregation in the states of the former Confederacy) and Ku Klux Klan terror tactics. Intimidation, segregation and violence reproduced many of the same effects as legalized slavery until (and somewhat less blatantly after) the 1960s Civil Rights Movement.[8] Despite the existence of anti-discrimination and equal pay legislation, women are still far from gaining political and economic equality. Whatever laws are in place, people will always find ways to discriminate.

Targeting oppression is a means to more general liberation for another reason: because oppression disables and disempowers its victims. Oppressive attitudes are to some extent internalized by those deemed by society to be inferior in the form of so-called 'self-oppression'. Self-oppression undermines the self-worth of its victims,

---

[7] Forms of political action associated with identity politics will be considered in more detail in the next section.

[8] On the African-American Civil Rights Movement, see above, chapter 3, pp. 64–6.

convincing them that they deserve their inferior status in society. It makes them less confident that they can achieve change by political means. Black Power activists argued on these grounds that an anti-racist movement must challenge not only unfair institutions and economic inequalities but also the racist assumptions underpinning them. To undermine oppression not only is worthwhile in its own right, it will also help to dislodge institutional and economic forms of subordination as well. Ending oppression will empower the constituency of potential activists and so strengthen the movement's ability to target all dimensions of subordination.

A number of other characteristics of identity politics flow from these basic features. In contrast to issues of economic distribution, conflicts at the level of identity and oppression, such as the conflicts between women and men or between ethnic minorities and dominant ethnic groups, are not straightforwardly 'zero-sum'. For class politics, it can usually be assumed that a gain for one group represents a corresponding loss for another. The poverty of the many can be eliminated only by extracting wealth from the few. With oppression, this is less obviously the case. Although women suffer from patriarchal attitudes and some ethnic groups suffer from racism, men and dominant ethnic groups do not *always* and *only* benefit from oppressing other groups. Men would be better off, at least in some ways, if they could engage in more equal relationships with women, which might be emotionally and sexually more satisfying. Men do not *always* and *only* benefit from patriarchal traits like aggressiveness and a lack of emotional sensitivity and self-awareness. Similarly, if racism were eliminated, dominant ethnic groups would no doubt be less wealthy and powerful, but they would benefit from living in a more harmonious and less violent society. Gay, lesbian and transgender people would undoubtedly benefit from greater acceptance of sexual diversity; others seemingly have nothing to lose but their prejudices.

Once it is recognized that identity and liberation from oppression are essential dimensions of political struggle, they can be seen to apply to economic conflicts as well. Working-class identity was itself, as we have seen, something that was achieved at an early stage in the movement. The formative stages of the working-class movement involved cultural challenges to oppressive stereotypes about the 'common people' and the value of manual as opposed to mental labour. Working people could raise demands for political rights and economic benefits only when they saw themselves as worthy of them.[9] It is important for political agents in general to recognize that the pursuit of even the most material interests and goals will be facilitated by changes of consciousness and identity. The pursuit of political goals by organizational

---

[9] See above, chapter 2, pp. 41–2.

and institutional means, which is now the main manifestation of working-class interests, is in danger of neglecting this dimension of change. So-called 'social movement unionism' recognizes the continuing importance of working-class activism. The alter-globalization movement can also be seen as a revival of social movement activism around essentially economic issues.[10]

At the same time, there is no reason for identity politics to neglect the institutional and material dimensions of subordination, which remain crucial. What is distinctive of identity politics is rather the recognition that material and institutional changes are always related to corresponding changes of identity, culture and consciousness. Similarly, class politics is not necessarily zero-sum or simply conflictual. Socialists would argue, in the first place, that capitalism is ultimately inefficient, because recessions and crises such as the global financial crisis of 2008 imply a dramatic underuse of productive resources. On the assumption that it could avoid periodic crises and slumps, socialist society would be more productive. So, although the rich might be less rich and the poor better-off, the changes to wealth would not be zero-sum. Secondly, socialism would maximize the satisfaction of needs rather than the production of 'exchange value'; much capitalist production is wasteful and/or serves distorted needs. Finally, since the economic mode of production is understood to influence the whole of society rather than just the economic sphere, its effects must be understood to be far more than simply economic. Alienation affects the whole of society and the lives of both capitalists and workers. So ending alienation would improve everyone's quality of life.

4.3 Strategy and Tactics of Identity Politics

New social movements have not only politicized new issues and established new ways for agents to identify themselves politically as women, as gay, lesbian or queer, as black or Muslim and so on. They have also made identity the explicit object of political strategy, tactics and action, challenging the usually negative and derogatory identities of subordinate groups. Thus, crucial to identity politics is the claim that politicized identities and the cultural assumptions associated with them *can be changed*. Identity politics aims to transform both the identities of the oppressed and the attitudes of their oppressors. This

---

[10] See P. Waterman, 'Social-movement Unionism: A New Union Model for a New World Order?' *Review (Fernand Braudel Center)*, 16:3, 1993, pp. 245–78; M. Novelli and A. Ferus-Comelo, eds., *Globalization, Knowledge and Labour: Education for Solidarity within Spaces of Resistance* (London and New York, Routledge, 2010) and cf. below chapter 7.

might occur *indirectly* as a result of changes to the oppressed group's legal, political and economic situation. Political, legal and economic changes may help to transform the self-consciousness and identity of the affected group and encourage a different evaluation of that group by the rest of society as well. The most effective way to change oppressors may be for the oppressed to change themselves: respect depends on self-respect; recognition by others depends on the oppressed having pride in themselves. But as the term 'identity politics' implies, particular identities and corresponding attitudes towards a specific group can be targeted *directly* as well. Supporters can be encouraged and mobilized to act. Opponents can be made to question their beliefs and attitudes and ultimately converted to (or at least reconciled with) less oppressive cultural assumptions.

Movements with a particular focus on oppression and identity employ distinctive strategies and tactics as well. These have, of course, much in common with those used by social movements in the past and, not surprisingly, the political repertoire they employ takes advantage of forms of political practice developed over previous centuries. They continue to strive for legal-institutional and economic changes and employ corresponding forms of action and organization. Even when addressing more distinctively identity-political goals of recognition, cultural transformation and pride, they organize demonstrations, lobby parliaments for legislative change, form political parties and promote ideas through books, journals and journalism. The distinctively cultural and symbolic concerns of identity politics do, however, have more specific implications for forms of political practice. Tactics designed to be deployed by a potential majority of the population in order to influence or coerce government are not necessarily useful modes of cultural politics. The militant style of nineteenth- and twentieth-century socialist politics achieved victories by force of numbers and demonstrations of strength. But where cultural transformation is involved, such tactics may be counter-productive, serving to entrench rather than undermine existing prejudices. The impact of sheer numbers, emphasized by Charles Tilly in his discussion of nineteenth- and twentieth-century social movements, is less critical for symbolic politics, although a disappointing turnout may have a negative symbolic impact on public opinion. Where a minority such as gays and lesbians is involved, then the sheer number of active supporters can, in any case, never be sufficient.

With the more open and activist campaigning since gay and lesbian liberation, it is the cultural message that becomes decisive. Political events organized and understood as a form of symbolic communication, such as the Gay and Lesbian Pride Marches in the UK and USA and the Gay and Lesbian Mardi Gras in Sydney, have been remarkably successful. The Sydney Mardi Gras began in 1978 as a conventional political demonstration, which was broken up by police who made a number of arrests. It has evolved into an extravagant cultural event that is widely celebrated far beyond the GLBT communities.[11] An important model for the identity politics of new social movements is Mohandas K. Gandhi's politics of 'truth-force' (*satyagraha*), which he developed in the first half of the twentieth century during the movement for Indian independence from the British Empire. Although the non-white, non-British majority in India might have overthrown British rule by sheer force of numbers, Gandhi advocated a campaign of strictly non-violent resistance, which relied only on the moral force of truth and moral conviction expressed through peaceful civil disobedience. Even in the face of violent repression, peaceful protests such as the Salt Marches both strengthened the resolve of independence movement supporters and undermined the British rulers' sense of entitlement and legitimacy.[12]

Although non-violence has been the preferred approach, confrontation and violence have sometimes played a role as well. Some activists were inspired by the confrontational and even violent tactics of some New Left organizations. But in the case of new social movements, acts of violence cannot really be serious attempts to enforce change or to take over the state. Such violence is intended to be symbolic rather than actually coercive. But it is often counter-productive nonetheless, undermining the movement's legitimacy and 'truth force' rather than strengthening it. From that perspective, terrorist tactics – adopted by the German Baader-Meinhof group and the Red Brigades in Italy – are particularly counter-productive.[13] At the same time, there are obvious limits to the non-violent, Gandhian approach. Against a ruthless, ideologically rigid and well-armed opponent, the ANC found itself compelled, despite its longstanding commitment to non-violence, to resort to armed struggle.[14] At the same time, the ANC's eventual victory would not have been possible without the moral and intellectual ascendancy achieved internationally by the anti-apartheid movement. The Civil Rights Movement in the USA achieved significant reforms

[11] See G. Wotherspoon, *City of the Plain: History of a Gay Sub-Culture* (Sydney, Hale & Iremonger, 1991), pp. 13–14 and 209–10, and cf. Jagose, *Queer Politics*, ch. 4.

[12] See above, chapter 2, p. 44. See M. Gandhi, *The Essential Writings of Mahatma Gandhi*, ed. R. N. Iyer (Delhi and Oxford, Oxford University Press, 1991), and M. Gandhi, *Hind Swaraj and Other Writings*, ed. A. J. Parel (Cambridge and New York, Cambridge University Press, 1997); and cf. Scalmer, *Gandhi in the West*.

[13] Violence was advocated by SCUM (Society for Cutting Up Men) and some contemporary Animal Rights activists. Terrorist acts were committed by the Baader-Meinhof group in Germany and the Red Brigades in Italy, but violence has more often been a tactic of the far right and agents of state power: see D. Bloxham and R. Gerwarth, eds., *Political Violence in Twentieth-Century Europe* (Cambridge and New York, Cambridge University Press, 2011).

[14] See Meredith, *Mandela*, ch. 9, esp. pp. 196ff., and cf. N. Mandela, *Long Walk to Freedom: The Autobiography of Nelson Mandela* (London, Abacus, 1995).

by essentially Gandhian means. But in 1968, both Martin Luther King and Robert Kennedy, a sympathetic Democrat candidate in that year's Presidential election, were assassinated and some activists turned to separatism and violence as a result. The movement for homosexual emancipation in some African countries is another case in point. The non-violent cultural politics of gay and lesbian liberation is not feasible in countries that inflict capital punishment on gay people and where homophobic violence is endemic.

The new social movements emerged in western liberal democracies where overt repression is sporadic and less brutal. The more positive or constructive cultural politics of movements of identity takes many forms. Demonstrations and other long-familiar political tactics are organized for cultural and symbolic effect rather than coercion or intimidation. The emphasis on personal transformation and radical identity encouraged novel modes of political action. Black Power's emphasis on the transformation of consciousness was taken up by second-wave feminism and the gay movement. Slogans like 'Black is beautiful' and 'gay pride' were symbolic assaults directed at the bearers of oppressive culture and those of its victims who had internalized it. Feminist 'consciousness raising' and gay liberation's insistence on 'coming out' as a demonstration of gay pride pursued parallel aims of cultural and psychological transformation. A controversial feature of consciousness-raising groups is the exclusion of those who are deemed to be oppressors – of men from women's groups, whites from anti-racist groups, heterosexuals from gay and lesbian groups. But it is difficult to see how a process of consciousness raising, which we have seen to be personal and even intimate, could take place under the gaze of those perceived to be oppressors. On the other hand, the exclusion of oppressors from consciousness raising does not equate to the separatist refusal of all common action or co-operation with people from outside the particular constituency.[15]

More congenial to the aims of consciousness raising were the non-hierarchical and sometimes anarchist organizational practices favoured by New Left, anti-Vietnam War and counter-cultural activists of the 1960s. Murray Bookchin describes the anarchist 'affinity group' as a loosely and informally organized group of people, often people who already know one another or belong to intersecting social networks. A number of observers of social movements have emphasized the role of informal networks as opposed (and sometimes in addition)

---

[15] On consciousness raising, see H. Eisenstein, *Contemporary Feminist Thought* (London, Unwin, 1984), esp. chs. 4 and 14, and S. Rowbotham, L. Segal and H. Wainwright, *Beyond the Fragments: Feminism and the Making of Socialism* (London, Merlin Press, 1979). Paulo Freire discusses 'conscientization' amongst illiterate peasants of Latin America: see P. Freire, *Education for Critical Consciousness* (New York, Continuum, 1973).

to hierarchical organizations.[16] Consciousness raising is thoroughly participatory in a way that conventional forms of organized politics are not. Unlike a conventional political organization, which may achieve its goals by mobilizing a large number of votes, an enormous petition or demonstration, consciousness raising is able to achieve its goal only through the active participation of each and every member of a group. It is essential that all participants share their experiences, if they are ever to succeed in transforming their consciousness. Leaders in consciousness-raising groups have a limited role in comparison to those in conventional modes of politics, because, although they may be more 'advanced' in their consciousness, their ideas can only be effective if they resonate with the experience of all participants.

Not surprisingly, the politics of language plays a key role in cultural and symbolic politics. Negative terms for people of colour were attacked by 'black' and then 'African-American' activists. In the 1970s and 1980s 'Asian' was favoured as an identity uniting the concerns of Indians, Pakistanis, Chinese and other groups, but it has now largely been replaced by terms for individual ethnic and religious groups. Second-wave feminism placed considerable emphasis on language.[17] In patriarchal society, words for women and all things female are frequently derogatory or demeaning. Terms for certain occupations, particularly prestigious ones, assume that the occupants will be male. Gay and lesbian liberation movements similarly rejected abusive terms often inspired by religion. Even the supposedly scientific term 'homosexual' is dubious, because it reflects the medical pathologization of homosexuality. The gay movement in Germany adopted the opposite tactic of substituting positive connotations for an originally insulting term *schwul* (equivalent to 'queer'). In the aftermath of the HIV and AIDS epidemic, English-speaking 'queer' activists reverted to that tactic under the influence of debates about the 'essentialism' of identity politics. The changing strategies and complex linguistic implications of the politics of language have given rise to conservative accusations of 'political correctness'.[18]

The cultural and symbolic ambitions of identity politics extend to political uses of music, art and other cultural forms. For the movements under consideration here, cultural and artistic manifestations of identity politics include Rock Against Racism, and rock and punk music.

---

[16] On 'affinity groups', see Bookchin, *Post-Scarcity Anarchism*, pp. 221–2. See M. Castells, *The Rise of the Network Society* (Oxford and Malden, MA, Blackwell, 2000), 2nd edn.

[17] See, for example, M. Macey and A. Carling, *Ethnic, Racial and Religious Inequalities: The Perils of Subjectivity* (Houndmills, Basingstoke and New York, Palgrave Macmillan, 2011); D. Spender, *Man-Made Language* (London, Pandora, 1990).

[18] See S. Dunant, *The War of the Words: The Political Correctness Debate* (London, Virago, 1994).

Popular music has been an important conveyor of rebellious and counter-cultural messages, although fascist and White Supremacist movements have also been able to exploit this medium. Style, clothes and image resonate with broader themes of youth culture to convey symbolic messages on behalf of a variety of movements. Once again, it is possible to find parallel strategies and tactics in class politics. The cultural expressions of working-class movements have a long and rich history. Trade union flags and insignia were important symbols of organizational cohesion, solidarity and tradition. Colour has played an important symbolic role in many historical movements. Just as the rainbow flag is associated with gay and lesbian politics, red has long been associated with socialism and the blood of workers. Black is the colour of anarchism, purple of women's suffrage and so on.[19]

An inevitable and problematic consequence of the focus on identity is the tendency for political identities to multiply and for movements to split. Because consciousness raising requires a context free of oppressors, problems are also created when there are overlapping and cross-cutting divisions. The early attempt to forge a unified anti-racist movement of all who identified as black gave way to movements of African-Americans and Asian, then Indian, Pakistani, Chinese, indigenous, Islamic, Hindu and Buddhist identities and movements. The women's movement was able to exclude men from consciousness-raising groups, but it experienced tensions between women of different class, ethnic, racial and religious backgrounds. The movement has since split into sub-movements related to different and hybrid identities of Muslim women, working-class women, lesbians and so on. Similarly, an originally unified gay movement split over divisions between (male) gays and lesbians, because women felt oppressed by gay men who occupied most of the leading positions and defined the movement's priorities accordingly. In the aftermath of queer politics, which sought to substitute an anti-essentialist, anti-identity politics of non-normative sexualities, there has ironically been a further multiplication of identities including (but by no means limited to) gay, lesbian, bisexual, transgender and intersex (GLBTI). In other words, the plurality of new social movements emerging in the 1970s has been succeeded by a further and seemingly endless proliferation of even newer identities and movements.

4.4 Varieties of Identity Politics

Diverse social movements have concerns with oppression, identity and empowerment, and employ (at various stages of their development)

---

[19] See M. Sawer, 'Wearing your Politics on Your Sleeve: The Role of Political Colours in Social Movements', *Social Movement Studies*, 6:1, 2007, pp. 39–56.

concepts of empowerment, radical identity and pride as well as related strategies and tactics. At the same time, there are significant differences between these movements as a result of differing relationships between the potential constituency and the natural opponents of the movement. These relationships can helpfully be compared to relationships typical of class politics, which had dominated both institutional and radical politics before the arrival of new social movements.

The definition of the working class is controversial, but by most definitions it is numerically much larger than the capitalist class. More recently, the Occupy movement has proposed a division between the 1 per cent and the 99 per cent.[20] The relationship of workers to capitalists in a capitalist society is mediated primarily by employment relationships at the site of production. Workers as 'wage labourers' are dependent on their employers for their income and, in societies without a welfare net, subsistence. In other areas of society, there is a degree of informal segregation in housing, entertainment, recreation and so on. Class relations are relatively permanent, persisting across generations, whilst still allowing a degree of mobility between classes. Some workers will ascend to positions of wealth and property ownership; some capitalists will lose their businesses and descend to the position of mere wage earners. These relationships between social classes in a capitalist society have obvious implications for the patterns of conflict between them. The numerical size of the working class supports both the electoral parliamentary politics of social democracy and the goal of revolution and state capture advocated by Marxism. The economic dependence but social independence of wage-labourers from their employers encourages strategies such as strike action and is compatible with class hatred. The possibility of social mobility and the importance of mobilizing working-class strength in numbers makes solidarity a prime value of workers' movements.

In ethnically or 'racially' divided societies like apartheid South Africa, divisions of race and ethnicity are more like divisions of class and caste, in that the members of different groups may interact economically but do not interact in most other ways. Interdependence exists only in the form of exploitation of one group by the dominant group. Separation takes the form of extreme differences of social status, as in the distinction between free citizens and slaves or indentured labourers. In other cases, racism eliminates most forms of contact by means of either legally enforced or informal segregation in areas such as housing, employment and education, and through bans on inter-racial marriage. In less segregated societies, ethnic differences may lead to informal separation with only marginal interaction. In contrast to the position of workers in a capitalist society, however, 'racial' and

---

[20] Some suggest that the division should be between the 0.1 per cent and the rest.

ethnic groups are often in a numerical minority, so they do not have access to the same electoral and revolutionary strategies as the working class. Capture of the state is not usually feasible, although nationalist secession (as, for example, in South Sudan) is sometimes an attractive option. Indigenous movements have sometimes adopted the goal of a quasi-nationalist secession within otherwise non-indigenous nation-states, although it is unclear what the status of any such arrangements would be in international law.

By contrast, relations of gender occur between groups who are evenly matched in numbers. But unlike differences of class, ethnicity and race, men and women are (when heterosexual) closely and even intimately related. Their relationships exist across all dimensions of life from the most impersonal (in public life and the workplace) to the most personal, emotional and sexual relations in marriage or de facto relationships. Men and women may have shared property in housing or business, although women typically have less control over it. More often, men are able to exercise power over women in both public and domestic spheres as a result of their greater access to wealth and income. The different relationship of women to men again results in significant differences of potential strategy. Women's numerical strength does not easily translate into coercive strategies, whether electoral or revolutionary, in part because the gender division cuts across competing divisions of class and ethnicity. The complex interdependence and intimate relations of men and women undermine any strategy based on outright hostility or (except for lesbians) separatism. Women's consciousness-raising groups (and the exclusion from them of men) are particularly central to second-wave feminism for related reasons. Women are constantly and pervasively subject to the influence of men and patriarchal culture, so consciousness raising is a difficult and ongoing task for a form of politics that directly impinges on the personal sphere.

Gays, lesbians and others who identify with 'non-normative' sexualities – sexual orientations stigmatized by traditional sexual morality – are minorities with no prospects of either majority rule or any kind of coercive takeover of the state. Like women, gays and lesbians live amongst other groups in society, in relationships which extend across a spectrum from legal, political and economic relations to family ties. A distinctive characteristic of sexual politics is the stigma attached to non-normative sexualities. This stigma – commonly if misleadingly referred to as homophobia – helped to enforce the invisibility of sexual minorities, who have become 'visible' only with the open assertion of their sexuality since gay liberation. 'Coming out' is both an assertion of the value of dissident sexualities and an essential step towards the formation of gay and lesbian communities, which are in turn a condition (or correlate) of emerging movements. Gays and lesbians (unlike bisexuals) do not usually have sexual relationships with people of the opposite sex and usually do not live in relations of economic dependence with them (except when they are children).

Of course, there are 'closeted' homosexuals, non-gay-identifying 'men who have sex with men' and non-lesbian-identifying 'women who have sex with women' who *do* live in such relationships. So separatism is an option for the gay and lesbian movement in a way that it is not for the (straight) women's movement, which only has the option of lesbian separatism. Sexuality is less directly connected with wealth and inequality than divisions of gender, ethnicity, race and religion. When members of sexual minorities are open and visible, they may suffer discrimination in employment and business. But socio-economic data suggest that lesbians are no more disadvantaged than women in general and that gay men are usually better off than average individuals from similar backgrounds. Movements of sexuality thus have better access to material resources, which to some extent compensates for their lack of numbers.[21]

There are interesting and complex contrasts between ethnic and sexuality movements. Most ethnic groups are visible and mutually aware, so they do not usually need to 'come out' and form a community as a first step towards the construction of a movement. Minority ethnic communities are able to develop their own self-assertive cultures and identities more easily than sexual minorities, because they live without constant and direct surveillance and interference from oppressor groups and cultures. On the other hand, visible ethnic groups are more easily excluded from economic opportunities and more liable to be subject to collective discrimination and punishment. The absence of social connections with members of dominant groups may lessen their political influence in comparison to sexual minorities, who exist at every level of society. By the same token, there are interesting parallels between movements of sexual identity and wholly or partially invisible ethnic and religious groups. Jews are not (despite racist stereotypes) physically identifiable as such. Muslims are often incorrectly assumed to be ethnically Arab, Asian or African and therefore visible, when there are in fact significant groups of ethnically Chinese and Thai Muslims as well as converts of all kinds. Assimilation to the dominant religion is a possibility for Jews in the face of anti-Semitism, just as homosexuals have had the option of repressing or hiding their sexual preference.[22]

---

[21] On the distinct situation of gay men, see C. Hewitt, 'The Socioeconomic Position of Gay Men: A Review of the Evidence', *American Journal of Economics and Sociology*, 54:4, October 1995, pp. 461–79.

[22] This is the basis for Proust's discussion of the relationship between anti-Semitism and prejudice against homosexuality in M. Proust, *In Search of Lost Time* (New York, Modern Library, 2003), 6 vols., trans. D. J. Enright, C. K. Scott-Moncrieff and Terence Kilmartin, Vol. IV, *Sodom and Gomorrah*.

In other contexts, Jews and Muslims adopt an ethnic model of identity which is, paradoxically, increasingly shared by sexual minorities who have now largely abandoned the anti-essentialist fluidity of queer identity.[23]

A related set of contrasts results from the difference between involuntary or ascriptive and voluntary or assumed social identities. Most obviously, gender and the characteristics that form the basis of race are not chosen. You are born male or female, white, brown or black. Sex is ascriptive but, in the era of sex-assignment therapies, can be changed.[24] It is impossible to change one's caste in India, although people campaign to remove the disadvantages of lower castes. Slaves may be liberated or may escape their servitude. Social mobility in class societies allows some people to move out of the working class to a higher socio-economic position or the reverse. Ethnic identities are usually ascriptive, but they sometimes allow for a degree of choice: you may choose to identify fully with your ethnic community or attempt to assimilate into the dominant culture. Religious affiliation is inherited from one's family or community, but it is possible to convert. Fundamentalist Muslims regard the abandonment of the one true faith as an apostasy that must be punished. Both anti-Semites and many Jews regard Jewish identity as something inherited and unchangeable and hence as a quasi-racial characteristic. The ascriptive or voluntary nature of sexuality is the subject of considerable controversy.

Equally complicated are the relationships between western new social movements and related movements in societies at different stages of social and economic development. Much discussion of new social movements assumes some kind of link between concerns with gender, sexuality and anti-racism and a certain level of development, affluence and education. Many of the activists in the western movements are 'new middle-class', educated to secondary and even tertiary levels, and enjoy easy access to varied sources of information, alternative values and ideologies. Ronald Inglehart's post-materialist hypothesis is a clear example of this approach.[25] By the same token, the emergence of similar movements in poor and less economically developed countries was not anticipated. This is ironic since, as we have seen, important sources of inspiration for the new social movements came from Gandhi's civil disobedience campaigns in India. The

---

[23] On the ethnic model of identity, see D. Altman, 'What Changed in the 70s?' in *Homosexuality, Power and Politics*, ed. Gay Left Collective (London, Allison and Busby, 1980), ch. 4.

[24] Sex-change operations are rarely considered to be a *political* strategy, although they have been criticized as gender-treachery. In Iran, sex-change operations are the preferred (and intensely homophobic) 'solution' for homosexuality.

[25] For more detailed discussion, see below, chapter 8, p. 181.

African-American Civil Rights and Black Power movements, which were also very influential, were supported by US citizens excluded from many benefits of the 'affluent society'. At the same time, there has also undoubtedly been a diffusion of ideas and forms of activism from western to less developed countries. Feminist, gay liberationist and anti-racist ideas have spread to the global South.

One common outcome is a tendency for the South's movements to have 'hybrid' characteristics combining identity-political concerns with more material issues, often giving greater emphasis to the latter. Deeper and more absolute, cross-cutting social cleavages of religion, ethnicity and race provide greater obstacles to unified movements than is the case in the West. Where movements from North and South have interacted directly, there are tensions and sometimes conflict. Some tensions reflect the different priorities women accord to particular issues: whether gender is the prime issue (as western radical feminists asserted) or class, ethnicity or religion. A particularly acute set of debates and conflicts surrounds the relationship between Islam and feminism – between those feminists who reject Islam as intrinsically patriarchal and those Islamic women who reject feminism as a secular and even immoral ideology. Other women attempt to negotiate the difficult path between Islam and gender equality.[26]

The gay and lesbian movements highlight different issues. Certainly, gay liberation emerged first in western countries like the USA, Britain and Australia, and similar movements have emerged in developing countries only more recently. But, although there are many links and much mutual influence between these different movements, the western ones have a tendency to ignore the dire situation of many gays in developing countries. Islamic countries are undergoing a revival of strict sharia law, which is interpreted to justify severe punishments for homosexual acts in countries like Iran. On a global scale, the death penalty and lethal violence are becoming more rather than less common responses to sexual diversity. Despite the severity of these repressions and the fact that in some African and Asian countries homophobia can be traced to the colonial-era export of Christianity, the western sexuality movements have largely reverted to an ethnic identity politics advocating legal equality for GLBTI people and the institutionalization of same-sex marriage.

Complicated North–South relations are also much in evidence around the issue of HIV/AIDS, which was originally perceived in the West to be a disease faced mainly by gay men, as well as intravenous drug users and haemophiliacs. Certainly, the HIV movement was largely initiated by gay men and lesbians. By contrast, in Africa

[26] On women and Islam, see H. Moghiss, ed., *Women and Islam: Critical Concepts in Sociology* (London and New York, Routledge, 2005).

and Asia the disease is either overwhelmingly heterosexual or indiscriminate in its impact.[27] The transnational links between related movements are further enhanced by processes of globalization, which have accelerated during the last decades. Cheap international transportation and rapid satellite and internet communications at the turn of the twenty-first century facilitate easier, more multi-dimensional and more frequent contacts between movements and the functioning of transnational organizations.[28]

4.5 Controversies and Critique

The region of politics conventionally labelled 'identity politics' turns out to be complex and multi-levelled. Issues of identity, culture and oppression are raised by a number of social movements, both new and old. Identity plays a role in two basic ways. For some movements – indeed, arguably for all movements – identity can be understood as the subjective pole of movement politics, the basis of allegiance and motivation. All participants must (explicitly or implicitly) identify themselves as members of a movement, which they see as representing their interests, values and goals. For some movements, such as anti-racist, women's and lesbian and gay movements, there is a more explicit concern to transform participants' identity. Activists aim to replace a more or less passive, hopeless and self-deprecating self-understanding with an active, confident, proud and empowered identity. But the transformation of identity is also a feature, whether consciously recognized and theorized or not, of the formative stages of all social movements. Any movement of the oppressed or exploited must first identify its particular constituency (as workers, the poor, the 99 per cent or whatever) and then challenge cultural assumptions that legitimize and entrench its subordinate status. The role of identity as the subjective pole of political action does not, of course, imply that 'objective' structural features do not play an essential role as well. Subjective identities always bear some relation to the distribution of resources, legal differences, events and so on. Even when the transformation of culture and identity are important and explicit concerns in their own right, identity politics represents only *one* dimension or level

---

[27] See M. W. Roberts, 'Emergence of Gay Identity and Gay Social Movements in Developing Countries: The AIDS Crisis as Catalyst', *Alternatives: Global, Local, Political*, 20:2, 1995, pp. 243–64; D. Altman, *Global Sex* (Chicago, University of Chicago Press, 2001).

[28] Another degree of globalization or internationalization is, of course, involved in the so-called 'alter-globalization movements' of the 1990s and 2000s: see below, chapter 6.

of movement politics: institutional, legal and economic concerns are inextricably involved as well. Identity interacts with underlying realities of interest, values and power, which provide an ongoing basis for and object of the movement's demands and activities. Any movement is likely to founder if its demands and analysis do not resonate substantially with the material situation of its constituency.

In fact, almost any difference, however trivial, can be the basis of discrimination and, by the same token, the basis of a political identity and a social movement. Jonathan Swift satirizes the tyranny of small differences in his account of the Lilliputian dispute between Big-Endians and Little-Endians, or, in other words, between those who open boiled eggs at the larger end and those who do the opposite. Swift has in mind the violent conflicts between Catholics and Protestants that ravaged Europe for two centuries after the Reformation. But differences that seem trivial to some have indeed provided the basis for destructive social conflicts and even civil wars between groups who take them very seriously. Skin colour is a good example of a difference that is intrinsically insignificant but socially significant.[29] Nor is this to deny that movements make mistaken and/or illegitimate demands. White Supremacists fight against perceived racial injustice, when *as whites* they are in reality more often the beneficiaries of racism. But the White Supremacist movement is still based on objective factors: such as the fact that its members are indeed white, that they may be educationally and economically disadvantaged and suffer low social status, poor education and so on.

Poststructuralist critiques of the 'essentialism' of identity politics are, in this light, only partially helpful. Essentialism here refers to the assumption that a particular (political) identity corresponds to some permanent underlying reality of essence – of sexuality, gender, race and so on. Critics of essentialist identity politics insist (as do, in fact, many proponents of identity politics) that there are no such correspondences and no such essences. The critique of the essentialism of identity is helpful, insofar as it reminds us that political identities are socially constructed.[30] Many identities depend on socially and culturally variable beliefs, values and attitudes. Differences that are noticed in one society may not be noticed in another. More importantly, the politicization of particular identities, even of identities based on physical characteristics such as sex or skin colour, obviously depends on socially

---

[29] Cf. Jane Elliott's blue-eyed/brown-eyed exercise to make school students aware of racism: see www.janeelliott.com/bibliography.htm.

[30] See, for example, L. Nicholson and S. Seidman, eds., *Social Postmodernism: Beyond Identity Politics* (Cambridge and New York, Cambridge University Press, 1995), and J. Butler, *Gender Trouble: Feminism and Subversion of Identity* (New York and London, Routledge, 1990).

and historically variable patterns of subordination and contestation. The politics of identity reflects society's prejudices and corresponding patterns of discrimination. When these patterns are politicized, so are the corresponding identities. For example, contemporary western movements concerned with sexual politics seek to legitimize sexual relations between members of the same sex, giving rise in the first place to gay and lesbian movements. Societies where sexual passivity rather than same-sex relations are stigmatized will inevitably give rise to different patterns of contestation. Again, Aboriginal politics is organized around a pan-Aboriginal identity which reflects the prejudices of white colonists. In Australia, pan-Aboriginal identity is a product of this repression: prior to European colonization, Australian indigenous peoples lived in diverse and sometimes mutually hostile groups, speaking different languages and subscribing to distinct religious beliefs and traditional laws.[31]

The socially constructed nature of identity also has consequences for the strategy and tactics of identity politics. In the first place, identities are strategic and transient rather than permanent and essential because, as the very notion of identity politics implies, the political status of particular identities is not fixed for all time.[32] The aim of anti-racist movements is to eliminate discrimination based on the illusory category of race (on skin colour, facial characteristics, etc.). Membership of a particular race would have no political significance in a society that ignored such distinctions. A society without sexual prejudices would not need a gay or lesbian movement. Differences between physical types and sexualities will always exist and may be recognized in the form of social identities. But in the absence of corresponding relations of subordination, these differences would have no intrinsic political significance – any more than eye colour and left- or right-handedness have such significance today. As other critics point out, there is a related risk, secondly, that the pursuit of identity politics will entrench people in – rather than liberate them from – their oppressed identities, reinforcing what Wendy Brown calls their 'wounded attachments'.[33] This risk is pertinent, because the movement's identity is the basis of its members' mutual solidarity, their emotional energy, courage and determination, which are required if the movement is to achieve its

---

[31] See J. R. Beckett, ed., *Past and Present: The Construction of Aboriginality* (Canberra, Aboriginal Studies Press, 1988).

[32] *Pace* over-hasty accusations of essentialism, the strategic nature of identity was recognized by early gay liberation theorists and activists. Cf. G. C. Spivak's notion of 'strategic essentialism': see S. Danius, S. Jonsson and G. C. Spivak, 'An Interview with Gayatri Chakravorty Spivak', *Boundary 2*, 20:2, 1993, pp. 24–50.

[33] Cf. W. Brown, *States of Injury: Power and Freedom in Late Modernity* (Princeton, NJ, Princeton University Press, 1995), and L. McNay, *Against Recognition* (Cambridge, Polity Press, 2008).

goals. But against this criticism, it is worth asking whether it is possible to avoid the risk without abandoning the social movement as a vehicle of activism and liberation.

Resistance to the essentialization of identity is important as well, thirdly, because essentialism encourages the degeneration of identity politics into an exclusive and separatist orientation to politics. An exclusive politics of identity treats a single overriding identity as pre-eminent, as what members of the movement really or essentially are. As we saw in the case of national and class identity, commitment to a single exclusive identity encourages the exclusion or subordination of other issues to the overriding priority of nation or economy and, as a result, the neglect and likely perpetuation of cross-cutting relations of subordination. When the universal claims of an exclusive identity are left unquestioned, then a separatist politics of identity is likely. For example, in the early years of gay liberation, (male) gay identity was prioritized, leaving lesbians, bisexuals, transvestites and transgender people further marginalized. In the separatist politics of identity, the exclusion of 'oppressors' from consciousness-raising and affinity groups is extended to other arenas of public life. The result is that the focus on personal transformation of identity is pursued at the cost of ignoring subordination in institutions, economy and the broader culture. Separatism isolates members of the movement from other aspects of their lives, from their other identities and allegiances: someone who is black may also be a lesbian, a lesbian may also be white and working-class; they cannot be liberated without pursuing all of these concerns. The fixation of separatist politics at the level of identity inhibits co-operation between diverse social movements and so fosters an irreducible fragmentation of opposition.[34]

The critique of identity politics is unhelpful, however, when it is taken to imply a wholehearted rejection of the role of identity in politics. As poststructuralists including Michel Foucault – one of the sources of the critique of essentialism – would probably admit, identity is a necessary basis for the constitution and mobilization of a movement of resistance against oppression. To insist that political action must avoid political identity altogether is to postulate a form of politics more diverse, diffuse and fluid than that of social movements. It may be appropriate to understand an individual's existential freedom as transcending particular identities. Individuals may indeed be free to move along 'lines of flight' between identities, convictions and attitudes.[35] But to base expectations of political transformation on this volatile and evanescent ground is to confuse the realm of personal freedom with

[34] See D. West, *Authenticity and Empowerment: A Theory of Liberation* (Brighton, Harvester Wheatsheaf, 1990), pp. 104–7.
[35] See P. Patton, *Deleuze and the Political* (London and New York, Routledge, 2000).

the necessarily (or at least commonly) collective engagements of extra-institutional politics and social movements. The experience of queer theory and politics illustrates this point. Queer theory emerged from a radical critique of the identity politics of earlier gay and lesbian liberation. Queer theorists made the valid point that sexual politics should include bisexual, transgender and intersex people, groups who were ignored and sometimes stigmatized by gay liberationists. Far from transcending the role of identity, however, queer politics has given rise (or, at least, given way) to a greater variety of increasingly specific and, in practice, essentialist identities. In Dennis Altman's terms, they function as *ethnic* identities: that is, as permanent and irreducible social and political constituencies. In this context, queer theory's anti-identity politics is more akin to utopianism; it posits an unattainable goal or limit of radical freedom.[36]

Like politics more generally, the politics of identity exists in the space between utopianism and fatalism. In order to avoid falling into utopianism, proposed forms of consciousness and identity must be feasible. The perennial political problem is, of course, how to identify feasible as opposed to utopian goals in advance. The only way to resolve such questions is by means of successful political action leading to desirable social transformation. For example, an important strand of the women's movement advocates gender neutrality on the assumption that all socially and politically significant differences between men and women derive from nurture or gender (under the influence of a patriarchal culture) rather than nature and sex.[37] The ideal of gender neutrality implies that boys and girls should be brought up to like and do the same things. But Martha Nussbaum questions whether this ideal is either possible or desirable. There may be differences of biology and neurobiology between males and females that make it impossible. It may not even be desirable to the extent that heterosexual desire thrives on gender differences. Feminism certainly implies that gender differences should not correspond to inequalities of power, wealth and status, but this does not mean that gender differences have to be eliminated as well.[38] The socialist tradition's attempt to replace the selfish and competitive individuals of capitalism with a model of 'socialist man' faces similar charges of utopianism. At least since the eighteenth-century Scottish philosopher David Hume, critics have

---

[36] For Altman, see above, footnote 23. The radical critique of identity thus resembles to some extent the radical existentialist freedom of J.-P. Sartre's *Being and Nothingness: A Phenomenological Essay on Ontology* (London, Routledge, 2003), trans. H. E. Barnes.

[37] By contrast, 'difference' feminists maintain that women and men are different but equal, or even that women are superior.

[38] See M. C. Nussbaum, 'Justice for Women!', Review of Susan M. Okin, *Justice, Gender, and the Family*, *New York Review of Books*, 8 Oct. 1992, pp. 43–8.

doubted whether human beings can be motivated to work and co-operate without the economic incentives of an unequal society, which implies that a socialist society would have to be authoritarian and coercive in order to be productive.[39]

The politics of identity also complicates the traditional objective of organizational unity. From the perspective of the 'old paradigm', effective action depends on the assumption of organizational unity, whereby a single organization (party or government) ranks policies and goals. Any departure from organizational unity undermines the strength of opposition and, for that reason, is vehemently resisted. However, an important result of debates inspired by the rise of new social movements is a rethinking of the assumption of unity. The theoretical and strategic discourses associated with new social movements are sceptical about the claims of any party or ideology to represent a historical project of universal emancipation. This scepticism was an important motivation for the formation of autonomous social movements in the first place. Only autonomous movements – of women, gays and lesbians, African-Americans and so on – are able to identify the complex roots of oppression, raise the consciousness of participants and challenge the broader culture. Only autonomous movements will act to end these forms of subordination immediately rather than postponing direct action to a distant future when other 'more fundamental' issues have been resolved.

At the same time, there are limits to the fruitful diversity and fragmentation of oppositional politics. Identity politics makes sense only as one pole of a dialectical process of differentiation *and reconstitution* of opposition. The diversity of movements and identities enriches opposition by uncovering previously hidden or neglected forms of oppression. But opposition is likely to prove ineffective, if movements fail to translate it into lasting and mutually reinforcing institutional, economic and cultural changes. Institutional reforms may be difficult and/or ineffective without corresponding changes to culture and consciousness. But conversely, changes to culture and consciousness will only have lasting effects if they are reproduced through education, cultural transmission and permanent institutional reforms. Whilst cultural and economic changes may be achieved by a diversity of agents acting independently, corresponding legal and institutional reforms require the organizational unity of governments and political parties. An exclusively anti-institutional approach to politics also raises normative issues. As Sheila Rowbotham has argued, the charismatic leadership of informal groups is potentially authoritarian, when it is not constrained

---

[39] See D. Hume, *An Enquiry Concerning the Principles of Morals* in *Enquiries Concerning the Human Understanding and Concerning the Principles of Morals* (Oxford, Clarendon Press, 1902), 2nd edn, ed. L. A. Selby-Bigge, §155, pp. 193–4.

by democratic mechanisms of accountability.[40] At a societal level, institutional protections such as liberal rights and democratic procedures
are essential for any legitimate political order. The organizational and
institutional levels of politics are, in that sense, never sufficient but
nevertheless indispensable.

That said, social movement activity within civil society is not merely
a formative stage preparing the ground for the later emergence of a
more mature form of organizational and institutional politics. Rather,
extra-institutional activism should be seen as a permanent level of
politics, which potentially persists alongside organized institutional
forms. So, for example, an electoral party may be persuaded to take
up some social movement demands, as has happened in the past with
some liberal, social democratic and now green parties. But that does
not mean that the social movement itself is redundant. The disappear-
ance of the movement only makes it more likely that the organization
will gradually retreat from its original goals. Contemporary labour and
social democratic parties, which owe their existence to earlier working-
class social movements and associated organizations, are now led by
professional politicians and advisers whose views and ideology are
far distant from those that they are supposed to represent. Even more
clearly, when a progressive party claims to represent the interests of
a variety of *other* constituencies – when labour and social democratic
parties claim to represent women, gays or ethnic minorities – it is clear
that continued pressure from the corresponding social movements is
required to ensure that the party remains faithful to its avowed goals.
Faced with a controversial issue such as same-sex marriage, members
of a progressive catch-all party will always be tempted to sacrifice idealist principles for the sake of pragmatic electoral considerations.

Further Reading

Identity politics is an intensely contested area within political theory
and philosophy. Some of the ideas presented in this chapter are
developed further in David West, *Authenticity and Empowerment: A
Theory of Liberation*. For discussion of related issues from a variety of
perspectives, see the essays in Linda Nicholson and Steven Seidman's
Social Postmodernism: Beyond Identity Politics. Iris Marion Young's *Justice
and the Politics of Difference* is an influential and wide-ranging discussion of some implications of identity politics. She defends a notion of
identity resistant to accusations of essentialism in her chapter 'Together

---

[40] On the potential for domination under informal leadership, see S. Rowbotham,
'The Women's Movement and Organizing for Socialism' in Rowbotham et al.,
Beyond the Fragments: Feminism and the Making of Socialism, esp. p. 41.

in Difference: Transforming the Logic of Group Political Conflict'. Positions more critical of identity politics are put forward by Lois McNay, *Against Recognition*, Judith Butler in *Gender Trouble: Feminism and Subversion of Identity* and Wendy Brown's *States of Injury: Power and Freedom in Late Modernity*. For readings on individual movements, see the suggestions made in chapter 3.

5

The Politics of Survival

Outline

The politics of survival is concerned with the survival of both human and non-human species in the face of emerging environmental threats. The rise of an environmental movement reflects a number of twentieth-century watersheds in the relationship between human society and nature. Ecological thought theorizes this relationship, challenging the short-sighted anthropocentrism at the heart of industrial society and defending natural ecosystems, biodiversity, animal welfare and sometimes animal rights. Emerging alongside other new social movements, however, contemporary ecological activism is also associated with a broad spectrum of characteristically 'green' (but not explicitly environmental) commitments to gender equality, the rights of gays, lesbians and other sexual minorities, social equality, participatory or 'grassroots' democracy, international justice, nuclear disarmament and peace. As a broad ideological coalition, green politics potentially spans the divide between institutional and extra-institutional politics. Green political parties exist alongside, and in complex relations with, diverse manifestations of green social movement activism.

5.1 Introduction: What Is the Politics of Survival?

Peace, environmental and green movements address what I shall refer to as the politics of survival. Although, like the women's, lesbian and gay and anti-racist movements considered in the last chapter, these movements have deep roots, they also have substantial claims to novelty. Although some of the issues associated with these movements have a long history, it is only from the 1960s that sizeable *movements* concerned specifically with these issues first emerged in western societies. What is more, their emergence at this time reflects a number of unprecedented historical developments and events, which help to explain why they are new.

Concern with nature, animals and the environment as well as action to protect them has a long history and can be traced to pre-industrial times, when local instances of pollution (if not the modern concept) were occasionally recognized as problems by rulers. Concern for the ill-treatment and abuse of animals is similarly longstanding. St Francis of Assisi, the early thirteenth-century founder of the Franciscan order, is well known for his love of animals. Closer intellectual precursors of environmentalism can be found in the Romantic reaction to industrialism at the turn of the eighteenth and nineteenth centuries. Klaus Eder describes the 'anti-modernist counter-culture' of German Romanticism advocating vegetarianism, the rights of animals and a return to rural ways of life. Romanticism in art, literature and philosophy railed against industrial society's polluted and ugly cities, the dire conditions of its factories, the obsession with 'industry' and neglect of the benefits of idleness. William Blake's poem *London* famously laments 'Every black'ning Church' and encounters everywhere 'Marks of weakness, marks of woe'. Thoreau's classic *Walden* celebrates a life lived in simplicity and closeness to nature.[1]

At the same time, contemporary environmentalism goes beyond any of its precursors in ways that reflect a series of historical events and thresholds. At the intellectual level, environmentalism in its contemporary form draws on two contradictory products of the Enlightenment. In the first place, ecological thought benefits significantly from the scientific heritage of modernity. Scientific ecology, which emerged early in the twentieth century, exploits the accumulated findings of sciences of zoology, botany, biology, organic chemistry and so on. At the same time, its holistic emphasis on the 'ecosystem' (a term introduced by Arthur Tansley) represents a departure from the analytical approach of post-Cartesian science. Secondly, however, environmentalism responds to cumulative effects – many of them negative – and historic thresholds of technological and industrial civilization. Whilst opposition to war is as old as war itself, the contemporary peace movement is significantly marked by the onset of the nuclear age. With the first nuclear explosions at Hiroshima and Nagasaki in 1945, the USA and then other powerful nation-states acquired for the first time the ability to destroy not only their enemies but human life itself. Even with the end of the Cold War in 1989, the

---

[1] See chapter 3, footnote 49. W. Blake, *Poems and Prophecies* (London and New York, Dent and Dutton, 1972), p. 31; H. D. Thoreau, *Walden* (1854), ed. J. L. Shanley (Princeton, NJ, Princeton University Press, 1971).

continuing proliferation of nuclear weapons represents a considerable threat.[2]

The human impact on the natural world has also passed a historic watershed. The depletion of resources such as oil and some precious metals will present severe challenges to industrial civilization, even if they may fall short of absolute 'limits to growth'.[3] Pollution is no longer a localized problem. Rather, the consequences of industrial civilization affect human and natural life at a global level. The world's human population expanded during the twentieth century from around 2 billion in 1927 to more than 7 billion in 2012, and is projected to expand to around 10 billion by 2050. Yet the 'ecological footprint' – the total impact on natural resources as a result of consumption and pollution – of the global human population is already estimated to be one and a half times the capacity of the Earth. If the degradation of land, fresh water and air quality were not sufficient, global warming represents an unmistakable and perhaps soon inescapable manifestation of humanity's burden on nature. This threshold has been described by some geologists as the onset of the *anthropocene* age – an era in which both climate and the evolution of species are determined predominantly by human factors.[4]

In the light of these events and developments, the emergence of a large-scale environmental movement is hardly surprising. In fact, a number of organizations have been concerned with the environment for more than a century. The British Commons Preservation Society, the Royal Society for the Protection of Birds and the US Sierra Club were all founded in the nineteenth century; the Wilderness Society was set up in 1935. But the 1960s saw the first stirrings of a mass social movement. A number of influential publications played a significant role in sparking the upsurge of activism. In *Silent Spring* (1962), Rachel Carson documented the damaging effects of widespread use of pesticides like DDT. Paul Ehrlich's *The Population Bomb* (1968) brought attention to the looming problem of an exponentially expanding world population, even if some of its scenarios of mass starvation were premature. The Club of Rome's widely publicized report on *Limits to Growth* (1972) argued that rapid economic growth is rapidly depleting essential raw materials and other natural resources. In the end, the clinching evidence of a mass environmental movement is provided by the sheer numbers of activists joining an array of groups and organizations, which have now become household names.[5] Greenpeace International

---

2 Cf. Bertolt Brecht's Postscript to *The Life of Galileo* (London, Methuen, 1964), trans. D. I. Vesey, and the Introduction to Arendt's *The Human Condition*.

3 Cf. D. H. Meadows and D. L. Meadows, *Limits to Growth: A Report for the Club of Rome's Project on the Predicament of Mankind* (New York, Universe Books, 1972).

4 On the anthropocene age, see above, Political Preface, pp. xi–xiii and footnote 4.

5 See R. Carson, *Silent Spring* (Boston, MA, Houghton Mifflin, 1962); P. Ehrlich, *The*

has grown rapidly from its Canadian origins in the 1970s to become a global organization with some 3 million supporters in more than forty countries. Friends of the Earth was set up in the USA in 1969 as a network of environmental organizations and is now also an influential world-wide organization. The result is that now far more people are members of green and environmental non-governmental organizations (NGOs) than are members of conventional political parties. The number of people who support environmental causes but do *not* belong to any particular organization is even larger but obviously difficult to quantify precisely.

Like the women's, lesbian and gay and anti-racist movements considered in the last chapter, the environmental and green movements have a number of distinctive features, which we will briefly examine in the rest of this chapter. Like movements concerned with gender, ethnicity, sexuality and religion, these movements challenge the materialist and class concerns of the 'old paradigm' of institutional politics. But unlike movements concerned with oppressed groups, environmental movements do not attempt to advance the position of some particular constituency or group of people. Nor is the politics of survival directly concerned with the politics of identity, although cultural assumptions about the value of consumption and materialism are important targets, and the movement aims to politicize a broad constituency who will identify with its goals. Environmental movements are strongly 'materialist', in the sense that they focus intently on the effects of production and consumption. But their concern with economics does not stem from self-interested or even altruistic demands for a greater share of goods for some group. Rather, they are concerned with the negative consequences of human productive activities on other species and the environment; they advocate either a reduction of or limits to production and consumption. For the first time, a major movement is primarily concerned not with relationships between human beings within society but rather with relations between human society and the rest of the natural world.

5.2 Ecological Thought: Nature as Subject of Politics

The politics of survival is concerned above all with the relationship between human societies and nature. The emergence of environmental and green politics in the last decades of the twentieth century repre-

Population Bomb (New York, Ballantine Books, 1968); Meadows and Meadows, *Limits to Growth: A Report for the Club of Rome's Project on the Predicament of Mankind*. Ehrlich's original, less sensational title was 'Population, Resources, and Environment'.

sents a marked shift from the inter-human concerns of the prevailing political paradigm. This shift is associated with a new ideology of ecology, which defines itself in opposition to the so-called 'dominant paradigm' of western modernity.[6] The latter term refers to a constellation of views associated with the secular and scientific world-view of western modernity, which displaced the predominantly religious thought of the European Middle Ages. Christianity placed humanity at the centre of a hierarchical cosmos and granted human beings rights of stewardship over the natural world. Its concept of stewardship implied the right to make use of animals and plants for our benefit, but also responsibility for the natural world. Although Christianity, like other religious world-views, regards human beings as the ultimate purpose of God's Creation, they are not regarded as separate or detached from nature. By contrast, the dominant paradigm of secular modernity no longer regards the natural world as a spiritualized realm that must be feared and revered as well as used. Instead, nature comes to be seen as a neutral resource to be exploited without limit or reserve in the service of human needs and wants. Whilst human beings are regarded as having intrinsic value, because they have eternal and immaterial souls, all other living creatures are no more than complex machines with only instrumental moral value. Animals are at our disposal, however painfully we might treat them and however trivial the benefit we derive from them – through, for example, vivisection, factory farming and the testing of new products on animals.

The modern world-view encouraged the rapid development of natural sciences, which equipped human beings with increasingly powerful tools for the manipulation and exploitation of nature. In the spirit of Francis Bacon's patriarchal remark that 'knowledge may not be, as a curtesan, for pleasure and vanity only, or as a bondwoman, to acquire and gain to her master's use; but as a spouse, for generation, fruit, and comfort', natural science has delivered an increasing technological grasp of natural processes and with that an ability to control them.[7] The translation of technological knowledge into control has been facilitated by the transition to capitalist forms of economy. The capitalist market and private enterprise (as both liberal defenders and Marxist critics acknowledge) provide strong incentives to develop new methods of production. The Industrial Revolution from the late eighteenth century and ongoing economic development are the result. Modern science, scientific medicine, industrial society and a range of manufactured goods have undoubtedly delivered significant

---

[6] See S. Cotgrove, *Catastrophe or Cornucopia* (London, Wiley, 1982). I will suggest in what follows that it is more accurate to regard ecology as post-ideological: see below, chapter 9, section 9.4.

[7] F. Bacon, *The Advancement of Learning* (London, Dent, 1915), p. 35.

material benefits. Advances in hygiene and medicine have dramatically reduced death rates, particularly among infants and children. Food production and a range of consumer products have contributed to the material welfare of an ever-increasing world population. The consequences in the twenty-first century, however, include the familiar and increasingly critical problems of pollution, environmental degradation and climate change. Concern about these consequences of industrial society's exponential growth is at the heart of contemporary environmentalism.

As the unintended consequences of industrial society became more apparent, some scientists were inspired to adopt a more holistic approach to the study of the natural world. In contrast to natural history and biology, which describe, analyse and classify animals and plants as isolated entities, the science of ecology studies natural species in all their complex interrelationships to their environment and other organisms. Ecology examines whole 'ecosystems' rather than just the biology of individual species. Scientific ecology shows that whole ecosystems may be transformed and even collapse as a result of human impacts on the environment. Because the relations between different species are so complex, these systemic effects may also be unpredictable. The science of climate change adds a new temporal dimension of possible variation to the complex interdependencies charted by the ecological sciences of the biosphere. Human impact on climate is evidenced by parallel rises in levels of atmospheric carbon dioxide and other 'greenhouse' gases like methane, and average temperature, since the Industrial Revolution. Climate or atmosphere, vegetation or biosphere, ocean chemistry and currents, polar ice caps and tropical rainforests, melting glaciers and rising sea levels, are all related in complex and as yet unpredictable ways. Indeed, we cannot assume that there is any simple, linear relationship between emissions and temperature, so accurate prediction may be in principle impossible. The holistic, systems approach of ecology and climate science alert us to the possibility of positive feedback mechanisms in the climate system. The melting of the Siberian permafrost may release huge additional amounts of carbon dioxide and methane. The loss of white Arctic sea-ice will reduce the albedo effect, whereby solar radiation is reflected back into space rather than absorbed by the Earth. Changing ocean currents may lead to unpredictable climatic effects. James Lovelock's Gaia hypothesis sums up this picture of the Earth as a single, complex and interdependent system, which is studied by Earth system science.[8]

Ecological thought takes its name and derives many of its distinc-

---

[8] J. E. Lovelock, *Gaia: A New Look at Life on Earth* (Oxford, Oxford University Press, 1987), rev. edn, and *The Revenge of Gaia: Why the Earth is Fighting Back – and How We Can Still Save Humanity* (New York and London, Allen Lane, 2006).

tive features from these scientific approaches. A radical strand of deep ecology or ecocentrism interprets the holistic perspective of scientific ecology in normative terms. As the name suggests, ecocentrism rejects the anthropocentrism of both religious and secular humanist traditions, which deem human beings uniquely valuable as either God's creatures or the only intelligent and rational animals. By contrast, ecocentrism insists that we should regard nature and all natural organisms as bearers of intrinsic moral value. They are valuable in their own right rather than merely as useful to human beings or, in other words, instrumentally.[9] Deep ecology typically also adopts a benign view of nature as a harmonious and balanced whole: nature is good both as a whole and in all its interdependent and complementary parts. Although deep ecologists place intrinsic value on every species and habitat, they differ over the relative value accorded different parts of nature. This raises many questions about the exact implications of this philosophy. Are all species to be protected, even ones that are harmful to human beings such as viruses, mosquitoes and tsetse flies? If human interests are given some priority, then a human scale of values is implicitly being used. What is the justification for giving human beings this priority? On the other hand, can we really get away from a human perspective on nature? Can an ideology that breaks so radically with the anthropocentric assumptions of previous political thought ever win substantial popular support? The task is especially demanding in developed societies whose populations have been deeply influenced by materialism and consumerism.

An alternative to deep ecology is humanist or shallow ecology, which advocates an enlightened instrumentalism regarding nature. In other words, it retains the anthropocentric assumption that only human beings have intrinsic moral value. Where deep ecology implies that we should protect ecosystems and species diversity because they are intrinsically valuable, humanist ecology implies that we should protect nature for *our* sake. But humanist ecology takes from scientific ecology a much more sophisticated and far-sighted understanding of the possible consequences of our actions. Once all the intended and unintended consequences of our actions are taken into account, it becomes clear that ruthless exploitation of nature is not in our long-term interests. So we should protect species diversity not just for its own sake, but also because we can never know which species might prove valuable to human beings. The most unglamorous species of mould and slime have been found to contain valuable pharmaceutical substances. Again, the pollution of the environment may also have unintended consequences for human and animal health. For example,

---

[9] See A. Naess, *Ecology, Community, and Lifestyle: Outline of an Ecosophy* (Cambridge and New York, Cambridge University Press, 1989), trans. D. Rothenberg.

minute traces of pharmaceuticals in the environment have led to the near extinction of some species of vulture in India, resulting in the spread to human beings of many diseases from decaying flesh that would have been consumed by the vultures. The requirements of intergenerational justice considerably reinforce the ecological implications of humanist ecology, which takes into account the interests of *future* generations. Those yet unborn obviously cannot be represented in parliamentary democracies, but they will undoubtedly suffer the long-term consequences of current patterns of production and consumption. We should consider the welfare of animals not only for their sake but also because cruelty to animals may encourage cruelty to other human beings. Human beings' aesthetic enjoyment of the beauty and fascination of nature implies that we should value the natural world in all its diversity: the loss of species and wilderness certainly reduces the quality of our lives. In all these ways, it is clear that even with its retention of anthropocentric assumptions, humanist ecology implies a radical transformation of industrial society.

In all its various manifestations, ecology demands a shift in the focus of politics away from the materialist commitment to economic and class issues that dominated party affiliations in western nation-states under the old paradigm. Ecology is anti-materialist insofar as it advocates limiting material consumption and encourages activities that do not impose a material burden on the environment. For example, enjoying natural habitats through eco-tourism does not, within reasonable limits, degrade the environment. Ecological goals nonetheless have a direct bearing on economics, since they can only be achieved by altering methods and reducing the scale of production. Unlike women's, gay and lesbian and anti-racist movements, ecological movements are directly concerned with the sphere of production. Ecological goals are not materialist in the conventional sense, however, because they do not directly aim for a redistribution of wealth or goods. Unlike class-based movements and parties, environmentalists do not argue that one group should get more and another should get less income, but rather that we should all want and consume fewer and less ecologically burdensome material products.

By the same token, ecology and the peace movement challenge the assumption that politics is largely self-interested and zero-sum, in the sense that gains for one group usually imply corresponding losses for another. To the extent that self-interested motivations persist, they are primarily concerned with *universal* survival rather than extracting benefits for one group at the expense of another. No one stands to gain from environmental catastrophe, although some have more to lose from measures designed to avert it. Everyone benefits from a healthy environment, although some may have more opportunities to benefit from it than others. In fact, many of the activities and enjoyments that would contribute to a less materialistic, less consumerist lifestyle – for example, conversation and sex, having a meal, creating and appreciating works of art, performing and enjoying theatre and music, playing sports and games – are intrinsically social, since they can be enjoyed only (or more fully) if others enjoy them at the same time.

Another contrast with women's, lesbian and gay and anti-racist movements is the fact that ecological politics is directly concerned with the economic sphere. Even though environmental activists do not aim for a larger share of wealth or goods for any constituency, they must obviously be concerned with the sphere of production. Ecology challenges neo-classical economics on the grounds that it ignores so-called 'externalities' of production: costs to the environment or community that are not included in the accounting of corporations. Figures for Gross Domestic Product similarly include only the value of goods produced, ignoring the loss of environmental habitats, depletion of natural resources and so on. As a result, they bias judgements in favour of environmentally destructive but (in conventional terms) profitable forms of production and growth. Environmental economists propose a 'triple bottom line' that would include such externalities. More ambitious ecologists have attempted to develop the economics of sustainable and steady-state economies.[10] With inequalities of gender or ethnicity, it may be enough for governments to enact anti-discrimination measures to encourage corporations to change inherited practices which have no direct or essential relationship to income and profits. Environmental demands, by contrast, often conflict with not only corporate interests but also the immediate interests of workers.

5.3 The Place of Ecology in the Green Movement

Ecological thought shifts attention to the relationship between society and the natural world and thus challenges the exclusively inter-human or intra-social focus of previous political thought and ideologies. Some strands of the environmental movement pursue ecological goals exclusively or, as some critics allege, as a form of single-issue politics that ignores other political issues and conflicts. However, an important strand of environmentalism contributes to a broader *green* movement, which adopts a range of positions characteristic of the concerns of new social movements. There are obviously local variations and internal differences, but in contemporary green movements there is a strong

[10] See, for example, H. E. Daly and J. Farley, *Ecological Economics: Principles and Applications* (Washington, Island Press, 2010), 2nd edn, and Paul Ekins, ed., *The Living Economy: A New Economy in the Making* (London and New York, Routledge and Kegan Paul, 1986).

association between ecological principles and commitment to peace and non-violence, opposition to nuclear power and nuclear weapons. Greens favour a participatory or grassroots style of democracy and often place strong emphasis on the role of extra-institutional social movements within civil society. They are critical of authoritarian, hierarchical and top-down styles of government. In addition, greens support women's equality in all areas of life. They defend the rights of gays and lesbians and support gay marriage. Greens favour cosmopolitan commitments to Third-World development and international social justice. Although not conventionally 'on the left', greens are critical of unregulated capitalism and unsympathetic to neoliberal globalization; they advocate greater equality both nationally and internationally.[11]

This raises the question of whether there is a systematic green ideology that can account for this range of positions or whether this constellation of positions is really a contingent product of historical circumstances. Ecocentrism or deep ecology does not provide an adequate basis for a broader ideology for a number of reasons. We have already seen that ecology has difficulty assessing the relative value of different species and other elements of the natural world. More generally, it is not obvious that scientific ecology can support the normative conclusions of deep ecology. From the perspective of science, which encompasses the universe's billions of galaxies, it is difficult to see what happens on Earth as particularly important or valuable. In any case, to attempt to deduce moral values from facts about the natural world involves what philosophers call the naturalistic fallacy. Even if we look to the natural world as a source of values, deep ecology's benign view of nature as a paragon of harmony is dubious. A scientific perspective on the natural world has certainly inspired less attractive moral visions. Darwin's theory of evolution through competition between species and survival of the fittest gave rise, in the nineteenth century, to social Darwinism and eugenics. According to this ideology, human society should be fashioned to resemble the ruthlessly competitive organization of nature 'red in tooth and claw'; the 'fittest' should be allowed to prosper without interference whilst the 'weak' should be left to die. Although deep ecologists do not, of course, follow this unattractive line, it is not obvious that they are entitled to their more benign normative conclusions.

The influence of the environmental movement has, in fact, encouraged the 'greening' of most major ideologies and the emergence of corresponding hybrids. But as we shall see, although each of these hybrids can point to some valid connections between ecology and

---

[11] On the green movement in Australia, see V. Burgmann, *Power, Profit and Protest: Australian Social Movements and Globalization* (Crows Nest, NSW, Allen and Unwin, 2003), ch. 4.

its inherited assumptions, these connections are not decisive. There was an early association between ecological ideas and anarchist or libertarian thought. A prominent exponent of this approach is Murray Bookchin. Having abandoned Marxism and Trotskyism, Bookchin proposed a 'social ecology', which emphasized the social sources of ecological problems and advocated the abolition of capitalism, decentralization of power and wealth, and face-to-face democracy at the municipal level as the solution.[12] Bookchin's ideas, which were in tune with the sixties' counter-culture and the New Left, undoubtedly had a significant influence on the emerging green movement's characteristic commitments to decentralization and grassroots democracy. Similar ideas were developed in France by André Gorz, who finds synergies between the anti-growth agenda of ecology and the early, humanist Marx's concern with the alienation of labour. The combination of rapidly developing technology and the ecological imperative to adopt a system of production geared to needs rather than ever expanding wants offers us, for the first time, the prospect of lives liberated from the alienation and drudgery of work.[13] It is less obvious, however, that anarchism has an essential (rather than merely contingent) relationship to ecology. Bookchin himself later became disillusioned with the individualism of much libertarian and anarchist thought, preferring the term 'Communalism'.

In fact, American libertarians have more often been sympathetic to capitalism, a tendency that has given rise to another hybrid ideology, namely eco-capitalism or eco-liberalism. These ideologies retain an overriding commitment to private enterprise and free markets, proposing private property rights and market mechanisms as the best means to achieve environmental goals. Eco-liberals point to the lesson of the 'tragedy of the commons', whereby property that is owned collectively tends to be exploited to exhaustion.[14] Every individual benefits from grazing more animals and no-one has an incentive to restrict their own usage of the common land, even though the inevitable outcome is overgrazing and ecological degradation. The eco-liberal solution is the creation of private property rights in the land and other threatened species and resources. Carbon emissions trading schemes are a currently prominent example. An obvious complication is the fact that such schemes can only be set up by government and, in the case of

---

[12] See Bookchin, *Post-Scarcity Anarchism*, and M. Bookchin, *The Ecology of Freedom: The Emergence and Dissolution of Hierarchy* (Palo Alto, CA, Cheshire Books, 1982).

[13] See A. Gorz, *Paths to Paradise: On the Liberation from Work* (London, Pluto, 1985), and *Capitalism, Socialism, Ecology* (London and New York, Verso, 1994), trans. C. Turner.

[14] See G. J. Hardin, 'The Tragedy of the Commons', *Science*, 162:3859, 1968, pp. 1243–8.

the global schemes required, by the agreement of many governments. With electoral constraints and competition between nation-states, such agreement is well known to be difficult to achieve. The more general problem with eco-capitalism is that private ownership and competitive markets generate increased production, consumption and use of resources. The power of large corporations is used to influence governments and to block policies that interfere with profitable enterprise. Eco-capitalism may be able to design eco-friendly mechanisms that might work in principle, but its ideology works against their adoption in practice.

Eco-socialism argues on the basis of these and similar arguments that capitalism is itself the main source of ecological problems. Capitalism vaunts itself on its ability to stimulate rapid technological innovation and economic growth. The social inequality promoted by capitalism encourages competitive consumption of 'positional goods'. By the same token, a socialist economy would focus on the satisfaction of intrinsically limited needs rather than potentially infinite wants or 'false needs' induced by marketing and competitive consumption. So a transformation to socialism would remove systemic factors intrinsic to capitalist economies, which promote continuous economic growth and ecological crisis. However, there are a number of problems with eco-socialist arguments as well. 'Actually existing socialism' was, if anything, more environmentally destructive than western capitalism. Even in social democracies, there are obvious conflicts between the interests of industrial workers, who have been its traditional supporters, and ecological concerns. The pursuit of jobs, wages and industrial expansion potentially conflicts with environmental goals of conservation, sustainability and the preservation of wilderness. If socialism is understood in ideal or utopian terms, there are currently few prospects of achieving it. The 'forward march' to socialism is everywhere halted or in retreat. The further development of capitalism on a global scale (with further growth in affluent countries and catch-up by less developed ones) is ecologically unsustainable, even if it could be expected to bring about an eventual transition to socialism. So although the ideal of an ecologically sustainable society resembles the ideal of socialism, there is little to be gained from tying ecological goals to socialist ideology.

Another example reinforces the point that green principles do not follow necessarily from ecological principles alone. Eco-feminism identifies some important connections between the 'dominant paradigm' (discussed above) and patriarchy. Scientific rationality is regarded as masculine. The patriarchal assumptions of early defenders of the dominant paradigm like Francis Bacon appear to confirm this relationship.[15]

---

[15] See above, p. 107 and footnote 7. Cf. A. Dobson, *Green Political Thought* (London and New York, Routledge, 2000), 3rd edn, pp. 189ff.

Bacon sees modern science as a powerful (and presumably masculine) tool for the exploitation and subjugation of a feminine nature. Eco-feminists accept this association between women and nature, seeing their role in childbirth and child-rearing as evidence of their closeness to nature. But although all of these points are true, eco-feminism is hard pressed to demonstrate any *essential* relationship between sex or gender and ecology. Women are as likely to be avid consumers, to own SUVs and to aspire to large homes. A view of women as natural child-bearers and mothers lies in some tension with the feminist critique of patriarchy, which confines women to just these roles. In some cases, this view has also led to ambivalence about women's right to abortion, virtually a shibboleth of the women's movement. These tensions are not relieved by some eco-feminists' apparent sympathy for pagan religion and mysticism.[16] Women's liberation from patriarchy might facilitate the transition to a more ecological society, but it would not make that transition inevitable.

The most interesting ideological hybrid is perhaps eco-conservatism, where conservatism is understood not as the ideology of free markets, private ownership and inequality – the tendency discussed above as eco-capitalism or eco-liberalism – but as the general disposition to resist radical change. Edmund Burke's reaction to the French Revolution and Oakeshott's criticisms of rationalism in politics set out the basic principles of this sort of conservatism. Existing institutions may embody a practical wisdom that has been slowly accumulated over generations. The rational ideals of modern ideologies are deceptively simple. When political movements set out to realize them – whether by revolutionary or reformist means – the results are often disappointing or even disastrous. There is no reason to believe that the historical process will automatically bring about a better society, so it is naïve and dangerous to support each and every change with dogmatic complacency. Although many changes since the eighteenth century – such as rapid advances in science and technology, the spread of affluence, state provision of education and health care, universal liberal and democratic rights – have surely brought great benefits, the contemporary ecological crisis suggests that a conservative disposition is now an unavoidable element in any viable common framework for contemporary social movements.[17]

In this context, green ideology must be seen as just another hybrid ideology, which combines ecological principles with a range of positions on a variety of issues that are characteristic of the new social

---

[16] On eco-feminism, see K. J. Warren, ed., *Ecofeminism: Women, Culture, Nature* (Bloomington, Indiana University Press, 1997); cf. the more materialist approach of M. Mies and V. Shiva, *Ecofeminism* (London, Fernwood Publications, 1993).

[17] See below, chapter 9, pp. 220ff.

movements on grounds other than strict ideological necessity. Rather, the constellation of green ideology corresponds to the range of new social movements that have been influential at the same time as environmentalism. As we saw in chapter 3, mass movements dedicated to the politics of survival emerged in the wake of the New Left, the counter-culture, anti-Vietnam protests and radical students' movements. They emerged alongside the women's, gay and lesbian and anti-racist movements of the 1970s. It is this historical context, rather than any necessary or essential ideological connections between ecology and a broader progressive agenda, which explains the contingent constellation of commitments that make up the green movement. In terms of the anti-essentialist Gramscianism of Laclau and Mouffe, green ideology can be described as a counter-hegemonic 'bloc', which 'articulates' historically associated but essentially independent issues and constituencies.[18]

One other possibility must be rejected: namely that the historical origins of green ideology and the green movement can be explained by some sort of historical necessity. An example of this sort of approach is Ronald Inglehart's post-materialist hypothesis. The anti-materialist and universalist emphasis of ecology leads Inglehart and others to suggest that the rise of ecology is a symptom of a broader 'post-materialist phenomenon', which can be explained by the growing affluence and security of western states delivered by the post-war economic boom, liberal democracy and the welfare state. The same period saw the expansion of universal secondary and free or subsidized tertiary education as well as the spread of electronic mass media such as radio and television. The post-materialist hypothesis is further supported by the mainly middle-class and 'new-middle-class' (rather than working-class) backgrounds of many new social movement activists. Inglehart's thesis is based on the psychologist Abraham Maslow's 'hierarchy of needs', which implies that once people have satisfied their basic physiological and security needs, they will focus on non-material ones: first the emotional needs of love and belonging, then self-esteem and self-actualization, and finally self-transcendence.[19] The substitution of 'post-materialist' for 'anti-materialist' is significant here, because it implies that the ideological shift we are considering has a particular causal explanation. Anti-materialism is explained as the effect of increasing affluence and security and, in the absence of any reversal of this increase, is presumed to be irreversible.

---

[18] Cf. below, chapter 9, pp. 212–13.

[19] See R. Inglehart, *The Silent Revolution: Changing Values and Political Styles among Western Publics* (Princeton, NJ, Princeton University Press, 1977), and *Culture Shift in Advanced Industrial Society* (Princeton, NJ, Princeton University Press, 1990). Cf. A. H. Maslow, 'A Theory of Human Motivation', *Psychological Review* 50:4, 1943.

However, the post-materialist thesis is questionable for a number of reasons. There are obvious problems with any assumption of a universal, cross-cultural hierarchy of needs, such as that proposed by Maslow in order to explain the transition from materialist to post-materialist modes of life. More specifically, there is no evidence that the shift from materialist to ecological concerns is psychologically or sociologically inevitable. Many materially poor and insecure societies are dominated by religious or kinship concerns rather than what we understand as economic ones. Conversely, experience of wealthy societies suggests that the pursuit of greed and self-interest is remarkably persistent. Affluence certainly allows for the satisfaction of basic material needs, but in a consumerist society affluence also generates new 'needs' or, more accurately, wants for new and ever more luxurious goods and services. Interestingly, many of these goods are actually marketed on the basis that they will satisfy emotional, psychological and spiritual rather than material needs. Typical products of consumer society promise to satisfy cravings for recognition, status, a sense of freedom and fulfilment, which partially confirms Maslow's hypothesis. But as long as the satisfaction of non-material needs is tied to material commodities, then the environmental impact is substantially the same. To cite just one example, over the last three to four decades, the average size of houses in Australia and the USA has doubled at the same time as the average household has almost halved.[20]

In fact, there is no reason to believe that increasing affluence will inevitably lead to a shift towards more ecological policies and values. What is worse, any attempt to explain future social movements as the inevitable by-product of historical development undermines the need to act politically and make choices now. So the concept of *post*-materialism is misleading and better avoided. It is more appropriate to see *anti*-materialism as an available political choice. Ecological politics is practically and normatively necessary as a response to looming environmental crisis. But it is by no means inevitable. The contingency of the ideological links between ecology and the other values comprising the green coalition is equally important for the same reason. If we cannot assume that environmental problems will generate an ecological response, we similarly cannot assume that an ecological response will inevitably take the relatively benign form of green ideology. If we fail to take action now to save the environment, we can be reasonably sure that there will be a severe ecological crisis or, more likely, a cascading series of such crises. But there is no guarantee that ecological crisis

---

[20] See C. Hamilton and R. Dennis, *Affluenza: When Too Much Is Never Enough* (Crows Nest, NSW, Allen and Unwin, 2005); and Australian houses have continued to grow after the 2008 financial crisis: cf. J. Curtin, 'Houses Too Big, Say Greens', *Sydney Morning Herald*, 1 December 2009.

will provoke a benign response, however belatedly: there is no reason
to assume that this response will be feminist, support sexual equality,
anti-racism, social and global justice and so on. There is no reason to
expect that participatory democracy will be favoured over more elitist
and authoritarian institutions. It is just as likely – indeed, in a situation
of crisis, it may be more likely – that belated responses to ecological
crisis will be elitist, authoritarian and even repressive. The ecological
concerns of Hitler's National Socialist regime testify to this possibility.
Ecological policies may ultimately be unavoidable if human beings are
to survive the present century, but *green* politics remains a matter of
collective political choice.[21]

5.4 Strategy and Tactics of Green Politics

In the contemporary context, ecological politics is, as we have seen,
a central component of a broader green movement, which includes
the issues of gender equality, sexual liberation and anti-racism, peace
and grassroots democracy, pursued as part of a broader alliance.
Accordingly, the strategy and tactics of the green movement include
those related to the movements concerned with identity and oppression
discussed in the previous chapter. At the same time, environmental
politics has some distinctive features, which are not shared by the other
strands of the green movement. This section will first consider strategy
and tactics that are distinctive of ecological and peace movements. It
will then look at forms of political action employed by the green bloc or
coalition as a whole. In contrast to feminist, lesbian and gay and anti-
racist politics, identity plays a less significant role in environmental
politics.[22] To belong to the environmental movement is not to have
an ecological identity in the same way that belonging to the women's
movement implies a feminist identity or that gay and lesbian people
affirm their identities. People who identify with, and support the aims
of, the environmental movement can, of course, be said to have an
ecological identity. But ecological politics is not directly concerned
with the transformation of an oppressed identity. Related to this point,
ecological politics does not aim to transform the status or esteem of
any particular group or constituency through the affirmation of pride
or cultural assaults on prejudice. However, ecological politics does
engage in cultural politics to the extent that it combats consumerism
and materialism.

The strategies of environmental politics are, for similar reasons, less
symbolic and more openly conflictual, in the sense that direct action

---

[21] See Bramwell, *Ecology in the Twentieth Century*.
[22] On the role of identity in politics, see above, chapter 4.

– sometimes in the form of civil disobedience – plays an important strategic role in the preservation of particular habitats and species, and in the prevention of pollution. Activists protect particular sites and associated species directly by standing in the way of loggers and bulldozers and by setting up camps in the canopy of endangered forests. Direct action is often illegal. Animal rights activists 'liberate' battery chickens and other animals reared for their fur or body parts. Sometimes direct action is potentially dangerous: environmentalist groups have destroyed sports utility vehicles (SUVs) in the USA; 'monkey-wrenchers' have spiked trees with nails, so that chainsaws cannot be used safely. Taking the willingness to endanger human life much further, the so-called 'Unabomber' committed acts of terrorism in his single-handed campaign against modern technology.[23] Other forms of direct action are more easily combined with symbolic and educational goals. Green consumerism is often criticized: as ineffective and easily co-opted by corporations, who sell products with green labels and pictures of dolphins; as little more than a way of salving one's conscience. But even if individual acts of green consumption make only a small contribution to ecological sustainability, their effects are significantly multiplied by their symbolic and exemplary value. Similarly, even though recycling only reduces pollution and waste to a small extent, it also helps to promote ecological goals more widely. More ambitiously, alternative communities devoted to self-sufficiency and less consumerist lifestyles both impose a smaller burden on natural systems and, as prototypes of alternative living, also have cultural and symbolic effects.

If symbolic politics plays a smaller (though still important) role, ecological politics is significantly concerned with science or systematic knowledge. Ecological awareness, as we have already seen, is strongly influenced by the holistic science of ecology. In contrast to the analytical and mechanical tendencies of much modern science, ecology investigates the complex interactions and interdependencies of ecosystems and, indeed, Earth or 'Gaia' as a whole. Contributions from scientists such as climatologists, hydrologists and biologists play an important role in ecological debates and campaigns. Current controversies surrounding climate science – between the 'believers' who affirm, and the 'sceptics' or 'denialists' who reject, claims of anthropogenic global warming – emphasize the degree to which science has been politicized.[24] The religious language of 'believers' and 'sceptics' is itself telling here. Nuclear power generates similar controversies

---

[23] See R. Young, '"Monkeywrenching" and the Processes of Democracy', *Environmental Politics*, 4:4, 1995, pp. 199–214; R. Arnold, *Ecoterror: The Violent Agenda to Save Nature: The World of the Unabomber* (Bellevue, WA, Free Enterprise Press, 1997).

[24] On Gaia, see above, footnote 8.

between scientific and economic 'experts' who proclaim its safety, environmental value and economic efficiency and alternative experts who argue that nuclear power is unsafe, unsustainable and inefficient. On these and similar issues, scientific experts and their interventions in public debate play an essential role in the environmental movement.

The close relationship between ecology and the economic sphere has important implications for strategy and tactics as well. Although ecology is not intrinsically concerned with distribution, its concern with the industrial mode of production leads to interesting parallels with socialism. As with the socialist movement, the environmental movement proposes both more and less radical remedies for environmental crisis. Andrew Dobson distinguishes between reformist environmentalism and revolutionary ecology, a distinction that is analogous to that between reformist socialism and revolutionary Marxism. Reformist environmentalism refers to a politics that advocates reform and regulation of capitalism in order to protect the environment. Some such reforms have already been implemented in the form of environmental protection agencies, clean air and water laws, national parks and ocean reserves and so on. Revolutionary ecology claims that such reforms will inevitably be insufficient, because current political and economic institutions and dominant forms of rationality and knowledge are incompatible with our ecological survival.[25] Only a radical transformation to a sustainable or even steady-state economy based on local small-scale production will save the planet. As with the contrast between reformist and revolutionary socialism, there is a complex relationship between radical *goals* and *strategies*. It might be thought that revolutionary ecologists are more likely to favour ecocentrism, whereas reformist environmentalists will opt for the less radical, humanist version of ecology.[26] But taken seriously (as we saw above), even humanist ecology implies a radical transformation of industrial society.

The breadth of green ideology – as compared to single-issue concerns with gender, sexuality or, indeed, the environment – means that green politics fits more easily into the institutional party politics of liberal democracy. Green ideology refers to a constellation of ethical and political positions that anyone can share, irrespective of their own individual characteristics and ascriptive identity. In addition, ecological commitments support a characteristic range of positions on the economy. Green ideology is able to compete with older ideologies such as liberalism, socialism and conservatism, which are rivals across the full range of social issues. For similar reasons, green parties are in principle able to attract a plurality or majority of voters. Green political parties have

[25] See Dobson, *Green Political Thought*, ch. 1.
[26] On the distinction between ecocentrism or 'deep' and humanist or 'shallow' ecology, see above, pp. 109–10.

prospects of electoral success not available to any of their constituent movements on their own. There have been a number of women's political parties, including Iceland's Women's List, but they are rare and have not achieved lasting success. The green movement has, by contrast, given rise to a number of ecology and green parties enjoying considerable and growing support. The German Greens (or *Die Grünen*), formed in 1979, have taken part at state level in governing coalitions with the Social Democrats. The Australian Greens are (at the time of writing) the third-largest party with the balance of power in the federal Senate and in coalition with the Australian Labor Party in the state of Tasmania.[27] Green parties can even aspire to be the alternative party of government.

Although green movements have given rise to successful electoral parties, a distinctive feature of their approach to political action is their only qualified reliance on electoral politics and enduring commitment to social movement activism. Reflecting their New Left and new social movement origins, green parties are inspired by the tradition of grassroots participation, Gandhian non-violent direct action and civil disobedience. They have correspondingly critical attitudes towards institutionalized and organized forms of politics, whether of left or right. So even when they take the electoral route to influence and power, green parties do not regard the green movement as a mere precursor of the mature institutional form, but rather as its essential and constant companion. German Greens have seen themselves as an 'anti-party' party. Social movement activism is a continuing level of politics alongside institutional politics, which aims to keep the party and its leaders faithful to the movement's aims and to prevent its co-option by the state and social elites.[28] At the same time, there is no doubt that green parties find it difficult to maintain effective links between party and movement. The pragmatism and compromises of electoral politics and government sit uneasily with the movement's idealism and antipathy to compromise. Green parties as a result tend over time to retreat from the idealism of the anti-party party.[29]

There are other tensions between green parties and institutional party politics, which result from the fact that green politics is essentially global or transnational in ways that other movements are not. Green politics shares with other movements participation in global civil society. But many environmental issues are *essentially* transnational in

---

[27] On the German Greens, see W. Hülsberg, *The German Greens: A Social and Political Profile* (London and New York, Verso, 1988), and T. Scharf, *The German Greens: Challenging the Consensus* (Oxford and Providence, RI, Berg, 1994). On the Australian Greens, see B. Brown and P. Singer, *The Greens* (Melbourne, Text Publishing, 1996).

[28] See Hülsberg, *The German Greens*, esp. pp. 118–24.

[29] See H. Wiesenthal, *Realism in Green Politics: Social Movements and Ecological Reform in Germany* (Manchester and New York, Manchester University Press, 1993).

ways that issues of distribution, gender and ethnic oppression are not.[30] In some cases, particular species and habitats are located entirely within one country or region and can be the object of a purely local or national campaign. But the solution of other environmental problems requires international action and organizations. The forests of much of Europe suffered from acid rain generated mainly in the industrial heartlands of Germany, the UK, France and the more 'successful' economies of former Eastern Europe. The survival of many species of fish and cetaceans depends on political action to prevent overfishing and whaling in international waters. The Antarctic raises significant environmental issues which are the subject of international treaties. The potential dangers of the nuclear power industry cannot be contained within national borders, as the Chernobyl and Fukushima disasters demonstrate. Airborne pollution is blown by the wind and spreads over wide areas beyond national borders and national control. Most familiar of all, global warming is a problem that requires concerted international action, if there is to be any effective solution. In effect, ecological politics is a hybrid of domestic and international politics, with significant consequences for strategy and tactics.

The intrinsically global nature of ecological issues has implications for organizational forms. The global nature of the politics of survival is reflected in a number of transnational organizations such as European Nuclear Disarmament (END), the World Wild Fund for Nature (WWF) and Greenpeace, which organize and act on a global scale. Their actions are wholly or partly beyond the control of particular nation-states – one example being the campaign of direct action by Greenpeace and Sea Shepherd against Japanese 'scientific' whaling in international waters. The global nature of many environmental issues presents acute collective action problems. As the issue of global warming demonstrates, it is particularly difficult to achieve effective and concerted action by independent nation-states to achieve a global public good. Any agreement that involves sacrificing profitable production is subject to the 'free rider' problem: the best outcome for any individual nation-state (in rational choice terms) is to gain the benefits whilst avoiding the sacrifices demanded by an international agreement. For that reason, world governments have (so far) conspicuously failed to build on the limited agreement to reduce emissions embodied in the Kyoto Protocol. Widespread civil society activism in a large number of countries has to date also failed to produce global action on climate change.[31]

---

[30] See L. Elliott, *The Global Politics of the Environment* (London, Macmillan, 1998). Obviously, in an era of corporate globalization, some economic issues are intrinsically transnational as well: see below, chapter 6, pp. 133–4.

[31] See A. Giddens, *The Politics of Climate Change* (Cambridge and Malden, MA, Polity Press, 2009).

5.5 Controversies and Critique

Environmental movements have certainly achieved some limited successes at the levels of consciousness, institutional reform and government regulation. With so far only minority support, green political parties have not yet achieved government except in coalition, usually with parties from the social democratic left. Prominent examples are green parties in Germany and Australia. As coalition partners, green parties have achieved some worthwhile reforms and policies: support for green energy, restrictions on carbon emissions, environmental protections and so on. But green parties have not yet reached levels of support required for permanent transformation of industrial society. At the same time, pressure from environmental and green movements has encouraged other political parties to adopt some environmental reforms. But these measures fall far short of what is required to ensure a healthy environment and flourishing human population. This failure is particularly obvious in the case of global warming, where international agreements have proved elusive or, when achieved, inadequate. There is a variety of diagnoses of this relative failure.

The ecological movement is accused of lacking an adequate theory of transition that would parallel the explanatory scope of scientific socialism. Despite (or perhaps because of) the closeness of radical ecology to revolutionary socialism, critics on the left argue that only socialism guarantees ecological survival and that only the strategic power of the working class as traditional agent of socialist revolution can ensure that transformation. But if the goals of the ecology movement depend on the success of revolutionary socialism, then its prospects are poor indeed. There are certainly some examples of working-class and trade union support for environmental campaigns and measures. The 'green bans' are a significant example in Australia.[32] Movements such as Chipko and the Zapatistas in developing countries demonstrate that ecological policies are sometimes compatible with economic goals.[33] There is no doubt as well that working-class support would be a great advantage to the environmental movement. But more often there has been conflict between environmentalists, workers and their trade union representatives. Workers in mining, forestry and nuclear power understandably oppose environmental measures that are seen to threaten jobs. The support of working-class people, who represent the majority

---

[32] For the socialist critique, see C. Boggs, *Social Movements and Political Power: Emerging Forms of Radicalism in the West* (Philadelphia, Temple University Press, 1986). Cf. M. Burgmann and V. Burgmann, *Green Bans, Red Union: Environmental Activism and the New South Wales Builders Labourers' Federation* (Sydney, UNSW Press, 1998).

[33] See below, p. 146 and chapter 6, footnote 36.

of the population by most definitions, is essential; it is less obvious that the working class will be significantly involved in their role or identity as workers.

If green ideology is to gain more widespread support, it must find a broadly persuasive answer to issues of distribution and social justice. As critics point out, there are in fact materialist and anti-materialist, universalist and conflictual or zero-sum aspects to *all* forms of politics, both ecological and non-ecological. Socialists would argue that everyone will benefit from a less exploitative, less conflictual and less alienated society. Feminists and anti-racists can claim that, although men and dominant ethnic groups might lose some benefits as a result of greater social equality, they would gain emotionally and morally. That case is even stronger in the case of prejudice against sexual minorities, which benefits no one, except perhaps the psychologically insecure. Conversely, ecological politics is not entirely either anti-materialist or universalist and non-conflictual. Some 'not-in-my-backyard' or NIMBY environmental activists are really concerned to protect their own amenities and the value of their own homes at the expense of the public good. Mostly well-educated and middle- or new-middle-class activists are unlikely to lose their jobs as a result of restrictions on forestry, nuclear power and other polluting industries. At the same time, less well-off citizens are more likely to live in heavily polluted areas near power stations, sewage treatment works, asbestos and mining waste dumps. They are also more likely to live in low-lying areas subject to risks of flooding and sea-level rise.

Relations between rich and economically less developed countries also present challenges. Anti-materialism and ideas of a steady-state economy do not transport easily from rich to poor countries. In poor and developing countries, ecology implies neither anti-materialism nor development as conventionally understood, but an *alternative* path to the fulfilment of essential material goals. This should perhaps be called *alter*-materialism. At the same time, ecological problems threaten the livelihood of people in developing countries more drastically and immediately than in rich countries. Loss of forests, deteriorating water supplies, degraded land and rising sea levels affect economically vulnerable people more acutely. This is reflected in the environmental activism of developing countries. The Indian Chipko movement defends forests essential for the survival of village communities. Environmental, economic and political concerns are combined in indigenous movements such as the Zapatistas in Mexico; forests are defended as an important source of food and other products for the sake of material survival as well as for their cultural value. Organizations like Survival International provide information about, and international support for, such activities. Environmental issues are also inseparable from issues relating to trade, production and consumption. In an unequal world, problems of industrial pollution are exported to poorer countries, which urgently need the income to be gained from waste-disposal and industries that are polluting.

Ecological thought thus stands to benefit from a cosmopolitan theory of social justice, which affirms the ecological value of social and economic equality in both domestic politics and international relations. Inequalities of wealth are sometimes defended on the grounds that they spur economic productivity and growth. On the same grounds, ecological politics can argue that equality is more compatible with economic sustainability and a 'steady-state' economy. Greater social equality would help to defuse the push for growth, ever-increasing consumption and competition for positional goods. Social inequality is tolerated when everyone has the prospect of increasing their individual shares of wealth and resources, even though others are increasing their shares much more rapidly. Once the prospect of ever-increasing wealth is removed, as ecological arguments imply that it must be, then social inequalities are no longer either tolerable or compatible with social harmony. Ecological thought does not face quite the same problem of combining economic efficiency and a dynamic economy with social equality that has beset the socialist tradition.[34] Efficiency in the use of natural resources and use value rather than exchange value may be served most effectively by a stable or steady-state economy.

A theory of social justice would help to locate ecological thought more securely within the field of post-Enlightenment ideologies. At the same time, it is important that ecology expunges any remaining Enlightenment faith in historical progress.[35] Progressive and radical visions of endless economic growth, which both left and right have shared in their different ways, are no longer plausible. The further development of industrial capitalism now threatens the diversity of species, the ecological health of the planet and human survival itself. But if ecology rejects assumptions of endless material progress, then ecological politics must also reject assumptions of a direction of history driven by economic and technological development. By implication, the ecological movement does not belong at any point on the conventional ideological spectrum from left to right.

As a popular green slogan has it, greens are 'neither left nor right'; but neither are they, as the slogan continues, 'in front'. If there is no

---

[34] The relationship between ecology and social justice is explored most often within broadly eco-socialist approaches: see T. Benton, *Natural Relations: Ecology, Animal Rights, and Social Justice* (London, Verso, 1993); D. Pepper, *Eco-Socialism: From Deep Ecology to Social Justice* (London and New York, Routledge, 1993); and M. Ryle, *Ecology and Socialism* (London, Century Hutchinson, 1988).

[35] Inglehart similarly places ecology within what amounts to a philosophy of history, which diverges from Marxism in seeing post-materialism rather than socialism as the outcome of capitalist development: see above, p. 116.

predetermined direction of advance, then greens are neither in front nor behind. In some ways, ecological politics is thus closer to the kind of conservatism that can be traced to critical responses to the Enlightenment and French Revolution.[36] Conservatives like Edmund Burke and, more recently, Michael Oakeshott reject the assumption that radical change is both inevitable and inevitably progressive. In contrast to traditional conservatives, however, the ecologists' commitment to social justice argues against the intrinsic value of hierarchy and social inequalities, which only serve to perpetuate environmentally destructive competition for status and goods. In that sense, ecology is not simply one ideology alongside other post-Enlightenment ideologies, which all take their stand in some way either for or against the presumed direction of history. Ecology belongs within a framework which places human agency rather than historical process at the centre of its thinking. Only political action can achieve an ecologically sustainable and genuinely humane society.

Further Reading

As its title suggests, Neil Carter's *The Politics of the Environment: Ideas, Activism, Policy* provides a comprehensive survey of ecological ideas, movements, parties and policies. Andrew Dobson's *Green Political Thought* is another useful introduction to these themes. A classic source of deep ecology is Arne Naess, *Ecology, Community, and Lifestyle: Outline of an Ecosophy*. Some connections between ecology and other ideological tendencies are explored in David Pepper's *Eco-Socialism: From Deep Ecology to Social Justice*, Martin Ryle, *Ecology and Socialism*, and by Karen J. Warren in *Ecofeminism: Women, Culture, Nature*. A classic text for liberal and neoliberal (or pro-market) approaches to ecology is Garrett James Hardin, 'The Tragedy of the Commons'. Alternative approaches to the economics of ecology are explored in Herman E. Daly and Joshua Farley, *Ecological Economics: Principles and Applications*, and Paul Ekins's edited collection, *The Living Economy: A New Economy in the Making*. The German model of green politics is analysed for a US audience in *Green Politics: The Global Promise* by Charlene Spretnak and Fritjof Capra, and from a German perspective in Werner Hülsberg, *The German Greens: A Social and Political Profile*. Global aspects of environmentalism are addressed in Lorraine Elliott's *The Global Politics of the Environment*.

---

[36] Radical ecology has been criticized as reactionary, to the extent that it advocates a return to a pre-industrial community more characteristic of rural than urban society. Cf. below, pp. 220–1.

6

The New Politics of Exploitation

Outline

Accelerating processes of globalization have transformed the context of social movement activism and given rise to an embryonic global civil society. At the same time, the currently dominant mode of neoliberal or corporate globalization has become the target of a new alter-globalization movement, which insists that another model of globalization ('another world') is possible. In the wake of the anti-materialist goals and identity claims of new social movements, alter-globalization represents a return to an essentially economic politics of exploitation. The movement is characterized more by diversity than by unity of purpose or ideology. Short of the world communist or anarchist revolution advocated by a minority, the movement more often proposes extending either minimal or more substantial social democratic institutions to the global setting. The new politics of exploitation supplements earlier socialist strategies of trade union activism and electoral or revolutionary state capture with strategies inherited from new social and pro-democracy movements or, in other words, social movement activism within the extra-institutional sphere of an increasingly global civil society. More recently, whilst the focus on globalization has waned, movements such as Occupy, the *indignados* and other responses to post-financial-crisis austerity policies maintain the concern with economic distribution and exploitation.

6.1 Introduction: A New Politics of Exploitation?

The alter-globalization movement, which came to prominence towards the end of the twentieth century, both reflects and reacts to a number

of independent but interacting developments associated with globalization. The prominence of the concept of globalization within
the social sciences bears witness to the importance of these broader
processes which, although they go back centuries, if not millennia,
are undoubtedly accelerating and in some cases reaching important
thresholds. The world is shrinking as a result of a number of interacting
processes, which have revolutionized communications, transportation and information technology. Economic relationships take place
on more levels, at greater distances and with increasing speed. A
growing number of political institutions cross national boundaries
and in some cases are global in reach. Social movement activism has
become increasingly global in response. But although the politics of the
alter-globalization movement is probably unprecedented, international
and transnational social movements are by no means completely new.
Early social movements were indeed primarily local and regional.
Before the nineteenth century, means of communication and transport
were, by contemporary standards, so slow that movements of greater
scope were impractical. The emergence of the modern nation-state and
nation-state politics began in the eighteenth and nineteenth centuries,
spreading from Europe to most of the developed world. The first
genuinely international movements were the anti-slavery movement
and revolutionary communism. Marxists contemplated revolution on
a world scale and saw communism as a social system that would no
longer need or tolerate differences of nationality.[1] Again, the new
social movements were already to varying degrees global in their
orientation, organization and activism. In a world already shrinking as
a result of spatial globalization, women's, gay and anti-racist activism
crossed national borders, even though the main targets of that activism remained within nation-state boundaries. For the peace, nuclear
disarmament and environmental movements, the globalizing tendencies common to social movement activism in the late twentieth century
are reinforced by the intrinsically global nature of their central issues.
Nuclear proliferation, many kinds of pollution and global warming can
only be addressed at the global level.[2]

   However, as its name suggests the alter-globalization movement
is global in the further sense that it directly and explicitly contests
the currently dominant mode of globalization. Because the movement does not necessarily oppose globalization as such, the term
'alter-globalization' will be used in what follows in preference to *'anti-*

---

[1]   Stalin argued against revolutionary communist orthodoxy for the possibility of
   'socialism in one country', i.e. the Soviet Union. See 'The Question of the Victory
   of Socialism in One Country' in J. Stalin, *Problems of Leninism* (Moscow, Foreign
   Languages Publishing House, 1947), 11th edn, pp. 156–66.
[2]   See above, chapter 5, pp. 121–2.

globalization'. The main target of the alter-globalization movement is neoliberal or corporate globalization, so it is obviously concerned directly with material and economic issues. This provides a contrast with the new social movements considered in previous chapters which, although they do not ignore them altogether, do relegate economic issues to a secondary status – after issues of identity and oppression, autonomy and survival. Unlike ecological and environmental movements, the alter-globalization movement is essentially concerned with inequalities of wealth and income. Belying claims of a new post-materialist politics, the alter-globalization movement is centrally concerned with issues of production, employment, trade, investment and distribution, demonstrating unmistakably that economic issues can still occupy the central ground of extra-institutional struggle. Members of contending social classes and people from countries enjoying unequal levels of wealth are affected in different ways by corporate globalization and they assume, not surprisingly, corresponding political stances towards it. In that sense, the alter-globalization movement represents a return to the politics of exploitation, which was associated with workers' movements and socialism from the nineteenth century.

However, although the alter-globalization movement revives issues characteristic of the 'old' politics of class, it does so in new ways. It is not just that, like many environmental issues, economic issues have now become unavoidably global in nature. After all, the international nature of both capitalism and revolution was a core principle of Marxism, which for that reason is often referred to as international socialism. But although revolutionary socialists are certainly one element of the movement, they are neither numerically nor ideologically predominant. The movement as a whole is not committed to socialism, even if it evidently opposes many aspects of capitalism. The aims of the movement are, if anything, closer to social democracy, albeit social democracy applied on a global scale. The main difference between the alter-globalization movement and both revolutionary socialism and social democracy is the movement's self-conscious emphasis on extra-institutional activism within civil society, which it has inherited from earlier waves of activism, including those of the new social movements.

6.2 What is Globalization and Why is it (Sometimes) a Problem?

As is perhaps already becoming clear, globalization is a complex and multi-dimensional phenomenon. It is important to understand the main dimensions of this phenomenon, if we are to understand the alter-globalization movement itself. It is necessary, if we are to understand both those sections of the movement that oppose globalization

altogether and the majority of the movement, which proposes alternative modes of globalization. In addition, it is important to understand
the complexity of processes of globalization, because they affect *all*
forms of extra-institutional politics, not just movements that directly
contest them.

Globalization can be defined as a set of social processes that displace
and/or supplement the predominantly national organization of economic, political, social and cultural space. The result of globalization
is that relations between human beings can be adequately understood
only by taking into account the global or transnational dimension.
Globalization is thus not just another way of referring to the familiar
topic of international relations, which has traditionally examined
relations between nation-states. Increasingly, human relations of all
kinds exist in ways that overlay, cut across and disrupt the binary
distinction between national or domestic politics and international
relations. Jan Aart Scholte defines globalization in these terms as the
spread of transnationality or 'supraterritoriality': 'globalization entails
a reconfiguration of geography, so that social space is no longer wholly
mapped in terms of territorial places, territorial distances and territorial
borders'. Globalization involves 'deterritorialization' and the 'growth
of "supraterritorial" relations between people'.[3] The concept of globalization is particularly significant in the humanities and social sciences,
because it challenges the assumption that political geography and
national boundaries provide the most useful conceptual framework
for understanding human affairs. The humanities and social sciences
have been dominated by the cognitive grid of nation-states, because
they emerged as disciplines in the modern period. From around 1500,
the 'civilizational' divisions between empires and religions, which had
already overlaid earlier tribal and nomadic groupings, gave way to a
national set of divisions based on the territorial boundaries of nation-
states. From about this time, politics and other aspects of human life
were understood mainly in national terms, supplemented by consideration of international relations, of diplomacy, war and trade between
states. But the national/international dichotomy has become less useful
as a result of a number of developments, some long-term and gradual,
some more recent and abrupt.[4]

In the first place, long-term but accelerating processes of what I shall
(for convenience) call *spatial globalization* affect the degree and speed of

---

[3] J. A. Scholte, *Globalization: A Critical Introduction* (Houndmills, Basingstoke and
New York, Palgrave, 2000), pp. 15–16 and 46–50.

[4] Scholte identifies three stages of globalization: the emergence of a 'global imagination' up to the eighteenth-century Enlightenment; 'incipient globalization'
from the 1850s to 1950s; and full-scale globalization from the 1960s to the present:
Scholte, *Globalization*, ch. 3.

contact and communication between different peoples. Human groups have always come into contact, sometimes in violent conflicts and wars, sometimes through trade and the exchange of goods, technologies, ideas and practices. As population increases, contacts become more frequent and less avoidable. World population reached 1 billion only around 1800, 2 billion some time in the 1920s and is now, less than a century later, over 7 billion. But the speed and intensity of human relationships is increased more predictably by improved technologies of transportation and communication. After millennia of relying on nothing more than human mobility, horses and sailing-ships, the first mechanized forms of transportation appeared only in the nineteenth century, with steam railways and steamships, then motorized vehicles and airplanes in the twentieth. Communications largely depended on transportation – messages had to be carried by messengers – until the invention and commercial development of telegraphy in the 1830s, telephone from the 1870s, radio from around 1900, television in the 1920s and the Telstar communications satellite in 1962. The internet, worldwide web, cell/mobile phones and social media have developed at an accelerating pace since the 1990s. The world is evidently shrinking faster and faster; the frequency and speed of contact between human beings is increasing exponentially.

The shrinking world helps to explain a second set of processes of *economic globalization*. Economic relationships between peoples in different parts of the world can, like spatial globalization, be traced back thousands of years to ancient spice routes and trade in precious stones, jewellery, pottery and tools. The ancient Empires of Egypt, Rome, China and Islam fostered dense economic relationships between distant regions as, in the modern period, did the European Empires of Spain, Portugal, the Netherlands, Britain, France, Italy and Germany. The nineteenth century was an era of relative stability in European international relations, which encouraged a flourishing of international trade before the catastrophic disruption of the 1914–18 World War and the Great Depression. Since the Second World War and during a prolonged period of relative stability, trade and other inter- and transnational economic relationships have increased once again. The intensity and range of these relationships has obviously been facilitated by the increasing speed and ease of transportation and communications. The contemporary form of economic globalization is, however, much more than a predictable result of cumulative economic developments and accelerating processes of spatial globalization. What is commonly referred to as neoliberal or corporate globalization is also a deliberate *ideological project*.

Neoliberal ideology has much in common with earlier, classical liberal economic doctrines. Neoliberal policies are by now familiar and, in basic outline, easily rehearsed. As Scholte puts it: 'Neoliberal approaches to globalization have . . . prescribed three general policies: liberalization of cross-border transactions; deregulation of market dynamics; and privatization of both asset ownership and the provision of social services.'[5] These policies imply a reduced role for states and for government regulation of the economy at both national and international levels. Neither classical liberalism nor neoliberalism are opposed to a strong state and state intervention in other areas of society – in particular, of course, property crime, the enforcement of contracts, law and order more generally, and defence against external aggressors. Thinkers associated with the neoliberal project include Friedrich Hayek and other members of the Mont Pelerin Society, Milton Friedman and the Chicago School of economists, and political philosopher Robert Nozick. Neoliberal ideas inspired Thatcherism in Britain, Reaganomics in the USA and 'economic rationalism' in Australia. Those who have pushed for neoliberal measures outside the academic domain include corporations and pro-business lobbies, governments and major political parties within most western countries, the commentariat of journalists (particularly financial journalists), economists and public servants in financial or economic departments of government. These are the proponents of what Michael Pusey has influentially (and critically) described as 'economic rationalism'.[6]

Like classical liberalism, neoliberalism advocates free markets, deregulation and the benefits of private ownership of productive assets. Like classical liberals, neoliberals are associated with business and finance or what the socialist tradition refers to as the interests of capital as opposed to labour. However, neoliberalism also differs from classical liberalism in a number of ways. The 'neo-' in 'neo-liberalism' refers to its more recent provenance and reactive nature. Liberalism in its formative years challenged the interests of landed property whilst attempting to keep wage-labourers in their subordinate position. Neoliberalism is an attempt to *reassert* classical liberal principles in the aftermath of social liberal and social democratic reforms, which had advanced the interests of workers and the less well-off. Neoliberal policies are designed to undo features of the organized, welfare state capitalism constructed in western states after the Great Depression and Second World War: the New Deal in the USA and welfare states in the UK, Western Europe, Canada and Australia.[7]

A further contrast with classical liberalism results from the fact that neoliberalism has been developed not just as a national ideology but as one designed for export to other countries. Elites who risked losing out to social democratic, socialist and other 'third way' models

[5] Scholte, *Globalization*, pp. 284–5.
[6] Pusey, *Economic Rationalism*, and cf. above, chapter 3, footnote 19.
[7] See above, chapter 2, pp. 59–63.

of development allied themselves with governments and corporations in western states in order to protect their positions of wealth and
privilege. Neoliberal reforms usually lacked popular support and were
introduced after either economic crisis, the collapse of communism
or the violent overthrow of democratic regimes considered hostile to
the West. What Naomi Klein calls the 'shock doctrine' was imposed
in a number of South American countries in the 1970s – this included
the coup against Chile's socialist President Salvador Allende in 1973.
Radical free market reforms were rushed through after the fall of communism in Eastern Europe and the Soviet Union after 1989. The same
collection of 'shock tactics' – in the form of the Washington Consensus
or conditions imposed by the IMF and World Bank – are now recom-
mended and often inflicted upon any country considered to be in crisis.
The austerity measures forced on the populations of Greece, Ireland,
Portugal and Spain in the wake of the global financial crisis are (at the
time of writing) a recent manifestation of the same approach.[8]

The overall impact of contemporary globalization, finally, is the
product of complex interactions between the various dimensions of
globalization described so far; and not all that is happening would be
endorsed by advocates of neoliberalism. Neoliberal policies, which
seek to break down any remaining barriers to a globalized market
economy, are being pursued at a time when they can have much more
profound effects. Accelerating processes of spatial globalization, technological advances and increasingly rapid communications combine
with longstanding (if uneven) processes of economic development over
more and more parts of the world to deliver what is arguably a qualita-
tively different level of corporate globalization. Because goods can now
be transported rapidly and (at least during periods of low oil prices)
cheaply, it is for the first time possible for production to be organized
globally. Corporations are able to take advantage of cheaper labour
and services and lower environmental and labour standards in many
developing countries. As a result, a product may now be assembled
in one place from parts manufactured in a series of countries and then
exported to consumer markets in Europe, the USA or Japan. A brand
owned by a US, European or Japanese corporation may be manufactured in an 'Export Processing Zone' in China, Indonesia or Malaysia at
a cost that represents a small fraction of the product's ultimate price.[9]
At the same time, because the internet allows almost instantaneous
sharing of information around the world, the movements of finance
and investment are virtually frictionless. Broadband internet facilitates
video conferencing in multiple countries, so management no longer

[8] See N. Klein, *The Shock Doctrine: The Rise of Disaster Capitalism* (New York, Henry
Holt, 2007).
[9] See N. Klein, *No Logo: Taking Aim at the Brand Bullies* (New York, Picador, 1999).

needs to be close to the actual sites of production. For the first time, there is not only extensive international trade but also a genuinely global organization of production.

6.3 The Contested Politics of Neoliberal Globalization

Neoliberal globalization is, as may already be obvious, an eminently political and contestable development. Crucially, it has fundamentally changed the balance of power between capital and labour. This is, of course, no coincidence. Neoliberal principles favour the freedom of capital and markets, not the interests of working people. It is often pointed out that, whilst the mobility of production and investment has dramatically increased, the mobility of labour, migrants and refugees is increasingly constrained. However, this is not really paradoxical, since it is precisely the globalization of production and investment that makes the mobility of labour unnecessary.[10] Waves of migration, which were encouraged in order to solve labour-shortages and provide cheap labour for unprofitable manufacturing industries in developed countries during the economic boom of the 1950s and 1960s, are no longer beneficial for capital. At the same time, the position of trade unions in both developed and developing countries has been weakened. Corporations are able to transfer production to the most profitable and compliant locations. Industrial action in any one location is no longer as effective. At the same time, the scope for profitable investment has been significantly increased, as newly privatized (or denationalized) industries and services become available as new sources of revenue.

It is a difficult task (and certainly beyond the scope of the present argument) to determine precisely the broader economic effects of corporate globalization on different sectors of the population in different parts of the world.[11] It is possible to concede, for the sake of argument, that pure market capitalism will promote competition, technological development and economic efficiency and therefore maximize aggregate economic growth. Neoliberalism claims to be the perspective of economic science and hence to advocate the best means to achieve these outcomes. Undoubtedly, some countries such as the 'BRICS' (Brazil, Russia, India, China and South Africa) have made dramatic economic

---

[10] An exception is often made for the migration of skilled and educated workers, for whom the costs of education and training are thereby effectively exported to another country, often a poor, developing one.

[11] For a largely favourable view see, for example, P. R. Krugman, M. Obstfeld and M. J. Melitz, *International Economics: Theory and Policy* (Boston, MA and London, Pearson Education, 2012), 9th edn; for a more balanced view, see M. B. Steger, *Globalization: A Very Short Introduction* (Oxford and New York, Oxford University Press, 2009), 2nd edn.

advances. Before the global financial crisis of 2007–8, it appeared that the world economy more broadly was in a very healthy condition. It is less easy to make that claim today. But even defenders of capitalism like Friedrich Hayek admit that markets distribute according to economic *value* rather than merit, let alone need or social justice. In other words, the distribution of wealth is determined exclusively by the market with no reference or relation to any other criteria.[12] Inequality is, by the same token, the predictable outcome in the absence of government regulation or intervention. Neoliberal globalization seeks to apply free market capitalist principles to the global context. To the extent that it succeeds, greater economic inequalities can be expected to occur across a wider range of societies. And, indeed, corporate globalization is associated with increases in inequality *within* both developed countries and developing countries such as China, India and resource-rich countries in Africa.[13]

At the same time, the contemporary context of corporate globalization does not spell the end of political and military conflict at the international level either. The rhetoric of free markets exists alongside the determined pursuit of national self-interest and *Realpolitik*. Free trade in manufactured goods and investments, which benefits rich and developed countries, is not extended to agricultural exports, which are the main source of income for many developing countries. Large trading blocs such as the European Union and super-states like the USA and China are able to exert disproportionate influence over international free-trade agreements and multilateral institutions, which accordingly tend to favour those countries' economic interests. As in the nineteenth century, the rhetoric of free trade has proved eminently compatible with a variety of essentially neo-colonial relationships.[14] Similarly discredited are arguments – advanced by Montesquieu and later liberal thinkers – that the spread of commercial society inevitably promotes the interdependence and peaceful co-existence of states. Certainly, it might seem that, since globalization reduces the significance and powers of nation-states, it must also reduce the likelihood of war, which during the last two centuries has mainly been the result of nationalist rivalries. But capitalist interests have encouraged wars of imperialism and colonization, wars for the control of scarce natural resources and lucrative export markets. Recent decades of

---

[12] Hayek, *The Constitution of Liberty*, ch. 6, 'Equality, Value, and Merit'.

[13] Inequalities *between* developed and developing countries are more difficult to assess: see above, footnote 11.

[14] Cf. M. Hardt and A. Negri, *Empire* (Cambridge, MA and London, Harvard University Press, 2000); R. Narula and J. H. Dunning, 'Industrial Development, Globalization and Multinational Enterprises: New Realities for Developing Countries', *Oxford Development Studies*, 28:2, 2000, pp. 141–67.

intensive globalization tell essentially the same story. The Iraq war of 2003–11 was in significant part an attempt to gain strategic control over the Middle East and its oil deposits. Wars in Iraq and Afghanistan and elsewhere have provided extremely profitable opportunities for corporations supplying not only mercenaries but also administrative, construction and many other services to US forces.[15]

Yet the political nature of neoliberal globalization tends to be obscured by neoliberal ideology which, like classical liberal ideology, presents the rise of global capitalism as an inevitable and unstoppable process. According to what can be described as the ideology of *globalism* corporate globalization is presented as the only rational option. The persuasiveness of any ideology is reinforced by the impression that there is no alternative to its recommendations. In the case of neoliberalism, this impression is promoted by failure to distinguish between globalization *in general* and *corporate* globalization. The neoliberal project is made easier, as we have just seen, by accelerating processes of spatial globalization which, in the absence of global catastrophe and widespread social collapse, will almost certainly continue. But this does not, of course, mean that corporate globalization itself is inevitable. Globalization should not be understood as an inevitable structural process but rather as a political process carried (and opposed) by agents, who are inspired by opposing ideas and ideologies. In effect, by ignoring the different dimensions of globalization, the essentially partisan political project of corporate globalization is presented as a straightforward rationalization or modernization of institutions. What *is* true is that once neoliberal measures are adopted, it becomes difficult to resist the power of global capital to influence government decisions (for example, through investment strikes) and thereby to outmanoeuvre labour organizations. Corporate globalization is, in other words, more easily constructed than dismantled.

The neoliberal project seeks to reduce the scope for politics in other ways. At the level of nation-states, neoliberalism implies that legitimate politics consists only in the administration of those policies required to sustain the legal framework of global capitalism. All interventions beyond those compatible with such 'minimal states' are, by the same token, illegitimate.[16] The ideally minimal government will be able to maximize aggregate production and wealth. Government's exclusive loyalty to what has been called economic rationalism means that other *non*-economic values should not be taken into consideration at

---

[15] Montesquieu claims that commerce naturally promotes peace: 'L'effet naturel du commerce est de porter à la paix': *De l'esprit des lois* in *Montesquieu: Oeuvres complètes* (Paris, Éditions du Seuil, 1964), Bk XX, §2, p. 651.

[16] A classic libertarian argument for the minimal state is R. Nozick's *Anarchy, State, and Utopia* (New York, Basic Books, 1974).

all.[17] So the social, cultural, educational and environmental costs of economic growth, inequality and instability are largely ignored or discounted – for example, when government services are privatized, 'outsourced' or reorganized in order to maximize productivity and efficiency. At the international level, the role of nation-states is simply to implement legal and technical measures required to facilitate corporate globalization. This involves transferring policy- and law-making powers from the nation-state to a variety of international institutions. Governments are 'encouraged' (pressured or coerced) by international lending organizations like the International Monetary Fund (IMF) and World Bank to privatize previously state-owned industries and services. Under the influence of neoliberal principles, states have removed controls over the movement of capital, investments and profits; transferred monetary policy from government to the boards of independent central banks; given up the right to subsidize particular industries. They have relinquished powers to impose tariffs and restrict imports on environmental, health and safety grounds.

At the same time, decision- and law-making powers have been transferred to a series of international bodies, which have largely been fashioned according to neoliberal principles and global *Realpolitik* rather than democratic norms, let alone ideals of social justice. The democratic credentials of the General Council of the United Nations (UN), set up in the aftermath of the Second World War, are overridden by the veto powers of the Security Council's permanent members Britain, France, the United States, Russia and China. Even when the UN is able to reach agreement on some position, it has (with rare exceptions) proved unable to enforce its will. Notable failures of the UN include the Belgian Congo, Iraq and Rwanda. Before the rise of neoliberalism and the Washington Consensus, the architecture of the post-Second World War economic order was determined by the Bretton Woods agreements, which were dominated by the victorious allies and, above all, the USA. These agreements set up the IMF and World Bank. Neoliberal ideology was more immediately implicated in the founding of the World Trade Organization in 1994. The Multilateral Agreement on Investments was a proposal – ultimately defeated by sustained social movement activism – to deregulate international investment. None of these international organizations is set up on democratic principles. Democratic accountability is assured only partially and indirectly through the intermediary of national governments. International organizations are dominated by the governments of rich states. As in state bureaucracies, officials and experts of international organizations often share social origins, educational background and ideological allegiances with more privileged social strata. The outlook

---

[17] On economic rationalism, see above, footnote 6.

of these officials and experts is strongly influenced, in particular, by neoliberal assumptions, neoclassical economics and the priorities of business and management. Most of them subscribe wholeheartedly to the Washington Consensus.[18]

The result at both domestic and international levels of politics is a serious *democratic deficit*. Economic issues that could once be decided exclusively by more or less democratic nation-states are now determined by global institutions wedded to neoliberal assumptions. In effect, the social democratic and welfare state compromises, which shared some of the risks and benefits of a market economy, have been either partially or wholly undone. What is more, because the reversal of social democratic gains has occurred at an international level and is combined with self-imposed but legally entrenched limits to state sovereignty, any return to more interventionist social democratic policies is extremely difficult.[19] In some cases, of course, nation-states could choose to reinstate national regulations and controls, but this would come at considerable short-term cost. One ambitious (and possibly utopian) option is to construct a 'cosmopolitan democracy' at the global level.[20] Corporate globalization obviously has implications for extra-institutional politics as well. To the extent that nation-state governance has been by-passed by processes of institutional and corporate globalization, it is simply not possible for exclusively national movements to achieve their goals. A major goal of neoliberal globalization, after all, was to neutralize the nationally based legislative and organizational power of labour. Conflicts concerning the sphere of production can henceforth no longer be confined to the national context. Only global activism can construct an alternative to corporate globalization.

6.4 Another World is Possible: Alternatives to Neoliberal Globalization

Against the anti-political and largely undemocratic implications of neo-liberalism, the alter-globalization movement asserts that there are indeed alternatives to neoliberal globalization. In the words of a popular slogan, 'Another world is possible.' As such, the movement serves to politicize the issues surrounding globalization and to resist their *de*politicization. However, as most observers point out, the alter-globalization movement includes a wide variety of diverse and often conflicting positions.

---

[18] Cf. Miliband, *The State in Capitalist Society*.
[19] See J. Habermas, *The Postnational Constellation: Political Essays* (Cambridge, MA, MIT Press, 2001).
[20] See D. Archibugi and D. Held, eds., *Cosmopolitan Democracy: An Agenda for a New World Order* (Cambridge, Polity Press, 1995).

Only a minority of the movement is opposed to globalization as such and so can accurately be described as part of an *anti*-globalization movement. These are what Scholte calls 'reactive radicals', who seek to avoid or undo all dimensions of globalization.[21] Short of the evidently utopian goal of reversing all processes of globalization on a global scale, groups opposed to globalization as such can only hope to avoid the consequences of globalization through various forms of economic independence and self-sufficiency or autarky. Such activists advocate a return to a world defined by nation-state boundaries. They take a variety of forms from economic nationalists, who want to reinstate economic barriers to foreign products, to religious fundamentalists who seek to impose Islamic, Christian or orthodox Jewish theocracy. Some radical ecologists propose a return to the largely self-sufficient rural communities characteristic of peasant agricultural societies. The problem with all of these forms of reactive radicalism is that they appear to accept a central tenet of neoliberalism: namely that *corporate* globalization is the inevitable consequence of *spatial* globalization. Because they wish to avoid the former, these radicals also reject the latter along with all its potential benefits.

By contrast, as its name suggests, the majority of the alter-globalization movement advocates a variety of alternative forms of globalization. Like the socialist movement before it (and with parallels in most social movements), a basic distinction can be made here between revolutionary and reformist approaches. What Scholte calls *proactive* radicals seek to 'take globalization further on a different structural basis'. Revolutionary approaches seek to overthrow the fundamental principles underlying processes of globalization. These have been understood variously as capitalism, western rationalism and industrialism. Global socialists return to the original internationalist agenda of revolutionary Marxism and seek global socialist revolution. Global postmodernism rejects the universal claims of western rationalism and the West's claim to represent the ultimate societal ideal. A variety of anarchist tendencies and groupings reject capitalism, all forms of state authority and traditionally authoritarian values of family and religion. In the global context, this naturally translates into a rejection of both national and international and global institutions.[22]

Reformist approaches, on the other hand, do not seek to destroy corporate globalization and its underlying assumptions root and branch, but rather attempt to mitigate some of its more negative effects by significantly modifying its trajectory. Reformist strategies do not challenge the basic or underlying principles of neoliberal globalization; they are designed to 'work within the bounds of capitalist production,

---

[21] Scholte, *Globalization*, p. 285.
[22] Scholte, *Globalization*, pp. 285–7.

bureaucratic governance, communitarian community and rationalist knowledge'. But these approaches do reject the implementation of neoliberal policies and, in particular, its restrictive view of the scope of legitimate state intervention in the economy. They seek instead to 'generate greater security, equity and democracy by means of proactive public policies'.[23] Obviously, as elements of a movement concerned with globalization, they pursue such measures not just at the national level but at the global level as well. They thus propose a combination of state policies and additional or transformed international and transnational institutions. There are more and less radical versions of this reformist agenda. What Scholte calls 'thin' reformism proposes a global basic welfare net, which would secure the lives of all people against absolute poverty, unemployment and insecurity. In effect, this would amount to something like the US or Japanese level of welfare provision but on a global scale. Modest though this level of social protection might seem, it would still be a radical departure from the current state of global governance, which tolerates starvation and abject poverty and provides only *ad hoc* and usually inadequate aid in the form of charitable donations, emergency aid programmes, disaster relief and the like.

A more substantial or 'thick reformism', on the other hand, would involve an even more radical break with the current state of affairs. Thick reformism would aim for something like global social democracy on the model of Scandinavian countries like Sweden or Denmark.[24] Scholte lists many possible policies including a Tobin tax on financial transactions, which would both raise revenue for global welfare programmes and reduce the likelihood of another global financial crisis. New, reinforced and democratic global governance institutions would serve to mitigate the democratic deficit of corporate globalization. At its most radical, some reformists have set out possible institutions for a global cosmopolitan democracy. There are two possible paths to this seemingly utopian outcome. Least likely, perhaps, would be for existing nation-states to agree to set up a world state through some kind of global social contract. Somewhat more likely is the possibility of a slow and unintended transition to global sovereignty. Just as most liberal democratic nation-states arose from dubious origins – for example, as a result of new leaders usurping power by means of coup or invasion – a global state might emerge from the imperial ambitions and hegemonic power of the USA or China. Global order, however illegitimately obtained, might then be transformed by a series of steps into genuinely cosmopolitan democracy.[25]

---

[23] Scholte, *Globalization*, p. 285.
[24] Scholte, *Globalization*, pp. 285–6 and 289ff.
[25] See above, footnote 20.

It is frequently observed that the alter-globalization movement lacks overall unity. As we have seen, there is undoubtedly substantial disagreement between elements of the movement, but a similar point can be made about most social movements. Unlike formal organizations and institutional bodies, movements harbour significantly different views under the aegis of one broad goal. The alter-globalization movement contains differing attitudes to globalization: some oppose globalization altogether, others only its dominant neoliberal mode; there is a wide range of proposed alternatives to corporate globalization. In addition, the movement inherits from new social movements a variety of supplementary issues, strategies and tactics. The alter-globalization movement combines opposition to neoliberal globalization with environmental, gay rights and feminist commitments. Demonstrations and sometimes violent protests are combined with styles of politics more typical of new social movements. The emphasis on expertise in economics and other scientific fields associated with environmental politics is combined with an emphasis on subjectivity and autonomy more characteristic of identity politics.[26] In that sense, the alter-globalization movement manifests a new politics of exploitation.

The range of the movement's challenges to corporate globalization reinforces the point that other worlds are indeed possible. Between autarkic isolation and a cosmopolitan democracy, there are evidently a number of plausible alternatives to corporate globalization that are feasible, at least in principle. It is possible to outline social democratic policies and even a democratic constitution for a new world order. However, all such alternatives remain merely utopian in the absence of a correspondingly plausible account of political agency. To the extent that the existing global order accurately reflects the current distribution of social power, it will surely be difficult to overturn. Neoliberal institutions and the broad contours of corporate globalization are, after all, the deliberate construction of the current array of social, economic and political powers in the world. So although a 'top-down' transformation of global institutions is no doubt possible in principle, it is surely unlikely to occur in fact, unless driven by the emergence of new centres of social power. Only an energetic and resourceful extra-institutional politics 'from below' – from those global citizens presently excluded both from influence over, and from the benefits of, globalization – has the ability to construct another world. The alter-globalization movement represents such an emerging challenge to corporate globalization, albeit a very diverse one.

---

[26] Geoffrey Pleyers identifies two major tendencies: the 'way of subjectivity' and the 'way of reason'. See G. Pleyers, *Alter-Globalization: Becoming Actors in the Global Age* (Cambridge and Malden, MA, Polity Press, 2010).

6.5 Strategy and Tactics of the Alter-Globalization Movement

The alter-globalization movement differs from earlier movements in its degree of 'globality'. The movement certainly operates in a more thoroughly globalized context. The 'political space' of the alter-globalization movement is as a result complex and multi-dimensional. But the strategy and tactics characteristic of the alter-globalization movement also reflect the nature of its objectives. Like the environment movement, the alter-globalization movement addresses intrinsically global problems and must act on a global stage. The addressees of political action are, as a result, unprecedentedly complex as well. They include conventional states and legislatures, but also international governance structures and organizations such as the UN, IMF and WTO. The movement targets multinational and transnational corporations such as Nike and McDonald's. Both national and global public spheres and media are directly addressed.

The repertoires of political action associated with the alter-globalization movement include both strategies and organizations associated with the labour movement, including demonstrations and trade union organization. An important role has been played by a variety of workers' organizations including some organizations from the socialist and Marxist left. In the twilight of Marxism and communism, however, most sectors of the alter-globalization movement are sceptical of a revolutionary politics that has proved rigidly statist and bureaucratic. For similar reasons, the alter-globalization movement cannot be seen as simply a global version of social democracy, as its activists are equally sceptical about the statist and bureaucratic means employed by social democratic reformism. The movement is characterized by opposition to both capitalism and the state. At the same time, the movement operates in an environment that has been affected by the activities of new social movements. The movement inherits from new social movements a deep suspicion of statist and bureaucratic politics and a corresponding emphasis on the participatory, grassroots and permanently anti-institutional politics of civil society. An interesting related development is so-called 'social movement unionism', which involves co-operation between trade unions and social movement groups and organizations in order to achieve social justice and environmental goals, including fair trade, debt reduction, adequate wages and working conditions, etc.[27] As in the 1960s, there is a significant revival

---

[27] See D. Jakopovich, 'Uniting to Win: Labour–Environmental Alliances', *Capitalism, Nature, Socialism*, 20:2, 2009, pp. 74–96; R. Munck, *Marx @ 2000: Late Marxist Perspectives* (London and New York, Zed Books, 2000); and cf. 'LaborNotes: Putting the Movement Back in the Labor Movement' (accessed at http://labornotes.org/).

of anarchist ideology within the movement, as well as a much more widespread appreciation of anarchist strategies and tactics to avoid hierarchical organizations and co-option. There is widespread recognition that overcoming democratic deficits of corporate globalization requires more than a combination of a revived nation-state democracy and democratized global institutions.

An adequate response to corporate globalization requires, in addition, a more active, expansive and powerful global civil society, which is arguably the primary site of the alter-globalization movement.[28] And, of course, civil society is itself undergoing processes of globalization. The relentless advance of spatial globalization means that the political space within which the movement acts is now unprecedentedly expansive, multi-levelled and complex. The fluid and networked structure of social movement activism associated with the alter-globalization movement is raised to a higher order by the availability of enhanced and accelerated global communications and infrastructure. Networking and organizing across national borders has become much easier as a result of new technologies. Cheap international air travel, the internet, worldwide web, email, blogs, mobile phones and social media provide the material infrastructure for an increasingly transnational practice of extra-institutional politics. Communications technologies are initially expensive and adopted most rapidly in rich countries of the global North. But some technologies can still have significant impact in the global South when earlier technologies such as landline telephone networks, which are dependent on expensive infrastructure, are bypassed by mobile telephony. The world-wide protests against the WTO in Seattle, Genoa and Melbourne are striking demonstrations of the apparently seamless transnational activism of the alter-globalization movement.[29]

Recognizing global civil society as the essential site of the alter-globalization movement does not, however, imply an uncritical stance towards it. At present the ideal of a powerful, democratic and accountable global civil society remains only a possibility. The movement may help to bring about a more adequate global civil society, but it does not operate on that basis already. Actually existing global civil society is certainly not just benign: it harbours as many dystopian as utopian possibilities. Civil society, whether at the national or trans-

[28] Cf. David Held and John Keane's model of 'double democratization', which can be applied at the global level: see D. Held, *Models of Democracy* (Cambridge, Polity Press, 1987); J. Keane, *Democracy and Civil Society* (London, Verso, 1988); and cf. Archibugi and Held's *Cosmopolitan Democracy*.

[29] See Canadian Security Intelligence Service, Archived Report No. 2000/08, 'Anti-Globalization: A Spreading Phenomenon' (accessed at www.csis-scrs.gc.ca/pblctns/prspctvs/200008–eng.asp).

national levels, is deeply penetrated by corporate influences and state power. If the hegemony of capitalism, neoliberal ideology and dominant nation-states subscribing to the Washington Consensus should persist, then global civil society will never be more than a thoroughly globalized market for the products of capitalism. What is worse, *global civil society is deformed by levels of social, economic and political inequality – both within many developing countries and between rich and poor countries – not seen in western societies since the nineteenth century. Despite claims of a 'level playing field' and a 'flat world', the social topography of global civil society includes dramatic highs and lows, stark differences of opportunity, health and well-being. Extra-institutional agents within global civil society may well be diverse and resourceful, but they face powerful opposition. The arena of civil society does not represent any kind of panacea; it merely transforms the field of conflict, raising the political stakes and complicating the politics of globalization.[30]

The alter-globalization movement also inherits from new social movements more self-conscious recognition of the politics of culture and identity.[31] In that sense, the movement provides an alternative to fatalistic variants of globalism, which treat changes to culture and identity (whether welcome or unwelcome) as automatic by-products of spatial and/or corporate globalization.[32] Spatial globalization leads to more frequent encounters between previously isolated human communities and so supplies an essential precondition of more cosmopolitan consciousness. It is easier for the world's citizens to recognize people anywhere as universally deserving of human rights. Recent campaigns against world poverty and indebtedness, support for disaster relief, Live Aid and so on can be understood as expressions of this benign form of cosmopolitanism. But it is by no means inevitable that globalization will replace the parochial consciousness of traditional societies with a benignly cosmopolitan identity and consciousness. Local and national identities and interests also persist and do so in far from benign forms. Ethnocentrism, racism and religious fundamentalism are just as much products of globalization. The only difference is that, in the face of constant exposure to cultural modernity, unthinking chauvinism and prejudice have been replaced by explicit ideologies of cultural, ethnic and racial superiority, which are deliberately and self-consciously defended'.

---

[30] See J. Keane, *Global Civil Society?* (Cambridge and New York, Cambridge University Press, 2003). The reference to a 'flat world' is from T. L. Friedman, *The World is Flat: A Brief History of the Twenty-First Century* (New York, Farrar, Straus and Giroux, 2005).

[31] Cf. above, chapter 4.

[32] On globalism, see above, p. 136.

Rather than being a globally uniform and inevitable development, the globalization of culture is, like the globalization of civil society, better characterized as a new field of conflict. Although sometimes benign, elements of the cosmopolitan perspective are imposed. The emergence of an increasingly universal culture can be seen (and is more often seen by non-Anglophone people) not as an inevitable and welcome by-product of globalization but as 'westernization' or even 'Americanization'. A burgeoning 'McWorld' spreads consumerist and materialist values, global brands and advertising campaigns, and lifestyles promoted by Hollywood films and US television networks. The spread of this western culture of consumerism, also referred to as 'Coca-colonization', has provoked a series of fundamentalist responses, which Benjamin Barber dubs 'Jihad'. Fundamentalist reactions can perhaps be seen as, in part at least, protests at the indifference to non-commercial values promoted by corporate globalization. But in the process, fundamentalist movements re-assert uncompromising religious values, ethnic and nationalist identities. But they do so in reaction to the 'detraditionalizing' challenge of modern ideologies.[33] As Anthony Giddens puts it, 'The point about fundamentalism is not its defence of tradition as such, but the manner of its defence. . . . Defending tradition in the traditional way means asserting its ritual truth in circumstances in which it is beleaguered.'[34] At the same time, fundamentalists employ the latest communications technologies and form networks and fluid organizations typical of many other social movements. Political Islamism and the Al Qaeda terrorist network are obviously prominent examples. Similarly, fundamentalist Christian and Islamic pro-family campaigns oppose abortion, homosexuality and gay marriage. The collapse of the former Yugoslavia after the death of Tito fed a toxic mix of national and sub-national identities and conflicts between Serbs, Croats and Bosnians. But as these examples make clear, fundamentalism often serves the purpose of subordinating other groups – of women or rival ethnic, national and religious groups. Cultures everywhere are media of social power and domination.

Cultures and identities are also, as we saw in chapter 4, potentially the object of extra-institutional action and resistance. Current processes of globalization open the way for a variety of forms of cultural and identity politics. Globalization weakens the hold of some national identities, at least in the sense that it encourages the proliferation of sub-national, transnational and hybrid allegiances and identities. There have been numerous ethnic challenges to nation-states and associated movements for national autonomy: for example the Basque movement

---

[33] See B. R. Barber, *Jihad vs. Mc World* (New York, Ballantine Books, 1996).
[34] A. Giddens, *Beyond Left and Right: The Future of Radical Politics* (Cambridge, Polity Press, 1994), p. 85.

in Spain and France, Tibetan and Turkic-speaking Uyghars in China and protracted religious and ethnic conflicts in Russia, Sudan, Somalia, Sri Lanka, Burma etc. The pursuit of sub-national identities (like, for example, Scottish and Welsh nationalism in the United Kingdom) is made easier by transnational blocs such as the European Union. Movements of indigenous people also cross national boundaries. The Zapatistas in Mexico are particularly interesting in this context, because they demonstrate a hybrid form of activism linking the politics of alter-globalization with indigenous issues. They have also employed a mix of strategies including early peaceful demonstrations, violent resistance to state repression and a recent reversion to non-violent global activism. They make use of computers and the internet to upload images and inform a broad global public of supporters and sympathizers.[35] But, however inspiring, there is no inevitability about the outcome of these various conflicts over culture and identity.

6.6 Controversies and Critique

The alter-globalization movement has been dismissed as a passing phenomenon. The movement arguably achieved some significant gains, including defeat of the proposed Multilateral Agreement on Investment and halting of the trade liberalization agenda of the WTO. Multinationals such as Nike, McDonald's and Apple have been put under considerable pressure by global campaigns.[36] But the politics of global civil society has proved vulnerable to other events and developments. Rising to prominence in the 1990s, the alter-globalization movement was eclipsed by the terrorist attacks of 11 September 2001, and the Global War on Terror and wars in Iraq and Afghanistan that followed. The anti-war movement, which sprang up in an attempt to prevent the invasion of Iraq in 2003, grew rapidly but was short-lived. Unsympathetic critics from a variety of perspectives see the eclipse of the movement as the inevitable result of its weaknesses and internal divisions. But diversity has not necessarily proved to be an obstacle to social movement success in the past.

Undoubtedly, the alter-globalization movement contains very broad and extensive internal divisions. Although there is broad agreement on the defects of corporate globalization, there is little or no agreement on an alternative model of globalization. Social democrats, Marxists and anarchists often disagree with environmentalists and advocates of

---

[35] Cf. the Chilean Mapuche movement: see D. Haughney, *Neoliberal Economics, Democratic Transition, and Mapuche Demands for Rights in Chile* (Gainesville, University Press of Florida, 2006).

[36] For example, see J. Vidal, *McLibel* (London, Macmillan, 1997).

indigenous people and women's rights and social justice. As a global movement, alter-globalization encompasses activists and constituencies from very different societies. Workers in developed economies experience very different conditions from workers in 'Export Processing Zones'. There are obviously also conflicts of interest between richer and poorer participants in the movement. The export of factories and jobs to developing countries disadvantages workers in developed economies and may benefit some workers in less developed countries, even if levels of pay and conditions are worse than in the North. The benefits for consumers in the form of lower prices are often claimed to compensate for these costs to workers in developed countries. Free trade and investment may indeed help people in certain regions, if it is implemented fully without the retention of protectionist measures by the European Union, the USA and Japan, despite lip-service to free trade principles.

However, although there are substantial differences, there are also shared interests between otherwise geographically, socio-economically and culturally divided people. The globalization of production, finance, trade and consumption means that the interests of actors from these different regions of the world are inextricably interconnected, albeit in complex and sometimes contradictory ways. The alter-globalization movement reflects this fact through its self-conscious concern with cross-border issues. But there is also widespread recognition of the shared interests between workers and consumers in different parts of the world. Workers in developed countries have an interest in supporting improved wages and labour standards in the global South. Otherwise a global 'race to the bottom', with different regions competing to provide the cheapest labour to attract inward investment, will inevitably undermine the wages and conditions of workers in rich countries as well.

Whilst there are no obvious or automatic solutions to conflicts of interest internal to the alter-globalization movement, it can potentially benefit from the legacy of new social movements and broader traditions of extra-institutional activism. Social movement activism is more tolerant of diversity than strictly organized and institutionalized forms of politics. Organized forms of politics resolve diverse interests and viewpoints by ignoring some issues and subordinating others for the sake of a single position and agenda. A diverse movement has the advantage of representing the actual diversity of interests and beliefs in its constituency. In addition, the alter-globalization movement benefits from the more specific cultural and ideological legacy of new social movements. The altruistic, universalist and anti-materialist values of peace and environmental movements of the 1970s and 1980s make a helpful contribution.[37] Social justice and anti-debt campaigners in the global North address poverty and exploitation in developing countries

---

[37] Cf. above, chapter 5, pp. 110–11.

and other social justice issues in seemingly altruistic campaigns. Both a commitment to social justice and suspicion of consumerism are central tenets of the peace, environmental and broader green activism of the new social movements. This is reflected in some of the cultural offshoots of the alter-globalization movement, for example criticism of McDonald's and other global chains, 'culture jamming' of advertisements and billboards, etc.[38] The values of equality, social justice and material sufficiency (as opposed to affluence and endless growth) are essential to any viable alternative global order.

A diverse movement is also able to recognize the value of individual autonomy and, in Geoffrey Pleyers's terms, the 'way of subjectivity'. Pleyers observes two distinct levels of the alter-globalization movement. A widespread concern with subjective autonomy is espoused by many activists and is most clearly apparent in small affinity groups and anarchist tendencies. This concern echoes themes of earlier new social movements such as the women's and lesbian and gay movements, alternative lifestyles and so on. Such concerns are most easily addressed through the diversity and free associations of civil society. The advocacy of autonomy is able to take advantage of some aspects of the liberal tradition, including the championing of religious toleration and political rights against undue interference in individuals' lives by either the state, culture or society.[39] On the other hand, supporters of the alter-globalization movement reject the liberal and neoliberal claim that the value of autonomy is best served by a free market capitalist system. The second level observed by Pleyers is the 'way of reason' and universal expertise. Although this level of activism interacts with the first, it is more often directed to state governments and legislators or, in other words, institutionalized dimensions of politics.[40] A more complex, multi-levelled account of political action has the advantage of alleviating the seeming utopianism of any attempt to realize something like a democratic global order. Even if a complete transformation of global institutions is at present hardly conceivable, it is possible to envisage meaningful changes in the direction of an alternative model of globalization. John Dryzek emphasizes the role of a plurality of discourses of global politics as essential components of democratization understood in gradualist rather than all-or-nothing terms. Democratization in that sense is achievable by degrees – through a series of steps whose size will depend on the strength and persistence of the movement.[41]

---

[38] See Klein, *No Logo*.
[39] Cf. Locke, *An Essay Concerning Toleration*, and Mill, *On Liberty*.
[40] Pleyers, *Alter-Globalization*.
[41] J. S. Dryzek, *Deliberative Global Politics: Discourse and Democracy in a Divided World* (Cambridge and Malden, MA, Polity Press, 2006).

Reports of the death of the alter-globalization movement have been greatly exaggerated. The tradition of extra-institutional activism teaches us, if nothing else, that the visible incarnations and organizations of a movement cannot be equated with the movement as such. If, for convenience, we nevertheless often refer to 'the' alter-globalization (or women's or environmental) movement, this should not mislead us as to their true nature. Social movements are composed of complex and sometimes dissonant patterns of activism. The crystallizations of these patterns – in the form of striking events, prominent political organizations and demands for institutional reforms – may subside and disappear from time to time. This does not mean that the movement does not continue invisibly, always ready to re-emerge and crystallize into new events, organizations and demands. The rapid spread of activism in the name of the Occupy movement in the USA, UK and Australia, the *indignados* in Spain and similar responses to financial crisis in Greece, Ireland and Italy bear strong family resemblances to the alter-globalization movement, even though they do not adopt the label. Indeed, the alter-globalization movement itself includes activists and organizations that played a role in social and labour movements. The politics of exploitation may assume a startling variety of new guises, but that very diversity makes it, if anything, likely to be all the more durable.

Further Reading

Jan Aarte Scholte, *Globalization: A Critical Introduction* provides a helpful overview of the topic. Geoffrey Pleyers achieves perhaps the most convincing overall synthesis of what he calls the 'way of subjectivity' and 'way of reason' or expertise in *Alter-Globalization: Becoming Actors in the Global Age*. Manfred B. Steger's *Globalization: A Very Short Introduction* considers arguments both for and against the economic benefits of globalization. Naomi Klein's *No Logo: Taking Aim at the Brand Bullies* and *The Shock Doctrine: The Rise of Disaster Capitalism* are highly readable and engaging introductions to some of the underlying economic, cultural and political issues raised by neoliberalism's corporate agenda. John Keane considers sceptically the potential of globalized civil society activism in *Global Civil Society?* A more optimistic view, emphasizing the contribution of civil society activism to democracy, is presented by John Dryzek in *Deliberative Global Politics: Discourse and Democracy in a Divided World*. Archibugi and Held's *Cosmopolitan Democracy: An Agenda for a New World Order* sets out an ambitious and controversial agenda for a decentralized model of globalized democracy.

Part III

Theories of Social Movements

7

Theories of Social Movements:
I. Normative and Formal Approaches

Outline

The rise of new social movements (described in previous chapters) has contributed to a normative shift in the evaluation of extra-institutional politics and an enriched understanding of democracy. Rather than always condemning social movements as illegitimate and disruptive, political theorists are more likely to recognize their contributions to democracy in this enriched sense. At the same time, social scientific studies have shifted from explanations of collective *behaviour* as a departure from rational political conduct (with a focus on crowds, panics, rumours and masses) to attempts to explain the distinctive rationality of collective *action* as demonstrated by successful social movements. Rational explanations must themselves be supplemented by accounts of the essential (and constructive) role of cognitive and cultural innovation, identity and emotion, narrative and performance, in collective political action. These social scientific approaches are all *formal*, in the sense that they concentrate on what social movements have in common as a form of political action. Formal approaches do not aim to provide any *substantive* explanation of the sources, distinctive features and possible outcomes of particular movements. Examples of such substantive approaches will be considered in the next chapter.

7.1 The Normative Shift: Recognizing the Legitimacy of Extra-Institutional Politics

In previous chapters we have examined a number of social movements, both historical and contemporary, with the emphasis on differing ideas of politics and agency. In the remaining chapters we will review some of the theoretical approaches to social movements and extra-institutional politics. As we shall see, these theories do not always compete on the same assumptions. They differ most clearly on what they are trying to achieve by theoretical means or, in other words, what questions they seek to answer. In this chapter, we will look at two approaches. First, *normative* or *evaluative* theories make claims about the legitimacy or justification, the moral rightness or wrongness, of extra-institutional forms of politics. A second set of approaches is *formal explanatory* theories, which apply empirical concepts in order to understand and explain social movements as a distinct mode of political action. In effect, they inform us about how extra-institutional movements do what they do: the emphasis is on the contrast between extra-institutional and institutional forms of politics. These formal approaches contrast with *substantive* theories (discussed in the next chapter), which examine and sometimes try to explain the distinctive features of particular movements: the emphasis there is on the differences between individual social movements. These somewhat abstract contrasts should become clearer in what follows.

The extra-institutional politics of social movements has frequently been condemned as illegitimate. This is hardly surprising because, by definition, extra-institutional politics takes place outside of recognized rules and procedures, outside of what are considered legitimate ways of conducting politics. Precisely because they challenge existing institutions and often give rise to new institutional forms, social movements inevitably break the rules prevailing at the time. At the same time, we have seen that extra-institutional forms of politics have played an indispensable role in the formation of institutions. Beyond any effects they might have in the broader society, social movements have helped to form the political institutions we enjoy today.[1] Institutions that we now regard as essential conditions of a just, liberal and democratic society owe their existence to actions that were once regarded as illegitimate. Normative political thought has usually focused only on the state of existing norms and institutions, endorsing and sometimes criticizing them. There has been less focus on evaluating the processes involved in the formation of institutional politics.

The default position for the evaluation of social movements, then, is disapproval. What are essentially conservative views of extra-institutional politics assume a variety of forms. An extreme (and now relatively rare) version of conservatism regards any kind of extra-institutional action as illegitimate, whatever the nature of the institutions prevailing at the time. From this perspective, the only legitimate forms of political activity are those allowed by the existing political system, whatever it is like. In traditional terms, any challenge

[1] See above, chapter 2.

to the ruler's sovereignty is wrong, even under conditions of tyranny or dictatorship. Although this position is now rarely defended, it was the dominant view during much of western history until the modern period. Monarchs and other rulers were thought to be ordained by God, so any challenge to their authority was considered shocking and even blasphemous. If all the ruler's actions are divinely sanctioned, then even actions that oppress the people are justified, for example as punishment of the people for their wickedness and sins. For much of European history, the political order was regarded as a divinely ordained microcosm within the larger cosmos. Challenges to this order were seen as evil and heretical. In the ancient world, Greek and Roman writers used terms like *demos* (Gk), *vulgus* and *multitudo* (Lat.), which, though they can simply mean 'people', also carry negative connotations of inferiority and irrationality. In modern times, conservative historians have been satisfied with explaining panics, riots and rebellions as the products of the intrinsic wickedness of human nature and the wild irrationality of the rabble or mob. Even during the Protestant Reformation in Europe, which led to widespread wars and insurrections, most rulers subscribed to the 'divine right of kings' and regarded rebellion as blasphemy.[2]

More commonly and plausibly, conservatives regard *their own* political institutions as legitimate and, accordingly, condemn all extra-institutional challenges to them. These conservatives are willing to countenance extra-institutional challenges to other political systems which differ in significant respects from their own. Some regard only non-violent protest as a legitimate form of action; others think that violent resistance may sometimes be justified, but only when it is directed against particularly unpleasant regimes. Reactions to the African National Congress's long campaign against the widely condemned racist regime in the former South Africa varied according to the ANC's changing policies on the use of violence. An early phase of non-violent direct action, which was directly inspired by Gandhi's doctrines of peaceful civil disobedience, was widely approved of internationally. After the apartheid government of South Africa brutally suppressed all forms of peaceful protest, the ANC abandoned its non-violent approach in favour of a policy of violent insurgency. This led many conservatives and even sympathetic liberal commentators to condemn the movement, despite their opposition to racism and support for the democratic principle of 'one person one vote'.[3]

---

[2] For much of his life, Martin Luther saw rebellion against instituted authority as unjustified, even though his doctrines helped to spark the upheavals of the Reformation: see Skinner, *The Foundations of Modern Political Thought*, Vol. II, ch. 7.

[3] See Meredith, *Mandela*, ch. 9, esp. pp. 196ff., and cf. Mandela, *Long Walk to Freedom*.

Conservatives stand on firmer ground when they argue extra-institutional challenge is not justified within constitutional liberal democracies. Indeed, until the advent of 1960s protest movements, the majority of liberal and democratic theorists supported this position. According to this standpoint, liberal democracy provides rights of association, freedom of thought and expression, the right to engage in lobbying and vote in elections. Democratic institutions allow people with different opinions and interests to form political parties and compete for public office. There can be little justification for extra-institutional action, because the constitution permits every legitimate form of political activity. Liberal democracies may not be perfect, but they will continue to improve as a result of reasonable protest, criticism and advocacy exercised through existing institutional channels. By implication, whatever the historical importance of social movements, they no longer have any legitimate role in correcting the defects of liberal democracy. Obviously, violent insurrection and revolution are condemned on these grounds. But advocates of this position would also argue that, even when social movements engage in non-violent civil disobedience and direct action, they go beyond the limits of legitimate politics. Citizens should express their opinions and pursue their interests through the institutional channels that are already available. As we shall see in the next section, this perspective encourages a view of social movements as pathological and irrational outbursts or, at worst, as subversive threats to democracy.

The arrival of 1960s protest movements and then new social movements made it clear that the institutions of western liberal democracies were not, in fact, perfect. They did not, as their apologists claimed, successfully represent all potential constituencies and issues. African-Americans, women, lesbians and gays, and ethnic minorities claimed – and have persuaded most observers – that they and their interests were effectively excluded from the prevailing institutional order. A number of fundamental legal and institutional changes extending liberal and democratic rights, which would not have been made without the actions of these social movements, were achieved as a result. Significant reforms include the Civil Rights Acts in the USA; equal opportunities, equal pay, anti-discrimination and anti-vilification legislation concerning gender, race and sexuality; and the decriminalization of homosexuality. The environmental movement has similarly challenged the institutionalized bias of western polities in favour of endless economic growth at the cost of the environment. This challenge has also resulted in changes of environmental policy, and regulation, and institutional changes such as the introduction of environmental protection agencies.[4]

---

[4] On these changes, see above, chapters 4–5.

At the same time, social movements helped to bring about associated shifts in normative political thought. Before the advent of the new movements, most liberal democratic theorists failed to recognize the distinctive claims of women, sexual and ethnic minorities. Representative in this regard is the American political philosopher John Rawls, who failed to consider issues of gender and sexuality in his very extensive work on the *Theory of Justice*.[5] The liberal mainstream faced theoretical challenges associated with the new movements, including a variety of feminisms, anti-racist and post-colonial theory, gay and lesbian studies and queer theory. Since the 1970s, however, Rawls and most other political thinkers in the liberal democratic tradition now devote considerable attention to issues of gender and ethnic equality, community rights and so on. Ecological thought and the position of nature in relation to society are similarly unavoidable topics in normative political theory, in part at least as a result of the activities of social movements.

Partly as a result of these surprising, yet in retrospect welcome, changes, there was also a significant normative shift in the evaluation of the extra-institutional strategies and tactics that helped to bring them about. Many liberal democratic theorists came to accept that, in these and similar cases, change could be brought about only as a result of extra-institutional challenges, including campaigns of civil disobedience. Racism, for example, was so deeply entrenched in the supposedly equal, liberal and democratic institutions of the USA and other western countries that only the Civil Rights Movement and equivalent movements elsewhere were able to achieve reforms. These campaigns transgressed the approved repertoire of institutionalized politics, relying on non-violent campaigns of civil disobedience, direct action and an ever-expanding repertoire of extra-institutional forms of protest. Normative theorists were consequently inspired to reconsider the legitimacy of these and other extra-institutional forms of social movement activity, and some at least were prepared to accept them as justified.[6]

At the same time, the activities of social movements have influenced normative political thought indirectly by extending the scope of what is regarded as political. New social movements in particular make clear that politics takes place outside of the institutional sphere as well as

[5] J. Rawls, *A Theory of Justice* (Cambridge, MA, Belknap Press, 1971), and cf. S. Moller Okin's critique in *Justice, Gender, and the Family* (New York, Basic Books, 1989, ch. 5).

[6] Rawls, *Theory of Justice*, pp. 363–91, and cf. P. Singer, *Democracy and Disobedience* (Oxford, Clarendon Press, 1973), and M. Walzer, *Obligations: Essays on Disobedience, War, and Citizenship* (Cambridge, MA, Harvard University Press, 1970).

within it. The emphasis on identity and cultural politics highlights the many avenues for the operation and formation of social power in areas beyond the institutional domain of official politics. Cultural oppression is not reducible to legal and institutional forms of discrimination and exploitation; it persists and must be fought in the sphere of culture and civil society as well as elsewhere through legal and economic changes. As the women's movement proclaimed, the personal is also political.[7] Institutional reforms are never sufficient for movements of liberation, which must directly address cultural oppression throughout society.

In this way, the successes of new social movements have also helped to revive interest in civil society as an essential dimension of a democratic political system. The formal political institutions of liberal democracy are only one (albeit essential) dimension of a fully democratic polity. The institutional forms of liberal democracy are incomplete, because no society can be fully democratic without the ongoing activities of social movements within civil society. The latter are necessary, because they allow for the formation of new political constituencies and interests, new centres of social power. Otherwise these interests either would not exist or would be excluded from institutions that have been captured by dominant centres of social power. In an early collaboration, David Held and John Keane argued in similar terms that genuine democracy requires a 'double democratiza-tion' of both state and civil society. Corresponding to this deepened understanding of democracy is a similarly extended view of the duties of democratic participation and citizenship. Citizens can and should participate not only by taking part in elections, joining a political party and lobbying their representatives. They should also become active within civil society on behalf of issues and constituencies that may not be adequately represented or even able to be represented within the current political order.[8]

7.2 Explaining Social Movements as Irrational Collective Behaviour

The shift from normative disapproval and neglect to recognition of the value of extra-institutional politics transforms the empirical study and explanation of social movements. This might at first seem surprising. Surely the scientific study of any phenomenon is factual and objec-tive, paying no regard to normative assumptions, values and biases. This is what is supposed to distinguish science from other kinds of

---

[7] On the politics of culture and identity, see above, chapter 4.
[8] See above, chapter 6, p. 145 and footnote 28. Cf. J. L. Cohen and A. Arato, *Civil Society and Political Theory* (Cambridge, MA, MIT Press, 1992).

explanation. But the example of social movements makes clear that normative assumptions persist in purportedly empirical social sciences. Paralleling the normative shift described in the previous section, the study of extra-institutional politics has changed from being a study of wrong-doing, deviance or pathology to a study of legitimate political activity, with corresponding differences in patterns of explanation and views of what needs to be explained. Understood as social deviance, *collective behaviour* must be explained as the result of social breakdown, state failure and irrational outbursts. Understood as a valid form of political action, social movements are explained as the rational achievement of *collective action*.[9]

The normative and associated methodological shift just described is also responsible for a shift in terminology. The neutral term 'social movement' now usually used to describe extra-institutional politics replaced the earlier term 'collective behaviour'. The latter term reflected the emphasis of the nineteenth-century discipline of sociology on the unintended effects of social change and, in particular, those associated with the emergence of modern industrial and urban society. The sociological studies of Émile Durkheim (1858–1917) set out from the assumption that individual actions are influenced by unconscious social factors or what he calls a 'collective unconscious' (*conscience collective*). His classic study of *Suicide* (1897) compares rates of suicide in different religious communities of Protestants and Catholics under a variety of social conditions. The implication is that the individual's very personal and momentous decision to take his or her own life is in fact influenced by unconscious social factors, which alone account for the different rates of suicide in different countries.[10] In the field of collective behaviour, Gustave le Bon's (1841–1931) work on *The Crowd* (1896) focuses on examples in which seemingly irrational behaviour is prominent: peasant uprisings and food riots, rumours and panics, sudden and violent revolutionary upheavals. In the twentieth century, the same approach to crowd psychology could readily be applied to the mass hysteria generated by Hitler's carefully staged Nuremberg rallies. Fascist and Stalinist propaganda was designed not to persuade individuals by means of rational argument but rather to exert influence by emotional and unconscious means over the 'mass mind'.[11]

The experience of fascism and Stalinism continued to influence sociological studies of extra-institutional politics. William Kornhauser's

---

[9] Cf. A. D. Morris and C. McClurg Mueller, eds., *Frontiers in Social Movement Theory* (New Haven and London, Yale University Press, 1992).

[10] É. Durkheim, *Suicide: A Study in Sociology* [*Le Suicide: étude de sociologie*] (1897) (London, Routledge and Kegan Paul, 1952), trans. J. A. Spaulding and G. Simpson.

[11] G. Le Bon, *The Crowd: A Study of the Popular Mind* (1896) (London, Benn, 1947).

declared aim is to understand fascism and to prevent the emergence of similar 'totalitarian' movements in the West. In *The Politics of Mass Society* (1959), he considers the 'widespread readiness to abandon constitutional modes of political activity in favor of uncontrolled mass action'.[12] The analysis of mass society contributes to the 'diagnosis of certain underlying tendencies' that make modern societies more vulnerable to totalitarianism. Rapid urbanization, industrialization and 'sudden and extensive changes in the structure of authority and community' erode the complex intermediate groups of traditional societies, producing an undifferentiated mass. The 'massification' of society makes it vulnerable to charismatic demagogues, irrational collective outbursts and even totalitarianism. Mass society is explicitly opposed to the 'pluralist society' of liberal democracies and, in particular, the USA. The organized interest groups and elite representation of pluralist democracy substitute for the intermediate groups that have been eroded by modernization. The remedy for mass society is, unsurprisingly, some form of representative democracy combined with pluralism on the American model.[13]

Neil J. Smelser's *Theory of Collective Behavior* (1962) similarly treats extra-institutional activity as a pathological threat to the existing social order.[14] Collective behaviour is the disruptive consequence of 'structural strain', which is caused by rapid social change as a result of societal modernization. Social change leads to rising aspirations and/or declining prospects for particular social groups, which makes behaviour within the institutional order intolerable for more and more members of these groups. When structural strain is combined with inadequate social controls as a result of a weakened state, economic crisis or external military threats, then these groups are likely to resort to unregulated forms of collective behaviour. Both delayed and over-repressive state responses may exacerbate such outbursts and make them more likely. Collective behaviour is throughout characterized in somewhat pejorative terms. Associated ideologies involve 'quasi-magical' belief systems, 'exaggerations, crudeness and eccentricity'. Collective behaviour is 'impatient' and often 'intolerant', 'based on rumors, ideology and superstitions'.[15] The early stages in the development of collective behaviour are marked by panics, riots and outbursts. The term 'social movement' is reserved for longer-term and progressively more organized expressions, as discontent

---

[12] W. A. Kornhauser, *The Politics of Mass Society* (Glencoe, IL, Free Press, 1959), p. 5.
[13] Kornhauser, *Politics of Mass Society*, pp. 229, 13 and 231.
[14] N. J. Smelser, *Theory of Collective Behavior* (New York, Free Press, 1962).
[15] Smelser, *Theory of Collective Behavior*, pp. 8 and 67–130, and cf. N. J. Smelser, *The Faces of Terrorism: Social and Psychological Dimensions* (Princeton, NJ, Princeton University Press, 2007).

is progressively institutionalized and there is a gradual return to normality.

If the mainstream sociological tradition, at least until the 1960s, thus appears biased in favour of institutionalized and organized modes of politics, it is important to observe that the orthodox tradition of Marxist social theory shares a similarly negative view of extra-institutional action. The rise of the working-class movement and associated organizations was, of course, the original inspiration for Marx's belief in the prospects of proletarian revolution. Marxism is strongly *anti*-institutional insofar as it advocates the abolition of private property and overthrow of the 'bourgeois' state. Indeed, it anticipates that revolution will almost certainly involve violent struggle, because the bourgeois ruling class can be expected to fight to the end to retain its power and wealth. Despite these anti-institutional credentials, however, Marxism is not in the end really sympathetic to social movement activism. Marx thought that the first stage of revolution would require a 'dictatorship of the proletariat' which, however loosely interpreted, implies hierarchical and even authoritarian rule during the period of transition to socialism. Marxism's authoritarian tendencies, already clear to nineteenth-century anarchist critics like Bakunin, are reinforced by Lenin's explicit view of revolutionary struggle. For Lenin, the working class provides only the 'elemental force', the disorganized energy of revolutionary transformation; the movement must be led by a disciplined and highly organized party of militants, who are experts in 'scientific socialism'. Although defenders of Lenin attempt to reconcile his position with democratic principles, it is hard to interpret Leninism as any kind of endorsement of social movement activism. Finally, once socialism has been achieved, Marxist theory foresees no further role for extra-institutional challengers. After class division has been eliminated and the state has 'withered away', socialist society can be administered without political conflict in the interests of all. There is no place for politics at all, whether institutional or extra-institutional. This hostility to social movement activism is reflected in the absence and/or repression of civil society in the countries of 'actually (now previously) existing socialism'.[16]

The sociological tendency before the 1960s, in both mainstream and Marxist theory, to treat social movement activity as either deviant or embryonic is matched by systematic neglect of this topic in contemporaneous political science. At first, this neglect reflected the fact that the dominant approach was *institutionalism*. The study of politics consisted, in other words, largely in describing and analysing extant political

[16] See Lenin, *What Is To Be Done?*, ch. 2. Cf. R. Bahro, *The Alternative in Eastern Europe* (London, New Left Books, 1978), trans. D. Fernbach, first published in German as *Die Alternative: zur Kritik des real existierenden Sozialismus*.

institutions and norms. More questionably, even empirical approaches modelled on the methods of the natural sciences – or what has been described as the 'American science of politics' – have neglected social movements as well.[17] Political scientists have largely relegated extra- and anti-institutional movements to a sphere beyond politics as they define it. Defining political behaviour as whatever takes place *within* the sphere of institutional politics, extra-institutional activities are seen as largely irrelevant to the proper conduct of politics. What is denied are not historical and contemporary facts concerning extra-institutional movements, but rather their immediate relevance to politics.

At the same time, political scientists have devoted considerable attention to the organized expressions of social movements and their relationship to core political institutions. However, the tendency of political science to treat organized interest and pressure groups as stand-ins for social movements must be rejected for two reasons. In the first place, this is to ignore a significant region of politics. It is impossible to understand interest and pressure groups – and by extension, the field of institutional politics as a whole – without addressing in addition the adjacent and overlapping spheres of civil society within which movements operate and from which new movements may originate in the future. The constitution of new political interests and centres of power takes place, almost by definition, outside of the institutional sphere. Organized interest and pressure groups usually emerge from, and often maintain continuing relations with, social movements; their influence and longevity depend on the size, state and extra-institutional activities of corresponding movements. Secondly, and more radically, the influence of extra-institutional movements is not just exerted *through* organized interest and pressure groups and directed *at* institutions. Social movements can also act directly on culture and society without the mediation of any institutions at all. They do so through the symbolic politics of identity and culture as well as by direct action within the sphere of production.

An expansion of the concept of politics implies, in turn, an expanded understanding of political rationality. No doubt many of the phenomena emphasized by the collective behaviour tradition do in fact take place. Social movements are indeed sometimes associated with panics, crowds, irrational outbursts, 'magical thinking' and even violence. But a broader understanding of politics allows us to see these phenomena as just one dimension of a broader and, crucially, potentially legitimate pursuit of political interests through collective action. Irrational collective behaviour is the occasional by-product and accompaniment of what is otherwise rational collective action to achieve legitimate political goals.

[17] Crick, *The American Science of Politics*.

7.3 Explaining Social Movements as Rational Collective Action

The Civil Rights, anti-war and student activism of the 1960s and the rise of new social movements after that have encouraged sociologists and political scientists to recognize extra-institutional political activities as both important and legitimate. There has been a shift from treating such phenomena as (irrational) collective behaviour to treating them as potentially rational collective action. This normative shift is reflected in the adoption of the more neutral term 'social movement', which now spans the disciplines of sociology and political science. Extra-institutional activities are thereby recognized as potentially rational means to achieve political goals. The legitimacy of any political action depends on both its goals and its methods, or ends and means. Conservative disapproval of extra-institutional politics presupposes the legitimacy of the institutional order. Conversely, recognition of the potential legitimacy of extra-institutional politics reflects the realization that society can never be presumed to be completely just. The new social movements have shown that liberal democracies still oppress and exploit certain social groups; their political systems exclude fundamental issues of peace and survival from effective consideration and resolution. In these circumstances, it is both legitimate and rational for social movements to challenge state institutions.

This shifts the focus from collective irrationality to collective rationality. Different approaches to the understanding of social movements then reflect different concepts of rationality. One major approach – dominant in north American social sciences and increasingly elsewhere in the English-speaking world – assumes an essentially economic view of rationality. Rational choice theory sets out from the assumption that individual actors seek to maximize their own welfare. In the economic context theorized by neo-classical economics, this means that individuals seek to maximize their wealth and material assets. These assumptions generate economic models with some explanatory value in economics. Rational choice theory extends these assumptions to human behaviour more generally. At the same time, it interprets individual interests more broadly to include the satisfaction of any kind of preferences including psychological, social, moral and political preferences.[18]

In the political context, the rational choice perspective emphasizes the importance of the so-called 'collective action' problem. This problem faces any set of individuals who have common interests and therefore have an interest in acting together in order to achieve their

[18] See M. Olson, *The Logic of Collective Action* (Cambridge, MA, Harvard University Press, 1965).

goals. The problem arises because the collective's interest in acting together does not automatically translate into every individual having a motive to act. This is because of the so-called 'free-rider' problem. If enough members of a group act to achieve some collective goal, then other members of the group have a (selfish) interest in doing nothing. They are able to 'free-ride' on the collective's actions: in other words, they gain all the benefits of collective action without incurring the associated costs. But if it is rational (in this sense of rationality) for one individual to free-ride on the efforts of others, then it is rational for all individuals to do so. In such circumstances, collective action is unlikely to occur or, if it does occur, must be irrational. But if no-one acts, then the collective benefits of action are lost.

For obvious reasons, collective action is even more difficult for exploited and oppressed groups, who not only suffer social deprivation and cultural oppression but may also not be represented by current political institutions. The exploited and oppressed face a number of additional problems. Members of such groups may be unaware of their common interests. They may not easily be able to identify all the group's potential members and to communicate with them. There may be social stigma and sanctions against 'coming out' as a member of the group. Members may disagree about the best course of action. In a repressive society, opposition is likely to be punished, so collective action will be costly and dangerous. But even in a liberal democracy that tolerates opposition, collective action is still difficult to achieve. Ignoring this difficulty encourages an over-hasty resort to theories of 'false consciousness' or ideological distortion to explain the absence of collective action. Yet social movements have, as we have seen throughout previous chapters, achieved considerable successes both historically and more recently. Even under difficult circumstances, social movements are evidently able to achieve the collective good of political action. It seems that social movements offer a potential solution to the collective action problem, even for politically excluded and seemingly powerless social groups.

A view of social movements as the potential solution to collective action problems is developed in the approach known as resource mobilization theory.[19] Resource mobilization theory focuses on the way social movements or, more precisely, some organizations and individuals within them are able to mobilize the human, financial and other resources required to achieve the group's collective goals. Bob Edwards and John D. McCarthy catalogue at least five kinds of resources: human resources in the form of active support; mate-

---

[19] See M. N. Zald and J. McCarthy, *Social Movements in an Organizational Society* (New Brunswick, NJ, Transaction, 1987), and A. Oberschall, *Social Conflict and Social Movements* (Englewood Cliffs, NJ, Prentice Hall, 1973).

rial resources including money and other assets; moral resources of support and solidarity; organizational resources including networks and formal organizations; cultural resources of ideology, values and traditions of political activism.[20] The key mobilizing role is played by social movement organizations and their leaders, who are described as 'political entrepreneurs'. From this rational choice perspective, the task of social movement leadership is understood in quasi-economic terms: as the organization of political resources and incentives in order to mobilize self-interested utility-maximizers with a given array of interests to act in support of collective action. In effect, the political entrepreneur looks for new opportunities in the social and political marketplace.[21]

Early resource mobilization theorists were criticized for failing to pay enough attention to the social and political context in which social movement organizations operate, which is emphasized in the work of Charles Tilly. The 'political opportunity structure' contributes significantly to the distinctive trajectory of success and failure, growth and decline, or 'life cycle', of social movements.[22] Differing political systems facilitate or inhibit particular social movement strategies and forms of organization. The availability of government funding encourages formal and legal models of organization.[23] Different electoral and party systems have implications for the strategies and tactics most likely to succeed in particular countries. Proportional representation makes it easier for social movements to form new parties and to gain representation. Such parliamentary strategies are doomed to failure, on the other hand, in first-past-the-post and strongly two-party electoral systems. In such systems, existing political parties may adopt new issues and constituencies in response to social movements, depending on their own ideologies and sources of support. Another factor influencing movement strategies is relationships between existing social and political elites: whether elites are united or divided and, if divided, in what configurations. These relationships are particularly important in repressive states, where collective action is only likely to

---

[20] See B. Edwards and J. D. McCarthy, 'Resources and Social Movement Mobilization' in *The Blackwell Companion to Social Movements*, ed. A. Snow, S. A. Soule and H. Kriesi (Oxford, Blackwell, 2004). On moral capital as a resource of leaders, see J. Kane, *The Politics of Moral Capital* (Cambridge and New York, Cambridge University Press, 2001), p. 4.

[21] See M. Taylor, *Rationality and Revolution* (Cambridge and New York, Cambridge University Press, 1987), and *Rationality and Revolutionary Collective Action* (Cambridge and New York, Cambridge University Press, 1988).

[22] See, for example, C. Tilly, *From Mobilization to Revolution* (Reading, MA, Addison-Wesley, 1978).

[23] See D. Della Porta and M. Diani, *Social Movements: An Introduction* (Oxford and Malden, MA, Blackwell, 1999), p. 155.

be successful if it can win support from elements of the existing state apparatus.

Rational choice approaches undoubtedly represent an advance over earlier studies that were unduly preoccupied with instances of irrational collective behaviour. They offer important insights into the nature of social movements considered as a distinctive form of political activity. There are, however, limits to their ability to explain what is distinctive about social movements. A general difficulty concerns the formation of interests or preferences. Rational choice theories are no doubt sometimes able to deduce theorems predicting the choices that particular agents will make on the basis of their existing preferences. But they are unable to cast much light on the formation or possible transformation of those preferences. Whilst this difficulty may not be a fatal problem in the area of economic behaviour, it is a major stumbling block in the explanation of social movements. Social movements are concerned not just with the pursuit of existing interests but also – and more specifically – with the formation of new interests and new definitions of identity. A successful social movement transforms the preferences of its constituency. Indeed, it will often bring about changes in the preferences of opponents. For example, the gay and lesbian movements have transformed how gay and lesbian people think of themselves, their attitudes to their sexual desires, their social aspirations and lifestyles. The success of the movement is reflected in substantial shifts in social attitudes to homosexuality more broadly.[24]

Although it is certainly worthwhile examining the entrepreneurial initiative of leaders and the individual incentives of participants in social movements, it is unlikely that a theory modelled on the self-interested and materialist motivations of *Homo economicus* will ever provide an adequate explanation of social movements. Social movements are important precisely because they are able to generate collective action in situations where it appears unlikely or, at least, not rational in narrowly self-interested terms. Rational choice approaches can only begin to explain such actions by extending the range of preferences to include the role of integrity, commitment to a cause and group, the role of identity in the self-interpretation of interests and the broader role of culture, community and solidarity. Some of these preferences may relate to (or develop in the context of) political action itself. People may enjoy taking action, engaging in risks; they may form social bonds and friendships that help to sustain their commitment. Only such considerations can begin to account for the otherwise inex-

---

[24] See B. Hindess, *Choice, Rationality, and Social Theory* (London and Boston, MA, Unwin Hyman, 1988). On the role of identity, see above, chapter 4, and cf. Della Porta and Diani, *Social Movements*, pp. 103–5.

plicable elements of solidarity, self-sacrifice and persistence in the face
of adversity, which characterize successful extra-institutional movements. But such evidently crucial determinants of social movement
success are not obviously susceptible to, or illuminated by, rational
analysis and formal modelling. Rational choice theories are better
equipped to explain actions within, rather than transitions between,
social value-systems, identities, conceptions of interest, culture and
ideology. Extra-institutional politics is centrally concerned with the
latter rather than the former, which is more relevant to institutional
politics. In that sense, the most useful contribution of rational choice
theory may be to reveal in stark outline what stands in need of further
explanation by other methods.

7.4 Beyond Rationality and Irrationality: Cognitive Practice, Framing, Culture and Emotion

A further set of approaches to social movements focuses on the cultural and cognitive creativity of social movements. In that sense, these
approaches recognize that social movements operate beyond any
simple distinctions between rationality and irrationality. Social movements are not (as the approaches discussed in the previous section
recognize) pathological phenomena defined by their irrationality, dis-
order and tendency to violence, although obviously such phenomena
may always intrude upon the movement. But neither can social
movements be explained as the predictable outcome of rational choice
– not, at least, when rationality is defined in the maximizing terms of
economic models. Rather, social movements are distinctive precisely
because they are innovative and creative in unpredictable ways.
They devise novel political tactics and strategies, form new identities
associated with original conceptions of interest, apply existing political concepts in new ways, propagate novel ideologies and values and
inspire institutional reforms. But crucially, these innovations are not
simply predictable permutations of existing preferences and beliefs.
Social movements create new social and cultural forms.

This creative role of social movements is emphasized by the cognitive approach put forward by Ron Eyerman and Andrew Jamison.
Changing identities, values and ideology are understood in these terms
as the result of learning processes. Crucially, however, a cognitive
perspective on social movements is not equivalent to a Marxist theory
of ideology, which posits a mismatch between the working class's
objective condition of alienation under capitalism and its lagging *subjective* consciousness of that condition. Marx assumes that the working
class will inevitably become conscious of its alienated condition:
that the objectively defined class 'in-itself' will become a subjectively

self-aware class 'for-itself'.[25] The cognitive process, which is reduced to 'becoming aware' of an already defined condition, is seen as the more or less inevitable by-product of the experience of life under capitalism and participation in struggle. This perspective is in danger of eliding the creativity of social movements, because the theorist anticipates the outcome of 'learning' in advance. In Eyerman and Jamison's terms, social movements should rather be studied 'as forms of activity by which individuals create new kinds of social identities' and 'as providing the breeding ground for innovations in thought as well as in the social organization of thought'.[26] As Eyerman and Jamison emphasize, political learning involves creativity, imagination and choice without any predetermined or predestined outcome. It is only in that sense that extra-institutional action can be understood as a form of 'cognitive praxis', which refers to 'the creative role of consciousness and cognition in all human action, individual and collective'.

Eyerman and Jamison focus attention, as a result, on the role of movement intellectuals. They distinguish between two kinds of intellectuals. The partisan intellectuals of the nineteenth century, 'intellectuals-in-movement', were, like Marx and Engels, already established intellectuals who entered into relationships of leadership with the working class. Contemporary 'movement intellectuals', on the other hand, are more organically related to the social movements to which they contribute. They emerge alongside and in interaction with the movement: 'they create their individual role at the same time as they create the movement, as new individual identities and a new collective identity take form in the same interactive process'.[27] The social movements considered in previous chapters offer many examples of significant intellectual contributions by feminist, gay, lesbian or queer, and anti-racist theorists. More broadly, the contributions of these movements can be understood (and in previous chapters have been considered) in terms of a series of novel ideas concerning such things as identity, consciousness, pride, culture, the value of nature, forms of strategy and tactics and so on. At the same time, these ideas are important, in large part, because they have been widely adopted and manifested in the extra-institutional politics of social movements.

The cognitive approach to social movements can also be expressed

[25] See K. Marx and F. Engels, *The Communist Manifesto* (Harmondsworth, Penguin, 1967), trans. S. Moore. Georg Lukács explores this distinction in *History and Class Consciousness: Studies in Marxist Dialectics* (London, Merlin Press, 1971), trans. R. Livingstone.

[26] R. Eyerman and A. Jamison, *Social Movements: A Cognitive Approach* (University Park, PA, Pennsylvania State University Press, 1991), p. 2.

[27] Eyerman and Jamison, *Social Movements*, pp. 3, 46 and 98; cf. chapter 4.

in terms of so-called 'framing approaches', which derive from the social psychology of Erving Goffman. Sydney Tarrow quotes David Snow and Robert Benford's definition of a frame as an 'interpretive schemata that simplifies and condenses the "world out there" by selectively punctuating and encoding objects, situations, events, experiences, and sequences of actions within one's present or past environment'.[28] Social movements typically challenge existing ways of framing social values, status and reward systems. Novel frames imply criticisms of the existing order and its associated interpretive frames as well as suggesting possible alternatives to them. Activists and social movement leaders promote new interpretive and cognitive frames, which imply improved status, greater rewards and autonomy for their constituency. Often a social movement promotes several competing frames. For example, second-wave feminism comprised both 'difference' and 'equality' frames. According to difference feminism, women are considered to be 'different but equal' (or perhaps superior) to men; according to the 'gender-neutrality' frame, women are essentially the same as, and therefore equal to, men.[29] Membership of the movement, which is not governed by the fixed rules of a formal organization, corresponds instead to an individual's willingness to adopt one or other of the associated cognitive frames. As the movement develops and grows, interpretive frames are diffused throughout the movement and, if it is successful, spread throughout the rest of society.

What distinguishes movement frames from ideology in the conventional sense – and implies a different emphasis from the cognitive approach of Eyerman and Jamison – is their less self-conscious and less discursive or intellectual character. The emphasis on the cognitive dimension and movement intellectuals risks ignoring the less conscious and more emotional aspects of social movement creativity. The interpretive framing approach recognizes that cognitive frames are not necessarily fully explicit and self-conscious.[30] Movement frames not only consist of arguments and novel concepts, they also convey alternative identities, distinctive styles of action and symbolism, liberating accounts of individual experience and suffering, etc. Works of art, music, theatre and literature, styles of dress and body decoration may all play an important role in conveying these non-discursive aspects of the movement's frames. A related advantage of framing

---

[28] Tarrow, *Power in Movement*, p. 110. See R. D. Benford and D. A. Snow, 'Framing Processes and Social Movements: An Overview and Assessment', *Annual Review of Sociology*, 26, 2000, pp. 611–39.

[29] See C. L. Bacchi, *Same Difference: Feminism and Sexual Difference* (Sydney, Allen and Unwin, 1990), and S. Gunew and A. Yeatman, *Feminism and the Politics of Difference* (St Leonards, NSW, Allen and Unwin, 1993).

[30] See E. Goffman, *Frame Analysis: An Essay on the Organization of Experience* (New York, Harper and Row, 1974).

approaches is their greater openness to the role of emotions. As we saw in the previous section, rational choice approaches cannot easily make sense of much political action according to their narrow conception of rationality. Political action in general and extra-institutional action in particular must be motivated by factors beyond narrow self-interest and calculating rationality. Emotional appeals are often conveyed through symbolic, artistic and stylistic means rather than through argument alone.[31] Movement frames accordingly place considerable emphasis on the expression of emotions such as anger (at the oppressor) and pride (of the oppressed in themselves). Emotions are, according to Axel Honneth, the motivational basis for struggles for recognition.[32] People take risks that cannot be justified by any calculus of probable costs and benefits, because they are committed to a cause. They brave the attacks of police and security forces, because they feel deep anger at the injustices they, and sometimes other people, suffer. A common expression of this kind of commitment is the claim that a life without freedom is not worth living. By the same token, an important condition of a social movement's success is its ability to generate and sustain appropriate emotions as a basis for the ongoing commitment of activists. As we have seen, emotion and identity play an indispensable role in the achievement of collective action by otherwise oppressed and isolated individuals. Movement leaders must work hard to maintain the morale and energy of members. Crucially, though, to insist here on the role of emotions is not to revert to the collective behaviour approach's assumptions of collective irrationality, which treat collective emotions as diversions from the path of sane and rational action. Such approaches treat extra-institutional politics as a symptom of breakdown or dysfunction. Rather, it is important to recognize that emotions can have a positive and constructive place within the rational conduct of life.[33] By the same token, rationality must be understood more broadly to include emotions, relationships and commitments.

Changes of ideology, culture and the framing of social and political conflict are most directly and readily understood at the collective level. At the same time, social changes must in some sense consist of, and be describable in terms of, individual choices and changes, as methodological individualism and rational choice theories imply. As

---

[31] See J. Goodwin, J. M. Jasper and F. Polletta, eds., *Passionate Politics: Emotions and Social Movements* (Chicago and London, University of Chicago Press, 2001), and cf. J. M. Jasper, *The Art of Moral Protest: Culture, Biography, and Creativity in Social Movements* (Chicago and London, University of Chicago Press, 1997), pp. 10–12.

[32] A. Honneth, *The Struggle for Recognition: The Moral Grammar of Social Conflicts* (Cambridge, MA, MIT Press, 1995), pp. 135–9.

[33] See above, section 7.2.

Foucault, Deleuze and other 'continental' theorists have also argued, there is undoubtedly a micro-analytics of power and a micro-politics of social and cultural transformation. Broad structural explanations abstract from the complex, multidirectional and often contradictory local events, individual thoughts and actions that make up the substance of any movement. It is less obvious, however, that much, if anything, is gained by insisting on a strict methodological individualism and the exclusive validity of this micro-level of analysis. As with other forms of reductionism, promises that collective phenomena are in principle analysable into, or reducible to, their elements are rarely seriously approached, let alone fulfilled. The complexity involved in any radical reduction defies current – and probably any conceivable – analytical techniques. Approaches that consider identity, culture and cognitive frames shift the methodological emphasis from individualism to collectivism and, in that sense, are closer to classic approaches in sociology and social psychology. An adequate explanation must inevitably connect the individual or micro-level with the collective, macro-level of description. Neither level is adequate in its own terms alone.

In any case, whatever the ambitions of scientific theory, political thought and action can hardly rely on reductionist approaches alone. Political critique and action must be informed by concepts and arguments that make sense to political agents, who in turn must identify with a variety of interests and causes, usually understood in terms of some larger collective, if they are to be motivated to act politically. At the same time, identity must connect with the subjective level of the agent's meanings and intentions. Theorists' claims about objective reality and the ultimate interests of particular social constituencies are never fully adequate in these terms. Attempts to theorize the role of identity, culture, cognitive frames and emotions within social movements reflect these difficulties and insights. These studies are empirically useful, providing a more flexible and comprehensive conceptual net for an understanding of extra-institutional politics than can be provided by more formal, deductive approaches like rational choice theory.[34] At the same time, to the extent that they depart from simple assumptions about motivation and strategy, interpretive approaches cannot achieve and surely should not aspire to rigorous, law-like generalizations, let alone predictions about the future course of social movements.

[34] Cf. H. Johnston and B. Klandermans, eds., *Social Movements and Culture* (Minneapolis, MN, University of Minnesota Press, 1995); Jasper and Polletta, eds., *Passionate Politics*.

7.5 From Formal to Substantive Theories of Social Movements

The theories of social movements considered in the previous sections might be thought to be helpful to social movement activists in general, because they are predominantly formal rather than substantive. They are concerned, in other words, with the 'how' rather than the 'who' or 'what' of social movements. Formal approaches focus on those features of extra-institutional politics that distinguish social movements generally from institutionalized and organized forms of politics. These approaches analyse the structures and patterns common to extra-institutional forms of politics and contrast them with those of institutional forms. They give us more precise concepts and clarify some of the techniques, obstacles and regular forms of extra-institutional politics. They may even generate interesting empirical hypotheses concerning the nature and prospects of particular movements.

However, there are two broad limitations to formal approaches. In the first place, formal theories inevitably fail to live up to the ambitious claims of explanatory empirical science. It is hard to see how such theories could ever make firm predictions and so confirm or refute the hypotheses they generate. The circumstances of individual movements are so complex, so historically situated and culturally determined, that they defy generalizations of the kind that form the core of natural sciences. A second, more mundane problem with formal theories of social movements is the abstraction and increasing abstruseness of their conceptual distinctions. The categorization of more and more subtle features of movements and distinctions between them does not obviously lead to greater understanding. It is doubtful whether movement activists in particular have much to learn from such abstract academic theorizing. The increasing discrimination permitted by a complex conceptual net comes at the expense of any communicable or usable insights. If the goal of law-like generalization and prediction is unattainable, then it is important to ask what purpose academic studies of social movements are designed to serve instead.

Furthermore, formal theories of social movements are not necessarily informative about the substantive features or content of particular social movements: in other words, those features that serve to distinguish one movement from another. Formal approaches do not consider systematically the constituency and activists, issues and identities, values and ideology that serve to identify and differentiate specific movements from one another. Rather, different movements are considered in terms of general characteristics and relationships – the role of political opportunity structures, resources and sources of motivation, identity, emotion and so on. Advocates of a formal approach to the study of social movements might claim that this is as it should be. The general findings of formal theories are designed to apply to each and every social movement. Beyond that, detailed histories and descriptions of particular social movements will give us whatever further knowledge is possible.

During recent decades, more descriptively inclined sociologists and political scientists have indeed gathered much information concerning the substantive characteristics – the emergence, structures, strategies, tactics, political opportunities, agents, goals, evolution or 'life cycle', successes, failures, persistence and decline – of a wide variety of social movements. Although they make use of concepts developed by formal theorists, their aim is to capture the distinctive and substantive characteristics of particular movements rather than to coin new and ever more refined concepts. The methodology of descriptive studies also reflects the shift away from normative disapproval of extra-institutional politics described above (section 7.1). They aim to provide an objective representation of movements without subsuming them under normatively loaded categories such as collective irrationality, manias, panics or outbursts. A small sample of their work has been drawn upon in the discussions of previous chapters. Within both English-speaking and European social science, there is a plethora of such descriptive and quantitative studies of the particular character of a wide range of movements in a variety of contexts: both 'new' and 'old'; progressive, conservative and reactionary; 'First', 'Second' and 'Third' or 'developing' world; national and transnational or global.[35] Such descriptive studies differ from the formal approaches considered earlier in this chapter, because they refrain from making broader theoretical claims and generalizations.

Neither formal approaches nor descriptive studies, however, claim to provide theoretical advice or guidance to contemporary movements and their agents. Neither formal theories nor descriptive studies seek to tell contemporary political actors what to do. By contrast, a series of ambitious substantive studies, which will be considered in the next chapter, combines detailed descriptions of particular movements and their social and historical context with claims about their future direction and possible contributions to society. These substantive theories, which resemble to varying degrees critical theories of Marxist provenance, promise more substantive guidance to social movement activists and supporters. Whether these ambitions are, or ever could be, fulfilled is, as we shall see, much less clear.

---

[35] See, for example, H. Kriesi et al., *New Social Movements in Western Europe: A Comparative Analysis* (Minneapolis, MN, University of Minnesota Press, 1995), and D. Rucht, ed., *Research on Social Movements: The State of the Art in Western Europe and the USA* (Frankfurt, Campus; Boulder, CO, Westview Press, 1991).

Further Reading

A comprehensive guide to the range of approaches to social movements is Donatella Della Porta and Mario Diani, *Social Movements: An Introduction*. Normative discussion of extra-institutional activism (and politics generally) has been deeply influenced by John Rawls's *Theory of Justice*. Jean L. Cohen and Andrew Arato provide a wide-ranging and historically informed account of the relationship of *Civil Society and Political Theory*. A good guide to earlier sociological approaches to social movements is Lewis Killian's chapter on 'Social Movements' in R. E. L. Faris's edited collection *Handbook of Modern Sociology*. Aldon D. Morris and Carol McClurg Mueller's edited collection, *Frontiers in Social Movement Theory*, introduces more recent sociological approaches. Other classic and influential discussions are Sidney Tarrow, *Power in Movement: Collective Action, Social Movements and Politics*; Mayer N. Zald and John McCarthy, *Social Movements in an Organizational Society*; Anthony Oberschall, *Social Conflict and Social Movements*; and Charles Tilly, *Social Movements, 1768–2004*. Susan Staggenborg's *Social Movements* is a good overall guide to current formal approaches.

8

Theories of Social Movements: II. Historical and Substantive Approaches

Outline

In contrast to formal theories (discussed in the last chapter), substantive theories of social movements focus on the differences between particular social movements. Particular movements – their main issues, constituency, ideas or ideology, strategy and tactics – reflect the kind of society and historical context in which they have emerged. Inspired more or less directly by Marxism's account of working-class responses to capitalism, substantive theories of contemporary movements offer a variety of interpretative frameworks in order to make sense of these characteristic issues, ideas, actors and strategies. Ronald Inglehart, Claus Offe, Jürgen Habermas, Alain Touraine, Alberto Melucci and Manuel Castells are prominent exponents of this approach. Theories inspired by poststructuralism and postmodernism relate contemporary movements to the crisis of modernity and/or rise of a postmodern culture. In their different ways, substantive approaches struggle to find a viable path between, on the one hand, dogmatically imposing on social movement activists *the* meaning of their conflict and, on the other hand, retreating to the level of mere description.

8.1 What Is To Be Done? Substantive Theories of Social Movements

The theories considered in the previous chapter focus on *formal* features common to social movements and extra-institutional politics in general. By contrast, *substantive* theories (considered in the present chapter) are concerned with the specific characteristics of particular movements – and in that sense with the content as opposed to form – which distinguish them from other movements. Specific movements are distinguished from one another by the fact that they represent distinct constellations of interests; they challenge defined social structures, forms of exploitation and oppression; they advocate social change and propose specific alternative values and institutions in order to achieve the goals of their particular constituency. In an obvious way, the women's movement differs from environmental and workers' movements, because it has distinct issues, interests and goals. Corresponding to these substantive differences are also differences of strategy and tactics, styles and forms of organization. Investigation of the substantive characteristics of social movements complements attempts to understand their formal features. But many substantive theories go further than that. They attempt to go beyond merely describing the substantive features of movements to a theoretical explanation of them.

An influential prototype for substantive explanations of social movements is provided by Marxian critical theory. However, the considerable ambitions of Marxist theory set a high (and probably unattainable) standard for critical theory. Marxism goes beyond mere descriptions of the substantive characteristics of the working-class movement and its historical context in fundamental ways. In the first place, Marxism seeks to explain the emerging movement through an analysis of its social and historical context in the Industrial Revolution. The relentless rise of capitalist relations of production intensifies class struggle between working class and bourgeoisie, which is understood as the essential and defining conflict of the age. The capitalist mode of production is situated, secondly, in the context of a broader theory of historical materialism, which conceives human history as an unfolding series of modes of production. The series of modes of production includes primitive communism, ancient slavery, feudalism and capitalism; it anticipates the arrival of socialism and communism. As this series implies, thirdly, Marxism even more ambitiously anticipates the *future* economic crisis of capitalism, its revolutionary overthrow by the working class and its replacement by socialism and ultimately communism. The classless society of communism will abolish the subordinate status of workers as wage-slaves and thereby complete human history understood as the history of class struggle.[1] Despite the radical nature of the communist ideal, Marxism claims, fourthly, that communism is not an unattainable or utopian goal, because it arises inevitably out of – or, at least, is made possible as a result of – the existing contradictions

---

[1] In fact, Marx refers to communism as the end of human *pre*-history, because only in communist society will a genuinely human existence and, therefore, history become possible: an existence and history no longer defined by material scarcity, alienation and class conflict.

of capitalism.[2] An important strategic implication is, fifthly, a powerful argument for the unity of all oppositional forces. Only the working class can achieve communism, and only communism promises to abolish scarcity, alienation and conflict. So other oppositional forces and movements should unite behind the leadership of the working class.

However, the practical ambitions of Marxist theory have not been fulfilled. Marxism has proved problematic both theoretically and practically and is widely recognized to have reached twin impasses during the twentieth century. Communist revolutions occurred in a number of countries in the East or Second World, but the results – Stalinist dictatorship, bureaucratic party rule and, after initial successes, economic stagnation – were anything but ideal. In the West, capitalism has appeared to thrive, notwithstanding a series of severe economic crises. The working class seems reconciled to capitalism; its oppositional activities are largely confined to trade unionism and social democratic reforms. Most significant in the present context is the fact that the impasses of Marxism – both the 'failed successes' of actually existing communism and the outright failures of revolutionary communism in the West – played an important formative role not only in the emergence but also in the self-understanding of the new social movements.

New social movements emerged, in part at least, as self-conscious successors to socialism and the left. The New Left's criticisms of the socialist tradition were renewed and radicalized by new social movements. Some thinkers and theorists saw them as a new (albeit intrinsically plural) agent of revolutionary transformation. New activists were pursuing new forms of emancipation in novel ways in an unprecedented historical context.[3] The substantive theories considered in the following sections attempt to explain these various dimensions of novelty. In the process, they effectively provide substitutes for some or all of the features of Marxian critical theory outlined above. In other words, they provide an analysis of contemporary society (often placed within an overall account of western or world history), which is designed to account for some or all of the emerging social movements. Central to this analysis is a diagnosis of society's main tensions, contradictions and crisis tendencies, which in turn implies a way to resolve them. The theory as a whole is intended to provide guidelines on strategy, tactics and possible alliances of contemporary social movements.

---

[2] The inevitability of communism is a matter of considerable controversy within the Marxist tradition.

[3] See above, chapter 3.

8.2 New Social Movements as Agents of the New Politics

Associated in particular with continental European approaches to the study of social movements, new social movement theory is one influential approach providing a substantive as opposed to merely formal explanation of the rise, role and prospects of contemporary movements. New social movement theorists explain the rise of new social movements as the result of systemic tensions and contradictions of contemporary western societies.[4] Significantly, these tensions are no longer seen to be centrally concerned with class conflict and economic relations.

For many intellectuals and activists already disillusioned with what Rudolf Bahro dubbed 'actually existing socialism', the failure of the New Left in the late 1960s was more than an event at the social and political level. It was the occasion of a final loss of faith in the industrial proletariat as the agent of revolution. A working class integrated into the institutional structures of welfare state capitalism was increasingly conservative, focusing exclusively on incremental gains within the system. In contrast to mainly middle-class student radicals and New Left protesters of the 1960s, working people and labour organizations were less likely to oppose the Vietnam War and, when they did oppose it, did so not as members of the working class or as a class issue. Although trade unions and other left organizations eventually became involved in the Paris Events of 1968, they were out of touch with the new style of protests and sought to co-opt the movement to their own ends. The eventual collapse of the 1968 protests, and with it the popularity of New Left ideas, helped to trigger a further substantial shift in thinking. The contrast between the successes of the new movements and a left that was splintered, factional and increasingly marginal encouraged many progressive thinkers, including many former Marxists and New Left activists, to see these movements as a new and promising basis for a radical challenge to western society. It was these thinkers who first described the new waves of activism as 'new social movements' in order to signal their role as a new transformative force replacing the working class.[5]

The term 'new social movements' is controversial and problematic, however, not least because it combines historical and normative claims.

---

[4] In that sense, new social movement theory is a variety of Marxian 'critical theory': see R. Geuss, *The Idea of a Critical Theory: Habermas and the Frankfurt School* (Cambridge, Cambridge University Press, 1981).

[5] See K.-W. Brand, D. Büsser and D. Rucht, *Aufbruch in eine andere Gesellschaft: Neue soziale Bewegungen in der Bundesrepublik* (Frankfurt and New York, Campus, 1986), 3rd rev. edn, and C. Jennett and R. G. Stewart, *Politics of the Future: The Role of Social Movements* (South Melbourne, Macmillan, 1989).

The normative connotations of 'new' as opposed to 'contemporary' align new social movement theory with the family of normative concepts inherited from Enlightenment conceptions of history. These terms reflect assumptions about the direction of history or social development and are closely associated with western claims to represent the height of modernity. New social movements are, in effect, conceived as 'radical' or 'progressive', because they are expected to contribute to the further development of western societies towards greater wealth, human rights, freedom and social justice. By the same token, religious revivals and nationalist, racist, sexist and homophobic movements are deemed 'reactionary', because they wish to halt or reverse that process of development.[6] From the same perspective, the working-class movement is described as 'old', because although it once played a progressive role in extending democratic rights and social justice to all members of society, it is no longer such a force for radical change.

Like Marxism and other critical social theories, new social movement theory relates the rise and nature of contemporary movements to the current state of western society. We have already considered how western societies were transformed during the course of the twentieth century. Pressure from the working class and its organizations combined with the influence of social liberal reformers and the impact of war and economic crisis to bring about a substantial transformation of liberal capitalism.[7] As we shall see throughout this chapter, this transformation is explained by different theories in different ways and terms. The resulting society is variously described as welfare state capitalism, late, advanced or organized capitalism, as post-materialist, postindustrial or programmed society, as the culmination of modernity or as the onset of postmodernity. There are, of course, important contrasts and distinctions between these different theories. But the differing theoretical constructions belie considerable agreement of sociological and political analysis.

Closest to the Marxist paradigm are theories that see new social movements as responses to the crisis of 'welfare state' and 'organized' capitalism.[8] A starting point for such theories is a revised class analysis of the contemporary state. The new institutional order can no longer be described as a 'bourgeois state', because it now includes the representatives of the working class, albeit usually in a subordinate position.

---

[6] See R. Williams, *Keywords: A Vocabulary of Culture and Society* (London, Fontana, 1976) , and cf. above, pp. 17–20.

[7] See above, section 3.3.

[8] See C. Offe, *Contradictions of the Welfare State*, ed. J. Keane (Cambridge, MA, MIT Press, 1987), and 'New Social Movements: Challenging the Boundaries of Institutional Politics', *Social Research*, 52:4, 1985, pp. 817–68; and S. Lash and J. Urry, *The End of Organized Capitalism* (Cambridge, Polity Press, 1987).

Trade unions and labour organizations are given an institutional role in the management of the economy alongside representatives of capital. At the state level, these arrangements typically involve tripartite bodies including representatives of government, capital and labour. Sometimes – for example, in Germany – corporate boards include labour representatives as well. These arrangements are described as neo-corporatism, because they give privileged access to representatives of particular social classes and functional groups.[9] Thanks to universal suffrage, social democratic and labour parties have also become major parties of government. In addition, organized capitalism involves the application of Keynesian economic policies to manage the capitalist economy. The state seeks through public spending to ensure continuous growth and full employment. It raises and distributes taxes in order to ensure greater material equality. Welfare state capitalism supplements civil and political rights with social welfare rights including universal medical care and free state education as well as unemployment, sickness and retirement benefits.

The incorporation of labour into the institutions of organized capitalism associated with a decline of working-class activism is reinforced by changes to the economic sector in developed capitalist economies. These involve, in the first place, the decline of traditional manufacturing industries and the rise of the services sector. Investment and employment in advanced economies occurs increasingly in the areas of research and development, finance and investment, marketing and retail. These activities are geographically more dispersed and industrially less thoroughly organized. Workers in service industries are less likely to identify as or with the working class. At the same time, state provision of welfare, health care and education creates a significant new class of state public service employees.[10] A further change in the post-Second World War economy involves a shift away from the Fordist model – so-called because of the success of Henry Ford's approach to the manufacture of automobiles – of assembly-line production of a relatively small range of standard products for mass consumption. The Fordist model is being replaced by a more diversified and decentralized organization of production and consumption. 'Post-Fordism' also promotes greater emphasis on individualized products tailored to individual identities and lifestyles, which are promoted through increasingly sophisticated and diverse marketing.[11] Both developments

---

[9] Corporatism refers to state forms that organize representation according to membership of social classes or functional groups rather than (or in addition to) the representation of geographical regions and ideological orientations.

[10] See Offe, 'New Social Movements', pp. 821–5.

[11] The Fordist model of production is also referred to as Taylorism, named after Frederick Taylor (1856–1915), who was a pioneer of the scientific management

undermine traditional forms of working-class identity, solidarity and organization.

The changing nature of the welfare state, capitalism and class helps to account for widely observed features of new social movements. The relative affluence and material security of welfare state capitalism supports a shift to altruistic and non-materialist political goals. Ronald Inglehart's 'post-materialist hypothesis' assembles evidence of a correlation between new social movements and a widespread generational shift of values especially among post-Second World War generations. This shift is related to the spread of mass media and state secondary and tertiary education. Concern for the environment, social justice and peace, and increasing cultural cosmopolitanism can all be related to this value shift. Supporters of new social movements have been shown to be younger, belonging to generations that have benefited from affluence, security and education. Also prominent are activists from the so-called 'new middle class' of technical experts, service workers and state employees in education and social services. Thus, although the post-Fordist welfare state pacifies the working class by satisfying some of its demands whilst disrupting traditional forms of class solidarity, it simultaneously gives rise to new forms of opposition.[12]

The *issues* raised by new social movements reflect the concerns of the new activists. These issues were effectively excluded from the class compromise of welfare state capitalism. Women and members of religious, ethnic and 'racial' minorities not only suffered widespread discrimination by employers, but also were at first ignored and sometimes discriminated against by labour organizations. Welfare systems were constructed on the basis of a man's right to earn a 'family wage', on the assumption that women were either secondary wage-earners or stay-at-home mothers. Public health and education services reflected similarly gendered assumptions. Even more starkly, homosexuality was legally persecuted in most western states until the 1970s. Working-class organizations and parties, even revolutionary Marxist parties, generally did not support the aims of gay and lesbian liberation. Even though attitudes on' the left were gradually transformed, it was the activities of the women's, lesbian and gay and anti-racist movements rather than working-class organizations that undermined these forms of discrimination.[13] The concerns of the peace and environmental movements were excluded from the welfare state compromise as well but in a different way. Welfare state capitalism institutionalizes the

and organization of production for the sake of maximum efficiency. See Lash and Urry, *End of Organized Capitalism.*

[12] See Inglehart, *The Silent Revolution* and *Culture Shift in Advanced Industrial Society.*
[13] See Offe, 'New Social Movements', pp. 825–32.

shared interest of capital and labour in continuing economic growth and industrial expansion. But there was little institutional recognition of environmental issues. The politics of nuclear deterrence and the burgeoning 'military-industrial complex' have similarly been accommodated to the interests of capital and labour, providing both profits and jobs within a largely shared understanding of international security. Labour parties and trade unions have, with significant exceptions, supported the US alliance and nuclear armaments with little critical distance or independence of foreign policy.

Claus Offe and others argue, in addition, that welfare state capitalism is subject to crisis tendencies analogous to the class division of liberal capitalism. The welfare state performs certain essential functions for business and finance: securing social stability, funding essential infrastructure and providing other public goods. But the need to finance its ever-expanding activities ultimately threatens capital's profitability. A 'culture of entitlement' leads to escalating demands from citizens for ever more welfare, education, health care and benefits. What is more, citizens' demands are only likely to grow, as the expansion of the state erodes such 'uncontested and non-contingent premises' of politics as the family, religion and the work ethic. If the welfare state denies or fails to satisfy these demands, it risks losing authority and legitimacy.[14] If it gives in to them, then ever-increasing taxes will undermine the profitable reproduction of capital. Offe considers three possible responses to the crisis of the welfare state. The response of 'old labour' is to defend and if possible reinforce the institutions of the welfare state. But, assuming the diagnosis of crisis tendencies is correct, this will only exacerbate the problem. The conservative or neoliberal agenda is to dismantle the welfare state and return to the model of nineteenth-century liberal capitalism. From Thatcher and Reagan to the Washington Consensus, this agenda aims to reverse the gains of labour, discourage the culture of entitlements, reduce the size of the state and provide greater incentives for enterprise.

For Offe, an alliance between new social movements and the social democratic left offers the most promising response to the crisis of the welfare state. New social movement activism revives civil society. These movements are associated with a politics of empowerment and a flourishing 'third sector' of self-help organizations, which offer to resolve societal problems without direct involvement of the state. At the same time, alliance with the social democratic left offers institutional support and the strategic power of labour organizations to achieve the goals of new movements. However, there are a number of problems with this prognosis. In the first place, it is not really plausible to see new

---

[14] See Offe, 'New Social Movements', pp. 818–20. Cf. J. Habermas, *Legitimation Crisis* (London, Heinemann, 1976), trans. T. McCarthy.

social movements as leading to a solution to impending fiscal crisis.[15] Although they are indeed associated with self-help, empowerment and the 'third sector', they have also reinforced campaigns for social rights for women and ethnic minorities. The activation of civil society tends as much towards increasing demands on welfare and government provision as towards autonomous third-sector solutions to social problems. Governments have also proved adept at exploiting the third sector and non-governmental organizations (NGOs) in order to offload their welfare obligations in the name of greater efficiency and client choice.

In other words, civil society activism has to some extent been co-opted by the neoliberal agenda. What is more, the considerable success of that agenda has subsequently overtaken much of the foregoing analysis of welfare state capitalism. Undoubtedly, the neoliberal project gained greatest momentum in response to the apparent unsustainability of the welfare state model of capitalism. Neoliberalism has proved remarkably successful, influencing many governments throughout the world to accept the ideals of neoliberal and corporate globalization. The successes of corporate globalization have in turn spurred the rise of the alter-globalization movement. As a consequence, as we have seen, that movement combines many of the concerns and values of new social movements with a renewed emphasis on economic and social justice issues.[16] Indeed, in addition to the upsurge of extra-institutional resistance to neoliberal globalization, there are other reasons to think that the neoliberal project may not be long-lasting. After all, welfare state capitalism first emerged in the twentieth century as a response to the systemic failures and crisis tendencies of nineteenth-century liberal capitalism. The harshness and instability of a society founded on efficiency and productivity alone generated significant and ultimately effective opposition. Transferring class conflict to the global level, the neoliberal model may nevertheless prove short-lived.

8.3 Jürgen Habermas: Social Movements and the Incomplete Project of Modernity

Jürgen Habermas's perspective on new social movements shifts the analytical focus from historical materialism and class analysis to modernity and processes of modernization. In the broad tradition of earlier members of the Frankfurt School, Habermas draws on Weber's account of societal rationalization to provide a sociological account of

---

[15] See Offe, 'New Social Movements', and cf. Samuel P. Huntington, 'The United States' in M. Crozier, S. P. Huntington and J. Watanuki, *The Crisis of Democracy* (New York, New York University Press, 1975).

[16] See above, chapter 6.

modernity. Central to Weber's contribution is his view of the modern bureaucratic state as a source of domination that is relatively independent of capitalism.[17] The state is not simply the tool of capitalism, as historical materialist accounts of the 'bourgeois state' imply. Both the state and capitalism are subject to independent but interacting processes of 'formal rationalization', which are characteristic of western modernity. Formal or, in Frankfurt School terms, merely instrumental rationalization has no bearing on the 'substantive rationality' of the ends we pursue. Formal rationality organizes efficient means (of production or administration) to goals or ends that are simply given. In fact, formal rationalization tends to displace judgements of the substantive rationality of ends. Capitalism maximizes efficiency and production with little regard for what is produced. State bureaucracies efficiently implement policies with insufficient regard to how beneficial or harmful they might be.

In Habermas's terms, formal rationalization creates quasi-autonomous social systems, which are increasingly independent of cultural and moral values governing ends. Both capitalism or 'money' and the state or 'power' represent developed forms of 'systems rationality'. Systems coordinate the actions of members of society not through the intersubjective processes characteristic of a 'lifeworld', which may involve both inherited religious and cultural traditions, moral and ethical reflection and critical dialogue. Rather, actions are co-ordinated in a quasi-mechanical way through markets and state structures, which operate 'behind the backs' – or without reference to the subjective perspectives, values and wishes – of people. With the advance of both capitalism and the modern state, these systems expand greatly and are increasingly 'uncoupled' from the lifeworld.[18] Or, as Pusey explains, the 'system refers to those vast tracts of modern society that are "uncoupled" from communicatively shared experience in ordinary language and co-ordinated, instead, through the media of money and power'. Worse, as these systems develop further, they begin to invade or 'colonize' the lifeworld.[19]

The systems' invasion of the lifeworld explains what Habermas sees as the ambivalent potential of modernity. As Weber's notion of 'disenchantment' also implies, the formal or instrumental rationalization of

[17] Offe also understands the issues of new social movements in terms of a 'modern' critique of modernization: 'New Social Movements', p. 850.

[18] J. Habermas, *The Theory of Communicative Action*, Vol. I, *Reason and the Rationalization of Society* (Cambridge, Polity Press, 1984), trans. T. McCarthy, esp. Part II, pp. 143–271, and *The Theory of Communicative Action*, Vol. II, *Lifeworld and System: A Critique of Functionalist Reason* (Cambridge, Polity Press, 1987), trans. T. McCarthy, Part IV, pp. 113–97.

[19] M. Pusey, *Jürgen Habermas* (London and New York, Tavistock, 1976), p. 107, and cf. Habermas, *Theory of Communicative Action*, Vol. II, pp. 301–73.

society undermines the unquestioned authority of substantive value-systems of both cultural tradition and religion. But on Habermas's more optimistic account, the disruption of traditional values and norms also opens the way for criticism and innovation. Traditional norms are often oppressive and authoritarian. Tradition and religion dogmatically assert values such as the inferiority of women, the superiority of certain ethnic or 'racial' groups and the wickedness of homosexuality and other forms of sexual diversity. According to Habermas's notion of communicative rationality, the disruption of traditional norms makes possible for the first time a process of rational discourse, through which just and universally acceptable norms can emerge. In order for these new norms to be universally valid, they must emerge through a discourse that is open, without artificial constraints and undistorted by social power. However, the emancipatory possibilities of western modernity are threatened by the aforementioned expansion of state and capitalist systems, which increasingly organize human life according to the instrumental logics of money and power. These logics threaten to overwhelm any possibility of communicatively achieved consensus and to reduce the lifeworld to an empty shell.

Habermas understands new social movements in these terms as an embryonic counterattack from the lifeworld against the colonizing systems of money and power.[20] As systems rationalization advances, conflict is displaced from within the economic and state systems themselves – from the political and economic conflicts characteristic of liberalism and socialism – to the lifeworld. More precisely, conflicts are displaced to the 'seam' between system and lifeworld: 'the new conflicts arise in areas of cultural reproduction, social integration and socialization. . . . the new conflicts are not sparked by problems of distribution, but concern the grammar of forms of life'.[21] This analysis is supported by the issues prominent in new social movements. The women's movement challenges patriarchal assumptions of male superiority and privilege, which permeate not only the workplace and public institutions but also the family, sexuality, literature, the arts and culture. Anti-racist movements challenge ethnic and racist assumptions about the superiority of certain peoples and racial groups, which similarly permeate every aspect of life including the most intimate. The gay and lesbian movements challenge traditional and religious prejudices against homosexuality. Sexuality, gender, personal identity and values, ethics and morality are all at stake in the conflicts engaged by new social movements.

In fact, Habermas is more ambivalent about contemporary

---

[20] See J. Habermas, 'New Social Movements', *Telos*, 49, 1981, pp. 33–7, and *Theory of Communicative Action*, Vol. II, pp. 391–6.

[21] Habermas, 'New Social Movements', p. 32.

movements than the foregoing comments might suggest. Contemporary movements respond to the disruption and colonization of the life-world in either 'defensive' or 'offensive' ways: they either defensively aim 'to defend or reinstate endangered life styles' or offensively 'put reformed life styles into practice'.[22] White supremacists defend the privileged position of white people against advocates of racial equality. Pro-life campaigners oppose abortion rights claimed by the women's movement. Campaigners for traditional family values, Christian and Islamic fundamentalists condemn homosexuality and oppose gay marriage. Focusing perhaps on deep ecology and radical self-sufficiency, Habermas describes environmental and peace movements in ambivalent terms as a more 'defensive' reaction, albeit one 'which already operates on the basis of a rationalized life-world and tries out new forms of co-operation and community'.[23] The universalistic normative orientation and ambition of Habermas's ideal of communicative rationality is difficult to reconcile with the substantive insights of particular movements. Movements' challenges to particular values, self-interpretations and identities do not contribute directly to the system of universal norms. They contribute only to the reform of lifestyles and identities which, as Habermas has come to recognize, cannot be generalized. He is surely too pessimistic, however, when he claims that the women's movement is 'the only movement that follows the tradition of bourgeois-socialist liberation movements. The struggle against patriarchal oppression and for the realization of a promise that is deeply rooted in the acknowledged universalist foundations of morality and legality lends feminism the impetus of an offensive movement, whereas all other movements are more defensive in character.'[24]

On closer inspection, Habermas's explanation of new social movements turns out to be less substantive than it at first appears to be. In response to criticism, Habermas has limited the scope of discourse ethics to intersubjective norms as opposed to ethical values and lifestyles. This means that his theory only applies to the normative framework of a liberal society. New social movements can be understood as contributing to a fully universal understanding of citizenship, one that includes men and women, diverse religious and ethnic groups and a variety of sexual orientations. Discourse ethics has nothing to say, however, about the specific values and forms of life adopted by social movements or, in the wake of their activities, by society as a whole. Habermas's theory thus effectively provides a historical explanation for the potential rise of a universal but largely abstract framework of individual rights and democratic norms. This framework

[22] Habermas, 'New Social Movements', p. 32.
[23] Habermas, 'New Social Movements', p. 35.
[24] Habermas, 'New Social Movements', p. 34.

is designed only to guarantee individual autonomy from unnecessary social constraints. It does not offer guidance on ethical judgements and forms of life.[25]

Put another way, Habermas charts the transition from a substantially constrained to a more open understanding of society. Habermas's early work on the *Structural Transformation of the Public Sphere* shows how the modern ideal of a public sphere emerges during the Enlightenment. In effect, he offers a historical account of the emergence of the possibility of genuine democracy, consistent with his early programmatic statement that the goal of critical theory should be to make it possible for humanity to escape a historical process that determines outcomes independently of collective human interests in order henceforth to make history 'with will and consciousness'.[26] Habermas understands the public sphere as a medium for the self-conscious and critical, rather than merely tradition-bound, formation of a 'public will'. It is, in that sense, closely related to the democratic ideal. His subsequent work aims to rescue the ideal of a rational public sphere from the contaminating and distorting effects of modern capitalism, the modern state and mass democracy.[27] The strategic electoral imperatives of opaque party bureaucracies, commercial mass media oriented to entertainment, the technical nature of many issues and the sheer complexity of society all stand in the way of Habermas's ideal of rational collective will formation. The difficult world-historical task facing social movements is, in effect, to escape from the substantive constraints of society and history.

8.4 Alain Touraine: Social Movement as Agent of Autonomy in Postindustrial Society

The work of Alain Touraine applies a quite different vocabulary to the task of understanding new social movements, but there are nevertheless strong parallels with Habermas's Weberian approach and more distant echoes of Marxism. Like Marx, Touraine identifies a single basic conflict as characteristic of contemporary society and conceives that

---

25 On the distinction between moral norms and ethical values, see J. Habermas, *Moral Consciousness and Communicative Action* (Cambridge, MA, MIT Press, 1990), trans. C. Lenhardt and S. W. Nicholsen, pp. 195–215: 'Morality and Ethical Life: Does Hegel's Critique of Kant Apply to Discourse Ethics?'

26 J. Habermas, *Theory and Practice* (London, Heinemann, 1974), ch. 6, 'Between Philosophy and Science: Marxism as Critique', pp. 195–252, esp. p. 252.

27 See Habermas, *Structural Transformation of the Public Sphere*; cf. R. C. Holub, *Jürgen Habermas: Critic in the Public Sphere* (London and New York, Routledge, 1991).

conflict in terms of the prevailing mode of production.[28] But Touraine departs from historical materialism in fundamental ways. In the first place, he rejects determinist interpretations of historical change including (on most interpretations) historical materialism and is similarly opposed to functionalism in sociology, which portrays society as a self-reproducing machine or system of structures. Social structures should not be reified in this way, because they are in fact made up of human actions, which continually reproduce but also, crucially, potentially transform them. On the other hand, he is equally opposed to 'action-ism' (*l'actionnisme*) or, in other words, any view that treats human actions as products of individual will or psychology without reference to surrounding social context and structures. The fundamental insight of Marxism and critical theory – that unless political action takes account of its social context it will never be more than utopian moral-izing – is correct. Touraine advocates instead a synthesis of 'structure' and 'action' that refrains from prioritizing either term. Social structure is seen as 'the changing and unstable result of relations between the actors who, through their social conflicts and via their cultural orienta-tions, produce society'.[29] The sociology of action attempts to combine critical theory's 'scientific' or materialist attention to existing society with a view that gives scope (and hope) to political action.

However, although human beings have always made history, they have previously done so largely unconsciously. This is because, in pre-modern societies, society's 'self-production' was restricted and obscured by unquestionable norms and assumptions – or what he calls 'meta-social guarantees' – imposed by metaphysical and religious systems. Modernity has eroded these arbitrary limits to society's self-production and so enhanced 'historicity', by which Touraine means society's 'capacity to produce its own social and cultural field, its own historical environment'.[30] Modern actors can, in principle, replace inherited norms and assumptions with new ones and act to transform society accordingly. Social transformation also requires knowledge which, in the modern period, is provided by the social sciences. With freedom to criticize and the knowledge to effect changes, modern actors have an enhanced ability to transform society. For Touraine the ultimate bearers of this potential are social movements: 'Men make their own history: social life is produced by cultural achievement

---

[28] Touraine's early study examined workers in Chile: see A. Touraine, *Conscience ouvrière* (Paris, Éditions du Seuil, 1966). For a range of essays on Touraine, see J. C. Dean and M. Diani, *Alain Touraine* (London and New York, Routledge, 1996).

[29] A. Touraine, *The Voice and the Eye: An Analysis of Social Movements* (Cambridge and New York, Cambridge University Press, 1981), trans. A. Duff, p. 30.

[30] A. Touraine, *The Self-Production of Society* (Chicago and London, University of Chicago Press, 1977), trans. D. Coltman, p. 16.

and social conflicts, and at the heart of society burns the fire of social movements.'[31]

Modernity's promise of autonomy and social creativity is, as Habermas's Weberian account also implies, threatened by other aspects of contemporary society. In what Touraine refers to as 'post-industrial' or 'programmed' society, technical knowledge has increasingly become a condition of social power. Like Daniel Bell in *The Coming of Post-Industrial Society*, Touraine emphasizes both the increasing importance of services relative to manufacturing and the growing power of business managers as opposed to owners. Manufacturing itself becomes technically ever more advanced and so dependent on the technical knowledge of experts. The role of technical knowledge extends further to expanding communications and media industries, universities and other institutions concerned with the production and transmission of knowledge. Significantly, *non*-technical knowledge also plays an important role in areas such as marketing, product design and the entertainment and culture industries. Creators of symbolic and cultural content are crucial to the postindustrial economy. In contrast to Bell's conservative approach, however, Touraine locates postindustrial society within an ambitious periodization of history with strong Marxist parallels, although he modifies the Marxist schema in significant ways. Touraine distinguishes between agrarian societies where 'investment is used only to produce surplus without altering the methods of production', merchant societies in which 'investment occurs at the level of the distribution and exchange of goods and services' and industrial society in which '[investment] is used to change work organization and the division of labour'. In postindustrial or programmed society, investment 'is used to change production itself, that is, to create the means of management and invent new products'. In addition, Touraine's model recognizes different 'patterns of development' for each mode. So, for example, in industrial societies there are capitalist, dependent, colonized, nationalist and communist patterns of development.[32]

Touraine also regards postindustrial society more critically as a new form of domination with correspondingly new modes of conflict. Just as Marx identified the conflict between capital and labour as the essential and decisive contradiction of capitalism, Touraine claims that the fundamental opposition of postindustrial society is between managers and managed. The newly acquired role of knowledge has replaced industrial society's central conflict between capital and labour by new conflicts, which focus on the management of society. The fundamental opposition of programmed society is between 'those who manage

[31] Touraine, *Voice and the Eye*, p. 1.
[32] Touraine, *Voice and the Eye*, pp. 102–3 and 106.

the apparatus of knowledge and economic transformation, and those who are caught up in change and are trying to regain control over it'.[33] Touraine initially saw the student activism of May 1968 in Paris as confirmation of this new pattern of conflict; student activists were resisting 'a structure of management, control, and manipulation of all social life'.[34] Being centrally concerned with knowledge and destined to occupy positions either as technical experts, knowledge workers or managers, university students undoubtedly occupy a crucial position in postindustrial society. Significantly, Touraine never simply assumes that new social movements as such *are* the progressive social movement of contemporary society. Rather, aspects of some contemporary movements can be aligned with resistance to the new domination. The anti-nuclear movement opposes an industry that benefits from a technocratic veil, which obscures the ethical and political issues it raises.[35] Environmental protesters oppose state and business managers who serve short-term imperatives of profit and electoral success. But equally, employees who resist management and attempt to gain greater creative control over their work are resisting technocratic imperatives as well.

In contrast to Habermas's overriding value of intersubjectivity, Touraine sees subjectivity and autonomy as the primary values informing resistance to programmed society: it is 'necessary to re-introduce the concept of the subject, not in a Cartesian or religious sense, but as the effort of the individual to act as a person, to select, organize and control his individual life against all kinds of pressures'.[36] However, Touraine understands the pursuit of subjectivity and autonomy in very broad terms. As he puts it in a recent work, 'The positive goal of today's social movements, which oppose both the reign of markets and the domination of communitarian-inspired movements, is the defence of the cultural and social rights of individuals and minorities.'[37] He points in this context to movements for 'cultural rights' including those of refugees or *sans-papiers*, the homeless and unemployed, as well as AIDS and anti-racist activists. But the 'recomposition' of industrial society also depends on the activities of the labour movement, colonial liberation movements, ecologism, the women's movement, children's rights and anti-paedophilia campaigns. Nor is the emphasis on subjectivity and autonomy incompatible with a collective approach.

---

[33] Touraine, *Self-Production of Society*, p. 156.
[34] Touraine, *The May Movement*, p. 347.
[35] A. Touraine, Z. Hegedus, F. Dubet and M. Wieviorka, *The Opposition to Nuclear Energy in France* (Cambridge and New York, Cambridge University Press, 1983), trans. P. Fawcett.
[36] Cited by Rucht, *Research on Social Movements*, pp. 390–1. Cf. Touraine, *Beyond Neoliberalism*, p. 48.
[37] Touraine, *Beyond Neoliberalism*, p. 51.

Contemporary movements fight for 'the right to a personal identity', but they are still collective political movements rather than symptoms of a retreat into an asocial and apolitical privatism.[38]

The creativity and autonomy of social movements is opposed to the dominance of both markets and the state. Social movements are essential to the deepening of democracy through direct political action within civil society: 'What we most need is neither more state nor more market, but less state and less market – we need more initiatives, more negotiations, more projects, and more truly social conflicts. . . . All social struggles, from the most defensive to the most innovative, are positive to the extent that they expand the political field, defined in the broadest sense as a public space.' This emphasis on social movements acting within civil society is the crux of Touraine's rejection of revolutionary Marxism:

> The difference between the two ways of interpreting popular movements and political interventions is, ultimately, a corollary of that between revolution and democracy. The basis for the revolutionary spirit is provided by the supposed powerlessness of actors, the central role attributed to the crisis, and the call for a vanguard leadership, while the democratic idea insists that all men and women must be regarded as potential actors who are capable of responsible actions despite the remoteness and strength of the dominant power.[39]

The revolutionary tradition ultimately disempowers, because it displaces the power of political transformation from social actors, who are in the end its only possible bearers, onto a system which, through the logic of economy and social crisis, is destined to bring about transformation through the unfolding of its own internal logic. By contrast, Touraine's democratic alternative is founded on the necessity and possibility of political action: 'We must resolutely reject all discourses that try to convince us that we are powerless.'[40]

There is a tension – one shared, it has to be said, with other versions of critical theory – between Touraine's democratic emphasis and his notion of 'sociological intervention', whereby critical sociologists aim to reveal the 'highest meaning' of contemporary social movements to their activists. This implies an ambitious and, some might argue, arrogant view of social-scientific knowledge. Touraine himself says that 'Sociology is an act of enlightenment ("connaissance") in the service of liberty. The latter cannot exist without the former.' He proposes to substitute sociology for political economy, which held the decisive theoretical position within Marxism: sociology 'holds a central place in

[38] Touraine, *Beyond Neoliberalism*, pp. 66–8 and 70.
[39] Touraine, *Beyond Neoliberalism*, pp. 80 and 78.
[40] Touraine, *Beyond Neoliberalism*, p. 116.

the programmed society just as economics did in the industrial society or political philosophy in merchant societies'.[41] Jean L. Cohen unsympathetically describes this approach as 'sociological Leninism'. Her criticism reflects the familiar dilemma of critical theory. The critique of utopian political thought and action implies that political actors must ground their action in some knowledge of society. This knowledge can only be supplied in rigorous form by the social sciences. But as the Leninist tradition of Marxism demonstrates, the subordination of politics to scientific expertise has potentially authoritarian implications.[42] As a critic of technocratic domination, Touraine should at least be aware of these dangers.

Another potential criticism of Touraine results from the increasing ascendancy of neoliberal globalization and associated academic discourses. The concept of postindustrial society does not translate easily onto a global context. In fact, what are described as postindustrial societies are really advanced economies that have exported much of their industrial production to developing countries with low wages and few regulations. There is obviously no corresponding reduction of the manufacturing sector as a whole *at the global level*. The globalization of production merely redistributes various kinds of productive activity to different geographical regions and to societies at varying levels of development. The rise of alter-globalization movements reflects this shift from the postindustrial politics of advanced societies to the politics surrounding neoliberal globalization.[43] Touraine's concept of postindustrial society captures only one dimension of these complex processes of globalization, essentially from the perspective of the nation-state.

On the other hand, Touraine's approach has the considerable advantage over other new social movement theories that it includes economic conflicts within the category of conflicts over the management of society. In that sense, it is less threatened by the alter-globalization movement's turn (or return) to material conflicts over distribution. Overall, despite their differences, Touraine's approach has much in common with that of Habermas. Both see modern society as ambivalent. On the one hand, the loosened hold of tradition and religion opens possibilities for greater autonomy and more expansive democracy. But this potential is countered by the relentless expansion of markets and states subject to managerial imperatives and purely instrumental crite-

---

[41] Cited by Rucht, *Research on Social Movements*, p. 370, n. 25.

[42] See J. L. Cohen, 'Between Crisis Management and Social Movements: The Place of Institutional Reform', *Telos*, 54, Summer 1982, pp. 21–40.

[43] Touraine himself has more recently sought to dispense with the concept 'society': A. Touraine, *A New Paradigm for Understanding Today's World* (Malden, MA and Cambridge, Polity Press, 2007), trans. G. Elliott.

ria of efficiency and control. Social movements offer some prospect of tipping the balance in favour of autonomy and democracy.

8.5 From Modernity to Postmodernity

A number of theorists move even further away from Marxian critical theory and modernist assumptions about the direction of history and the development of society. Touraine and Habermas remain committed in their different ways to classically modern values of autonomy and rationality and both are, in that sense, theorists of modernity, even though they distance themselves from 'hard' or dogmatic interpretations of modernity and its values. Alberto Melucci's more critical and sceptical approach whittles away the remaining modernist elements still further, bringing him even closer to the formal approaches considered in the previous chapter.

Melucci closely follows Touraine's injunction to transcend the opposition between 'action' and 'structure'. But Melucci thinks that this involves focusing more closely on the internal dynamics of social movements. It is essential to avoid any tendency to reify social movements or, in other words, to treat the social movement as a thing. To speak of 'the' women's or environmental movement is a convenient abstraction rather than an accurate reflection of reality. We must focus on 'how a "collective actor" is formed and maintained', 'how the process of constructing collective action takes place'.[44] We should not be misled into thinking that a movement has some predetermined essence, that it had to exist in its present form. Social movements are 'action systems operating in a systemic field of possibilities and limits'. The collective identity of movements is important, but it is only 'built through a complex system of negotiations, exchanges, decisions'.[45] By the same token, the boundaries of social movements are not absolute or unchanging either. Movements are patterns of relative stability in a flux of networks and interactions.

Melucci also follows Touraine in his emphasis on the symbolic nature of contemporary social movements. The new movements are new, because they are concerned with the production of 'information and meanings' rather than being directly concerned with the internal working of economy and state.[46] This focus reflects the current

---

[44] A. Melucci, *Nomads of the Present: Social Movements and Individual Needs in Contemporary Society* (London, Hutchinson Radius, 1989), pp. 20 and 198.

[45] A. Melucci, 'The Symbolic Challenge of Contemporary Movements', *Social Research*, 52:4, 1985, pp. 789–815: pp. 792 and 794. Melucci is accordingly more sympathetic to the resource mobilization paradigm: see above, pp. 164–6.

[46] Melucci, *Nomads of the Present*, p. 5, and cf. Melucci, *Challenging Codes*.

condition of 'complex societies' where conflicts develop 'in those areas of the system which are crucial for the production of information and symbolic resources, and which are subject at the same time to the greatest pressure to conform'.[47] Melucci defines exploitation in symbolic terms as well: 'In the contemporary context, we can define exploitation as a form of dependent participation in the information flow, as the deprivation of the control over the construction of meaning.'[48] The problems movements respond to are what Melucci describes as 'metapolitical', involving dilemmas that cannot be settled by institutional political means.[49] Social movements are 'laboratories of experience', through which new 'cultural codes' and forms of life are developed and then spread throughout society by a molecular process. Related to this symbolic focus, Melucci notes an increasing concern with the formal aspects of movements: with political methods or means rather than ends. As social movements aim to produce effects principally at the symbolic and cultural level, they cannot ignore the symbolic meaning of their own activities.[50] Put in different terms, the actions of contemporary movements must 'prefigure' the social values they represent.[51]

Since social movements are primarily concerned with cultural codes rather than state and economy, the most significant activities of a social movement may escape the attention of most observers and theorists. Melucci stresses the importance of personal politics and the politics of everyday life as opposed to what takes place in the formal public domain: 'Movements are only part-time participants in the public domain, precisely because they practise new forms of everyday life.'[52] By the same token, movements may have effects that are not immediately apparent. A movement may bring about important changes in society that cannot be observed by conventional social sciences and media. There may be small-scale molecular changes, which permeate society gradually without being noticed. The partial invisibility of social movements also helps to account for their often surprising effects. The collapse of the communist states of Eastern Europe at the hands of democracy movements and the recent Arab Spring in the Middle East and north Africa demonstrate how suddenly and unexpectedly social movements can erupt and effect change. In both cases, the abrupt overthrow of longstanding regimes depended on less visible changes of attitude and allegiance over a much more protracted

---

[47] Melucci, *Nomads of the Present*, p. 55.
[48] Melucci, *Challenging Codes*, p. 182.
[49] Melucci, *Nomads of the Present*, p. 222.
[50] Melucci, *Challenging Codes*, p. 6, and *Nomads of the Present*, p. 60.
[51] On prefigurative politics, see above, pp. 66–7.
[52] Melucci, *Nomads of the Present*, p. 6.

period. Similarly, movements like the women's and alter-globalization movements may persist long after they have apparently disappeared, ready to return to public prominence should the opportunity arise. The resurrected movement may not have the same slogans and leaders; it may not see itself as a continuation of the earlier manifestation. In fact, as the ban on reification of social movements implies, the identity of social movements is always relative and contentious.

Melucci's later work, *Challenging Codes*, takes account of processes of globalization in ways that qualify his earlier claim that contemporary movements are exclusively concerned with symbolic codes. Rather, there is a range of different movements with different kinds of issues, concerns and styles of political action. As Melucci puts it, 'The inner differentiation of action is reinforced by the fact that in a planetary system social reality becomes synchronic: in the contemporaneity created by the media system, all the "geological strata" of human history are simultaneously present.' There is no global uniformity of issues, as a result of what the Marxist tradition describes as 'uneven development'. At the same time, ideas and issues are communicated at ever-increasing speed between the most socially and culturally diverse settings. Gay marriage is legalized in South Africa at the same time as the death penalty is enforced for homosexual acts in other parts of Africa and the Middle East. The village women of the Chipko movement fight simultaneously, in effect, for women's rights, basic material security and environmental conservation. Changes are small-scale and cumulative rather than systemic. Small movements can have a significant role in changing meanings, where they would be unequal to the task of major structural change.[53] More to the point, it is difficult, if not impossible, for the theorist to formulate an overall goal of social transformation without violating his insights into the diversity of movements. If the objects of 'planetary' movements are diverse, then Melucci's vision of an alternative global order must be correspondingly formal rather than substantive as well.

As with Habermas and Touraine, Melucci thus refrains from any ambitious (and substantive) teleology, which would be incompatible with any genuinely democratic project. His vision of an alternative society is thus necessarily (but frustratingly) sketchy: 'A new society, then, is not a society which will, or even could, succeed and wholly substitute the present one, but rather a different set of values and political goals which can be established through action to influence the ways of organizing the world system, its social structure, its political priorities, its transnational relations.' Like Touraine, Melucci insists on the central role of political action: 'The future depends solely on our action

---

[53] Melucci, *Challenging Codes*, pp. 5 and 94.

purged of all teleological connotations.'[54] Once again, the substantive settings of contemporary movements are seen as the condition of liberation from social structures and constraints.

8.6 The Limits of Substantive Explanation

The approaches considered in previous sections maintain a commitment to the values of modernity, albeit in nuanced and self-limiting ways. By contrast, postmodernism declares thoroughgoing scepticism about all universal values and 'grand meta-narratives' and in particular those associated with modernism. It proposes instead a single-minded celebration of diversity. In this spirit, postmodernist social theorists and philosophers frequently refer to new social movements as proof of the irreducible plurality of 'voices' in the aftermath of the unifying, universalizing and essentializing projects of liberalism and capitalism, socialism and Marxism. There is, however, some vacillation within broadly postmodern approaches between two tendencies. One tendency risks violating its own ban on historical meta-narratives by treating contemporary developed societies as a distinctively postmodern stage of western history. This tendency differs from modernist theorists mainly in attributing to this new stage a decisive break from modernist culture and values. The other tendency is more consistent with postmodernist assumptions in that it eschews all historical narratives but, as a result, risks failing to provide much theoretical illumination. Postmodern approaches face the dilemma of *either* producing another substantive theory of western society (albeit one that disavows unity, universalism and the authority of theory) *or* alternatively confining itself to rigorously sceptical but ultimately uninformative descriptions of irreducibly diverse phenomena.

Pursuing the first tendency, despite scepticism about attempts to impose theoretical unity on the diversity of social life, a number of theorists present a more general account of new social movements as responses to postmodernity. In fact, postmodernity is characterized in terms of social and economic developments already familiar from modernist theorists. Thus Jean-François Lyotard identifies the 'mood of postmodernity' as involving scepticism about all grand historical meta-narratives, both Enlightenment narratives of reason and progress and dialectical narratives of crisis and revolution. But the setting for this mood is described as postindustrial society. In terms already familiar from the work of Alain Touraine, postindustrial society is defined by a mode of production in which technical knowledge, information technology and the production of symbolic goods play the decisive role.

[54] Melucci, *Challenging Codes*, pp. 190 and 196.

Technical knowledge is applied to the production of new commodities, fostering new needs and new cultural values. In terms also similar to Marcuse, Lyotard sees postindustrial society as dominated by the 'spirit of performativity' and relentless attempts to reduce society to an efficient system. The main difference from Habermas's theory is Lyotard's insistence that rational consensus is no longer a viable option. Indeed, he claims that to aim for consensus is inevitably authoritarian. Rather, we should celebrate diversity and the multiplicity of incommensurable 'language games'.[55]

Lash and Urry provide a more detailed and sociologically informed version of a similarly substantive approach in their theory of 'disorganized capitalism'. Capitalism is currently undergoing processes of 'disorganization', to the extent that social and economic forms characteristic of organized capitalism – roughly equivalent to welfare state capitalism – are being displaced. In organized or welfare state capitalism, production is dominated by large-scale manufacturing on the Fordist model and mass consumer markets. Workers are organized in trade unions, which are incorporated into governmental and sometimes management structures. But Fordism is being replaced by 'post-Fordism' which involves the internationalization of production and finance, decline of manufacturing relative to the service sector and diversification of production and consumption. Related social developments include the weakening of traditional working-class organization, the rise of the new middle class and a shift to the new politics of new social movements. Also familiar by now is their emphasis on the increasing salience of culture as a site of both domination and resistance: 'domination through cultural forms takes on significance in disorganized capitalism which is comparable in importance to domination in the sphere of production itself'.[56]

Lash and Urry differ from modernist theorists mainly in their explicitly postmodernist view of contemporary culture, although they themselves avoid adopting the anti-historical and sceptical position of philosophical postmodernism. Disorganized capitalism is just another stage of capitalist development, albeit one not anticipated by Marx himself. It is associated with the 'appearance and mass distribution of a cultural-ideological configuration of "postmodernism" [which] affects high culture, popular culture and the symbols and discourse of everyday life'. Postmodern culture is 'transgressive' of intellectual boundaries between what is considered 'rational' and 'non-rational' and of aesthetic boundaries between 'high' and 'low' culture. Drawing on the work of Walter Benjamin, Lash and Urry describe postmodern culture as 'post-auratic': the work of art is no longer an eternal object of

---

[55] Lyotard, *Postmodern Condition*, pp. 45–6, and cf. above, section 8.5.
[56] Lash and Urry, *End of Organized Capitalism*, pp. 311 and 14.

contemplation and quasi-religious reverence but just another element of the 'economy of pleasure', a 'means of distraction like any other'.[57] At the same time, communication increasingly occurs through images, sounds and impulses rather than the spoken and written word. As a result, postmodern culture is resistant to the rational and discursive forms of critique characteristic of modernity.

Culture itself is an increasingly important site of struggle in disorganized capitalism. It is the potential site for the imposition of an 'authoritarian populism' closely identified with the politics of the New Right and Thatcherism. The right has responded to the challenge of the new movements with a re-emphasis on cultural issues, family values and opposition to gay marriage in the so-called 'culture wars' of the last decades. At the same time, the commitments to private property, free markets and inequality persist in largely unaltered form. As a result, a significant proportion of the educationally and economically deprived are persuaded to vote for governments that deprive them further. On the other hand, developments like the counter-culture, popular music and film point to an alternative possibility of 'anti-authoritarian radical democracy'. This progressive alternative involves 'genuine dialogue' between 'new social movements' and the old left.[58] In effect, new social movements inject an irreducible diversity of struggles and a radical cultural focus into the longstanding socialist agenda of the left.

Laclau and Mouffe offer a broadly similar account of contemporary society and culture in their early collaborative work, *Hegemony and Socialist Strategy*, but they combine this account with either post-structuralist or postmodern philosophical principles. Their approach emerges from a sustained critique of Marxist essentialism, which insists that there is a single true theory of exploitation and liberation. Marxist essentialism is implicated in the authoritarian fate of revolutionary communism, because it leaves no room for political difference and contestation. Antonio Gramsci reintroduces some scope for politics into Marxism with his notion of moral and intellectual hegemony, which implies that the struggle for socialism is not determined in advance. The working class must construct around its leadership a contingent alliance of democratic social forces that is appropriate for the particular circumstances of a particular country. But Gramsci is still guilty of essentialism, because he assumes that the working class must lead this 'counter-hegemonic bloc'. Laclau and Mouffe insist instead that there is no given logic of revolutionary transformation placing either the working class or new social movements at its heart: 'There is no

---

[57] Lash and Urry, *End of Organized Capitalism*, pp. 7 and 286.
[58] Lash and Urry, *End of Organized Capitalism*, p. 312. Cf. J. Urry, *Global Complexity* (Malden, MA and Cambridge, Polity Press, 2003).

uniquely privileged position from which a uniform continuity of effects will follow, concluding with the transformation of society as a whole.'[59]

Neither particular social interests nor the possible alliances that can be constructed between them are given in advance in the way essentialist theories assume. Rather, both the unity of particular interests or 'subject positions' and their 'articulation' depend on uncertain political processes. Articulation is defined as 'any practice establishing a relation among elements such that their identity is modified as a result of the articulatory practice'. Unity is never 'the expression of a common underlying essence but the result of political construction and struggle'.[60] By the same token, the goal of political struggle cannot be defined in advance, whether as communism or in any other fixed terms. Laclau and Mouffe describe the aim of struggle more fluidly as 'radical and plural democracy', which can be achieved only if we abandon notions of objective political truth: 'there is no radical and plural democracy without renouncing the discourse of the universal and its implicit assumption of a privileged point of access to "the truth", which can be reached only by a limited number of subjects'.[61] Radical and plural democracy remains a somewhat vague and undefined ideal, though it evidently involves radicalization of both the liberal democratic commitments to autonomy, pluralism and democracy and social democratic concerns for social justice.

Laclau and Mouffe's position serves to highlight the dilemma faced by postmodern approaches to social movements. Certainly, they rightly resist the temptation to impose a binary logic of struggle – positing one defining conflict between a single emancipatory agent and the prevailing structure of power – on the diverse social creativity of new social movements. But in doing so, they risk making only a negative theoretical contribution to the politics of contemporary societies. Their emphasis on the constructed and contingent nature of political constituencies and alliances is a salutary antidote to both fatalism and voluntarism. Nor, as some critics allege, is the commitment to difference simply equivalent to a vacuous relativism without political import. Laclau and Mouffe's 'agonist' advocacy of radical and plural democracy implies, at the very least, a positive normative commitment to diversity, toleration and political engagement.[62] But, understood in this way, postmodern agonism differs from Habermas's deliberative

---

[59] E. Laclau and C. Mouffe, *Hegemony and Socialist Strategy: Towards a Radical Democratic Politics* (London, Verso, 1985), p. 169.

[60] Laclau and Mouffe, *Hegemony and Socialist Strategy*, pp. 105 and 65.

[61] Laclau and Mouffe, *Hegemony and Socialist Strategy*, pp. 191–2.

[62] In their later work, Laclau and Mouffe develop versions of an agonistic theory of politics, which insists on the irreducible place and usefulness of conflict: see C. Mouffe, *The Return of the Political* (London and New York, Verso, 2005).

democracy only by degree. Agonistic conflicts are still assumed to take place within an agreed institutional framework, if only in the sense that conflicts should be conducted in a way that respects the other party and avoids descending into violence. Conversely, even deliberative democrats are able to accept the values of diversity and political contestation without abandoning their ultimate aim of rational consensus. Shorn of even such minimal normative commitments, postmodern scepticism could offer, in practice, little more than a purely descriptive or empirical approach: namely a detailed cataloguing of specific social movements in all their contingent detail. Substantive description would then, in effect, replace critical theory's original and more ambitious goal of substantive explanation and emancipatory intervention.

Further Reading

There are many works on Marxism (both orthodox and in a variety of revisionist guises) and other substantive approaches reviewed in this chapter. An alternative but still highly compressed account of the range of approaches is provided in David West, 'New Social Movements' in Gaus and Kukathas, eds., *Handbook of Political Theory*. Ronald Inglehart's *The Silent Revolution: Changing Values and Political Styles among Western Publics* will be congenial to those of a more empirical disposition. Some of the more helpful primary texts from a European perspective include Claus Offe's article, 'New Social Movements: Challenging the Boundaries of Institutional Politics', and articles in the same volume of *Social Research* by Jean L. Cohen, Klaus Eder, Alain Touraine, Charles Tilly and Alberto Melucci. Alberto Melucci's *Nomads of the Present: Social Movements and Individual Needs in Contemporary Society* is a helpful preparation for *Challenging Codes: Collective Action in the Information Age*. Habermas's short article on 'New Social Movements' is a dense but useful alternative to the two volumes of *The Theory of Communicative Action*. The most succinct introduction to Alain Touraine's ideas is his *The Voice and the Eye: An Analysis of Social Movements*. Useful texts from poststructuralist and postmodern perspectives are Scott Lash and John Urry, *The End of Organized Capitalism*, Jean-François Lyotard, *The Postmodern Condition: A Report on Knowledge* and Ernesto Laclau and Chantal Mouffe's *Hegemony and Socialist Strategy: Towards a Radical Democratic Politics*. For discussion of a variety of postmodern perspectives (including those of Lyotard, Judith Butler, Michel Foucault, Donna Haraway and Cornel West), see Steven Seidman's edited collection, *The Postmodern Turn: New Perspectives on Social Theory*.

9

Conclusion: A Critical Theory of Social Movements?

Outline

By way of a conclusion, the present chapter identifies some elements of a critical theory of social movements. Critical theory in the Frankfurt School tradition has the ambitious goal of combining social analysis and normative critique with a practical orientation towards the transformation of contemporary society. Although it can benefit from the formal and empirical approaches discussed in chapter 7, a critical theory has more affinities with the substantive approaches of chapter 8. Like those theories, it attempts to steer a path between, on the one hand, dogmatic ('modernist' or 'totalizing') claims to knowledge of society and, on the other hand, an ultimately unhelpful postmodern scepticism. Finding a way between these extremes involves recognizing the *concrete* and *contingent* (rather than abstract and universal) limits of theoretical knowledge. At the same time, elements of a common set of values for contemporary movements emerge from consideration of the approaching environmental limits to the further material expansion of human societies. With limits of both kinds in mind, critical theory can be seen to have an essential but always corrigible role in social movements and societal transformation.

9.1 Introduction: Social Movement Theory Between Modernism and Postmodernism

The aim of this final chapter is to outline some essential elements of a critical theory of social movements. This task follows directly from the discussion of the last chapter. All the theorists discussed there have some affinities with the Frankfurt School tradition of critical theory. In other words, they seek to combine empirical knowledge of society and politics with an emancipatory vision of social transformation. Rather than simply describing or seeking to explain social reality, they aim to illuminate and facilitate the progressive transformation of society. Marxism provides the prototype of critical theory in that sense, as it combines sociological observation, economic theory and a political programme in an allegedly scientific socialism, which is designed to both inform and advance the revolutionary overthrow of capitalism. At the same time, the theorists discussed in the last chapter depart in significant ways from Marxist assumptions. They develop a series of differing accounts of contemporary society, albeit ones of recognizably Marxian provenance. Within this set of approaches, there is a broad contrast between modernist and postmodernist tendencies.

Modernist theorists of new social movements such as Habermas and Touraine still conceive of a substantial alternative to present society as the destination of a historical process of modernization. By diagnosing *the* contemporary social pathology, they also posit a single remedy. They are sometimes accused, as a result, of being too close to Marxism or, at least, guilty of modernism. They are also accused of pre-empting the diverse social creativity of social movements, which are left only with the task of discerning their allotted transformative task. However, as we have seen, the alternatives both Habermas and Touraine envisage are in fact in significant respects formal and abstract, leaving considerable scope for creativity and diversity. Although their visions imply a possible alternative society, it is one where the determinism of social structure would be largely replaced by more self-conscious human direction. Marx, after all, saw communist revolution as the way of escaping a human *pre*history constrained by economic scarcity and class domination into a 'realm of freedom', where history would in future be made by human beings freely and self-consciously. Touraine and Habermas similarly see the progressive potential of modernity as preparing the way for a society of communicatively rational and individually autonomous self-determination: in Habermas's words, a society in which human beings make history 'with will and consciousness'.[1] This would be a form of society in which human needs are formed and fulfilled free of the distorting effects of both capitalist markets and bureaucratic states, liberated from limitations of instrumental knowledge and technocratic domination. With all their differences, both theorists are sympathetic to a more extensive and deepened democracy and an enriched and extended public sphere.

Postmodern theorists, on the other hand, criticize the remaining modernist commitment of theorists like Habermas and Touraine. Indeed, strict commitment to postmodern assumptions would seem to

---

[1] See above, sections 8.1, 8.3–4, and cf. chapter 8, note 26.

imply a radically different position. If we can achieve neither reliably objective knowledge of existing social reality nor generally applicable norms and values, then political theory can hardly make a significant contribution to social and political emancipation. On these assumptions, even the methodical *description* of social movements, as pursued by empirical social sciences such as political science and sociology, is strictly impossible since there can be no description of reality independent of theoretical assumptions. We are left, on these strict postmodernist principles, with an endlessly proliferating array of interpretations and perspectives. In this spirit, Foucault and Deleuze reject all 'totalizing theories', which they associate with modernism, and advocate instead a view of political theory as a 'local and regional practice'. The critical theorist should avoid the 'representative' and totalizing pretensions of the Marxist intellectual. She should refrain from prescribing any substantive goals, let alone devising detailed utopian blueprints. A critical theory of social movements can never aspire to the status of absolute or totalizing theory. A critical theory can never justifiably support the kind of authoritarian political projects that complacent modernists have sometimes hatched. More positively, the critique of the authoritarian uses of theory is itself an essential element of any critical theory.

Rather than aiming for a single and seamless, totalizing theory of society, the theorist should be committed to acknowledging multiple perspectives, experiences and voices. Theory should provide a 'political toolbox' for social movements. Foucault's 'archaeology' and 'genealogy' of discursive practices and institutions contribute to this task by uncovering hidden or 'masked' and 'subjugated knowledges' and discourses, contributing in this way to the 'efficacy of dispersed and discontinuous offensives'.[2] Theorists can at best look to the experiences of social movement activists in order to uncover what Sarah Maddison and Sean Scalmer call 'activist wisdom', the practical knowledge required to pursue political action.[3] In its most sceptical form, a strictly postmodern approach would mean abandoning the substantive commitments to liberation characteristic of critical theory. The 'political toolbox' of 'activist wisdom' is in principle available to all movements and activists, however unattractive their goals and values.

In practice, however, postmodern theorists do typically propose some substantive positions, which are based on norms and values that

---

[2] See M. Foucault and G. Deleuze, 'Intellectuals and Power' in *Language, Counter-Memory, Practice* (Ithaca, NY, Cornell University Press, 1977), trans. D. F. Bouchard and S. Simon, pp. 205–9 and 208, and M. Foucault, *Society Must Be Defended: Lectures at the Collège de France, 1975–76* (London, Penguin, 2004), trans. D. Macey, pp. 5–7.

[3] S. Maddison and S. Scalmer, *Activist Wisdom: Practical Knowledge and Creative Tension in Social Movements* (Sydney, UNSW Press, 2006).

turn out to be surprisingly close to those of their modernist opponents. The authority of conceptions of freedom and autonomy inherited from humanism and modernism may be undermined, but it is difficult not to see the more radical substitutes proposed by postmodern theorists as expressions of a similar underlying stance. The ban on 'totalizing' theories and universal normative frameworks typically co-exists with (whilst not being allowed to *ground*) commitment to something like the 'radical and plural democracy' espoused by Laclau and Mouffe. Broadly left-wing commitments to social justice and material equality (or at least redistribution) are frequently invoked as well. Postmodern social theorists differ mainly in their greater sympathy for non-discursive and non-rational modes of discourse and engagement, their embrace of popular culture rather than 'high' or 'intellectual' culture and art, and their appreciation of symbols, imagery and emotion as well as argument.[4] In that sense, they offer useful correctives to the excessive intellectualism of a modernist theorist like Habermas, who places too much trust in the reasoned discourse of citizens susceptible only to the 'unforced force of the better argument'.[5]

Postmodernism is less useful, however, to the extent that it encourages a generalized scepticism about the possibility of objective knowledge and universal values and norms and, as a result, undermines commitment to political action. Paradoxically, a generalized scepticism of this kind serves only to divert attention from the *concrete* limits of both knowledge and ethics. It is, after all, only unreconstructed modernists who would claim that it is possible, for the purposes of a critical social theory, to establish an absolutely objective and 'totalizing' theory on the basis of definitive knowledge and universal moral values. It is, indeed, relatively easy to show that it is impossible to establish universal, absolute and eternal foundations for empirical knowledge and morality in the ambitious sense that such a goal would require. Radical postmodernist sceptics are tempted to conclude (at least in theory) that the only alternative is some form of relativism: that there can be no objective science, only rival interpretations of the world; that there can be no universal moral truths, only rival and equally valid moral and ethical world-views.

It is possible, however, to abandon the ambitious claims of unreconstructed modernists without relapsing into the undifferentiated 'grey

---

[4] See, for example, Laclau and Mouffe, *Hegemony and Socialist Strategy*; W. E. Connolly, *The Ethos of Pluralization* (Minneapolis, University of Minnesota Press, 1995). It is worth noting, though, that poststructuralist and postmodernist philosophers such as Foucault and Lyotard maintain the high modernist commitment to serious art as opposed to mere entertainment.

[5] See J. Habermas, 'Wahrheitstheorien' in *Wirklichkeit und Reflexion: Walter Schulz zum 60. Geburtstag* (Pfullingen, Neske, 1973), p. 226 (my translation).

on grey' of cognitive and moral relativism. In order to do so, we need to settle for a less ambitious model of knowledge and morality. We can accept the anti-modernist point that the goal of a timeless and universal social theory is indeed unattainable. But the timeless philosophical and epistemological grounds for this impossibility should not divert us from the concrete and contingent limits of our knowledge and theories. The crucial further point is that we can only determine these concrete limits once we have denied the radically sceptical position. If we remain at the level of generalized scepticism, we are not in a position to identify the substantive limits to any critical social theory, because only knowledge of social and political reality can inform us of these limits. Our tendencies to moral and ethical absolutism should likewise be constrained by our recognition of the differing ethical values of others. But a thoroughgoing scepticism would undermine the latter just as much as the former. As critics of postmodernism have pointed out, absolute relativism is as compatible with the 'might is right' philosophy of Mussolini as it is with a sensitivity to moral difference and otherness.[6] Generalized scepticism undermines focused critique.

A similar conclusion can be reached by a somewhat different path. Critical theory is designed to apply to the contemporary context and to serve the needs of existing and future movements of emancipation. From the practical perspective of these movements, it is decidedly not a question of whether we can achieve absolute and eternal truths and universally valid norms. Still, social movements face certain problems that only theory – empirical knowledge, critique of ideology and moral innovation – is able to resolve. Movements need to avail themselves of some sort of theory, even if that theory cannot be validated absolutely from an epistemological point of view. Gramsci makes the related point that it is not possible to live without some philosophy of life, some set of assumptions and values, even if they are often largely unconscious, not always consistent and impossible to ground in absolute and incontestable rational terms. Some philosophy is implicitly adopted, even if its status is always less than certain.[7] The task of the critical theorist (like the task of the life-philosopher) is surely not to refuse all involvement and responsibility until the time – distant, if not infinitely so – that absolute knowledge can be guaranteed. Rather it is the task of the theorist to engage with the actually existing theories and values of agents, in the hope that critical reflection and investigation will at least make them more adequate and more effective.

---

[6] See S. Gaggi, *Modern/Postmodern: A Study in Twentieth-Century Arts and Ideas* (Philadelphia: University of Pennsylvania Press, 1989) p. 177.

[7] Gramsci, *Selections from the Prison Notebooks*, Part III, 'The Philosophy of Praxis'; cf. R. Rorty, *Philosophy and the Mirror of Nature* (Princeton, NJ, Princeton University Press, 1980), esp. ch. VIII, 'Philosophy Without Mirrors'.

Laclau and Mouffe point in the right direction with their notion of 'articulation', which is consonant with this less ambitious, more situated and contingent understanding of the role of theory.[8] The role of an articulating theory is to undertake the linked and interdependent tasks of both constituting particular social and political interests and providing links between them. An articulating theory makes connections between the concerns of different movements, for example finding common values or principles, conceptions of rights and entitlements, which permit the construction of broader 'counter-hegemonic' blocs of activists and movements. Only such a counter-hegemonic bloc is able to contest the dominant or hegemonic array of interests and ideology. Whilst it seeks to accommodate the needs of a variety of social movement actors (though, of course, by no means all), the articulating framework must renounce potentially authoritarian claims to absolute, general and authoritative truth.

Theory understood as articulation is always contingent, just one of a number of possible alternatives. This implies, crucially, that the role of theory is to *supplement* rather than to *displace* the different critical discourses associated with particular movements. A totalizing theory such as Marxism (at least in its orthodox incarnations) claims to account for all other theories and discourses: all social conflicts and ills are deduced from class struggle and, in the contemporary context, the capitalist mode of production. By contrast, an articulating theory sets out to form links and relays between diverse theoretical perspectives without absorbing or reducing them to a monocular vision. In concrete terms, an articulating, critical theory should not aim to replace or encompass the theoretical insights of feminism, queer theory, post-colonial theory and so on. At the same time, an articulating theory – as well as those discrete and diverse critical theories that it seeks to articulate – must surely still be based on some substantive material and evaluative claims, however tentative and corrigible. Whilst rhetoric and cultural innovation clearly play an important role in political discourse and social transformation, they are hardly sufficient. A critical theory that is purely rhetorical would surely, in the end, be inadequate even as rhetoric. Rhetoric is powerful only when it maintains some rational and cognitive purchase on both material reality and the moral and ethical values of those it addresses.

9.2 The Concrete Limits of a Critical Theory of Social Movements

In order to operate on the more fruitful terrain that lies somewhere between absolute objective certainty on the one hand and subjectiv-

---

[8] Laclau and Mouffe, *Hegemony and Socialist Strategy*, ch. 3, esp. pp. 105ff.

ism and relativism on the other, a critical theory of social movements must be able to negotiate the concrete or substantive limits and possibilities of knowledge. The concrete limits of social theory derive from a number of considerations.

In the first place, human societies are made up of highly complex patterns of action and interaction that are unpredictable in practice and, almost certainly, even in principle. This idea should not be too surprising; indeed, it has been defended by a wide range of social theorists.[9] Even many natural systems – the objects of physics, chemistry and biological sciences – are complex in ways that make them impossible to predict. The movement of fluids and the behaviour of weather systems are just two examples. They are unpredictable even though it is possible in principle to quantify all the relevant variables. As the development of the mathematics of chaos theory demonstrates in a rigorous way, some non-linear systems are subject to 'catastrophic' transformations, whereby an infinitesimal change of initial conditions results in a disproportionate and non-linear difference of outcome.[10] A further infinitesimal change of initial conditions in the same direction might bring about the opposite outcome just as abruptly. This is what makes the prediction of climate change as a result of global warming so uncertain: a gradual increase in global mean temperature may translate into diverse and chaotic climatic shifts in different parts of the world.

Social systems are surely at least as complex as natural systems like the climate. For example, in the realm of economic behaviour, a small shift in sentiment can lead to a catastrophic loss of confidence, triggering perhaps the collapse of share and financial markets or even the onset of economic depression. A similarly small shift in a different direction might contribute to the return of what Alan Greenspan described as 'irrational exuberance', a similarly resilient commitment to optimism. We have seen over previous chapters that social movements sometimes involve similarly 'catastrophic' events, which may be beneficial or harmful to the movement's prospects. An uprising against an oppressive regime may suddenly and unexpectedly occur, leading to the overthrow of that regime. Centuries-old prejudices may erode over the course of one or two decades, as has occurred in attitudes to homosexuality, ethnic and 'racial' differences and the position and capacities of women.

Social systems, however, display further dimensions of complexity and potential non-linearity in comparison to natural systems. Even though natural systems such as the climate are complex and often chaotic, they are based on relatively simple and unchanging physical laws. By contrast, the regularities or 'laws' of social systems are

[9] Cf. Popper, *The Poverty of Historicism.*
[10] See J. Gleick, *Chaos: Making a New Science* (London, Heinemann, 1987).

themselves subject to change. Social 'structures' are, as theorists like Touraine, Melucci and Giddens emphasize, in fact made up of only relatively stable patterns of action and interaction. Structures may persist for many years and have seemingly substantial effects. Slavery blighted the lives of many generations. The capitalist economic system is driving the world towards environmental collapse. But in fact both slavery and capitalism depend on the actions of many individuals who, knowingly or unknowingly, deliberately or unintentionally, reproduce those structures. This means that social systems can change in at least two different ways. They can change as a result of the complex dynamics of the social system, of the functioning of its existing structures. Or they can change because those structures (and associated ideas and actions of social agents) are themselves transformed.

Further layers of social complexity and unpredictability result from the role of social theory itself. The self-understandings of social actors – their beliefs about their interests, needs, values, capacities and so on – are evidently important factors in the ongoing self-production and variation of society. But these self-understandings are sometimes influenced by thinkers and theorists, including critical social theorists. This point is, once again, quite a familiar one. Theorists of the social sciences have long pointed to the possibility of self-fulfilling and self-negating predictions.[11] Predictions based on current understandings of human behaviour may, if they become known to those to whom they apply, provoke changes of behaviour which either reinforce or contradict the theorists' expectations. Empirical studies show, for example, that students of neo-classical economics, which assumes that economic agents are 'self-interested maximizers', behave in more self-interested ways than other people.[12] Marxist theory has had an enormous impact on twentieth-century history, inspiring both revolution and reaction. Closer to home, the strategies and discourses of new social movements reflect widespread awareness – deriving from critical studies and theoretical argument – of the deficits of the 'actually existing socialism' to which Marxist-inspired revolutions gave rise. It may be an exaggeration to claim that every 1960s activist carried a copy of Marcuse's *One Dimensional Man* (1964) or, as David Halperin has suggested, that every anti-AIDS activist in the 1980s brandished a copy of Foucault's *History of Sexuality*.[13] But it is certainly impossible to understand either of these

---

[11] Popper, *Poverty of Historicism*, esp. pp. 121ff.

[12] See, for example, Y. Bauman and E. Rose, 'Selection or Indoctrination: Why Do Economics Students Donate Less than the Rest?' *Journal of Economic Behavior and Organization,* 79, 2011, pp. 318–27.

[13] See D. M. Halperin, *Foucault: Towards A Gay Hagiography* (Oxford and New York, Oxford University Press, 1995), pp. 15–16.

waves of activism without taking into account the broader climate of ideas to which these works contributed.

Beyond acknowledging these mutually reinforcing levels of complexity and unpredictability, it is important to recognize that political action is itself unpredictable at a deeper level. This is because, as Hannah Arendt has emphasized, human action, whether individual or collective, implies the possibility of creation and innovation. Here, in effect, Arendt transposes to the social and political domain the existentialist insight that for human beings 'existence precedes essence'. In other words, human individuals and societies do not simply realize a pre-given nature and fixed interests, but rather in acting and living they redefine their nature and form new interests.[14] At the political level, Arendt discusses the American and French revolutions as each founding a new institutional order – a *novus ordo saeclorum*. The Hungarian uprising of 1956 is another inspiring but ultimately unsuccessful example of revolutionary innovation.[15] Of course, innovation occurs within the realm of institutional politics as well, but it is inescapable in the extra-institutional domain. More generally, although the actions of social movements are inevitably constrained to varying degrees by existing realities and the actions of other agents, as social movements they always strive to transcend these constraining and conditioning factors. This tendency to surpass current social and political realities corresponds to the transformative potential of extra-institutional politics.

This raises the question of what form of knowledge, if any, is appropriate to political action. The fact that there can be no epistemologically well-founded prediction of future actions implies that we can only have knowledge of political actions retrospectively or, in other words, as history. In fact, according to Arendt, it was the unfolding of the French Revolution as a seemingly unstoppable process that quickly escaped the control of its leading actors which gave rise to the Hegelian and Marxist philosophies of historical necessity. The problem with such 'grand meta-narratives', which according to Lyotard are characteristic of modernism, is not that they present historical events in the context of a meaningful story, which is surely legitimate. It is rather that they project that story into the future. A meaningful narrative of past events should not be mistaken for the uncovering of a necessary course of events, let alone one whose future course can be anticipated in advance.[16]

---

[14] See Arendt, *On Revolution*, pp. 27–8 and 209–11. On Arendt, see M. Canovan, *Hannah Arendt: A Reinterpretation of her Political Thought* (Cambridge and New York, Cambridge University Press, 1994).

[15] Cf. Arendt, *On Revolution*, ch. 5, and *Origins of Totalitarianism*, ch. 14, 'Reflections on the Hungarian Revolution'.

[16] H. Arendt, *Between Past and Future: Eight Exercises in Political Thought* (London

One important contribution of critical theory to action (which avoids the temptation of prediction or prophecy) is essentially phenomeno-logical. A political theory or discourse is, in other words, what enables us to recognize a particular category of experience and related situations, events and actions as political. Such a theory thereby also helps us to identify the ways in which we can act – and, indeed, may already be acting – politically. From this perspective, the fundamental goal of theory is politicization. This goal is evidently closely related to the extra-institutional emphasis of social movements. Social movements politicize previously ignored issues and identities, enabling otherwise isolated and unorganized constituencies (who may even be unaware of their oppressed or exploited condition) to achieve consciousness, solidarity and collective action. They thereby bring about cultural shifts, which substitute active and empowered identities for subordinate and disempowered social positions. Feminist consciousness, for example, involves the realization that many aspects of woman's 'condition' are really the effects of women's contingent and alterable political situation. That realization is essential to women's active transformation of that situation. In that sense, too, the *first* task of theory is not to put political tools or instruments into the hands of already formed political actors, but rather to transform the passive human victims of inherited social structures into self-consciously transformative agents. At the same time, political thought must always struggle to counter its own and broader countervailing tendencies to *de*politicization. It is difficult for people to maintain the surprise and intensity of becoming-aware. To persist with the example of feminism, now that gender issues high-lighted by feminism are recognized within institutional politics, it is easy to forget the politicizing achievement of the women's movement. An exclusively institutional focus on politics encourages such forget-fulness. A focus on extra-institutional politics, by contrast, not only encourages us to remember the formative role of social movements, it should also make us more receptive to new and emerging issues and constituencies, which are only just in the process of becoming political.

Further insights into the substantial but limited scope of a critical theory of social movements derive from a fundamental feature of the politics of identity. As we saw in chapter 4, essential to the politics of identity is the claim that particular constituencies have ultimate authority in defining their own experience and interests.[17] Even a sympathetic and empathetic external observer can never claim to know the interests of an oppressed constituency with certainty. In fact, even *within* a particular movement it is dangerous to assume that a shared

and New York, Penguin, 1977), ch. 2, 'The Concept of History', and cf. *On Revolution*, ch. 1, section 5, pp. 47–57.

[17] See above, chapter 4, pp. 88 and 100.

core of oppression can be identified by leaders or intellectuals of the movement. Any such assumption is liable to inspire an authoritarian style of leadership, which overrides the expressed wishes of its constituency for the sake of their 'real interests'. The politics of liberation is thus best understood in terms of notions of autonomy and authenticity that exclude in principle the possibility of a neutral and objective knowledge of personal interests and identity.[18] Identity and interests should reflect, instead, emancipatory discourses which are specific to particular movements and which remain subject to challenge and revision even there. These insights support a further core principle of liberation movements: since only the oppressed can really know the nature of their own oppression, in the end the oppressed must always define their own liberation and then liberate themselves.

9.3 The Potential Contributions of Theory to Practice

The concrete contributions to practice of a critical theory of social movements stem from the practical political needs of the movement. In the first place, the very identity and unity of any movement depends on a related movement discourse and theory – or, more likely, a series of such discourses and theories. Once we refrain from reifying – or, in other words, treating as a thing – the fluid, diverse and cross-cutting patterns of activity that make up 'a' or 'the' movement, we are more likely to see that the unity and identity of any movement is never simply given by supposed facts or any 'reality of the situation'. Rather, unity and identity are important achievements, ones owed in considerable part to associated movement discourses and theories. The movement's internal relations are just as much contingent achievements as are its relations with, and impact upon, the broader society. Just as there is no given, thing-like movement, there is no pre-existing guarantee of mutual intelligibility and shared truths amongst its members. It is movement discourses that help to establish mutual comprehension, agreement and (just as importantly) characteristic disagreements amongst members. In these terms, feminism, queer theory, anti-racism and ecology are prominent examples of movement discourses which, for all their internal differences and tensions, are inseparable from the existence and effectiveness of the corresponding movements.

It follows that a critical theory of social movements must allow for, and co-exist with, an irreducible plurality of movement identities and discourses. Critical theory thus exists, in the first place, at the level of the distinct critical theories of particular movements. Feminism, queer theory, post-colonialism and green theory can be recognized as

---

[18] See above, chapter 4, and cf. West, *Authenticity and Empowerment*.

so many critical theories combining empirical observation, theoretical analysis, normative critique and political engagement. These theories have an irreducible place in any overarching critical theory. They are essential to any understanding of the nature, directions and possibilities of new social movements, which can be found only by attending to their diverse narratives and experiences, values and history, literature, music and art. In these terms, the discourses of women, lesbians and gays, ethnic minorities and indigenous people, greens and peace activists have surely served to enrich the political, cultural and moral universe of both western and non-western societies over the past decades, even in the absence of any convincing overall (or 'totalizing') theory. What is more, at the level of the socially embodied and concrete critical discourses of new social movements, the mutual relations between oppression and liberation, between 'theory' and 'practice', are less problematic than at the level of a more general theory. Movement discourses are developed in the context of an ongoing movement and both inherited and improvised strategies and tactics. The dialectic between theory and practice takes place, in the first instance, within the ongoing activism (or practice) of the social movement; at the same time, as we have just seen, the movement itself would not and could not exist without its associated discursive and theoretical claims. Recognizing the concrete critical discourses of existing social movements thus helps to resolve the otherwise problematic relationship between critical theory and emancipatory practice.

At the same time, it would be a mistake to regard plural social movements and discourses as radically incommensurable entities without any common or connected interests and concerns. This would be to remain arbitrarily at a level of analysis just as abstract as that which would reduce differences between movements to some overarching unity. It would be to ignore the fact that movements themselves are made up of potentially unique individuals, who have cross-cutting identities and correspondingly diverse interests.[19] People typically participate – or, at least, have an interest – in a variety of movements and identities. So, even though we must accept that the relations between movements do not follow inevitably from some objective structural basis – the variety of conflicts cannot, for example, be reduced to the single contradiction of class – we nevertheless cannot avoid constructing some relations between different struggles. The movements' discourses and concerns must be to some extent commensurable in practice, if not in terms of strict structural relations or abstract theory.

---

[19] Even the notion of the self-contained and consistent individual is arguably an abstraction from the internal complexity and inner contradictions and inconsistencies of 'the' self: cf. D. Parfit, *Reasons and Persons* (Oxford, Clarendon Press, 1984).

Politics in a complex society inevitably depends on the articulation of logically independent but contingently interdependent movement discourses.[20]

The limited authority of any general critical theory vis-à-vis specific movement theories reflects the principle of autonomous organization affirmed by new movements.[21] Different dimensions of oppression can no more be reduced to some overarching formula than can the corresponding critical discourses. Any links between identities, interests and movements are contingent rather than necessary, constructed rather than given in advance. Such links can only be the products of theoretical innovation and political action. There can thus be no universal primacy of class as asserted by Marxism; neither can gender, sexuality, ethnicity or religion be posited as primary contradictions in the place of class. There is no overarching logic of exploitation and oppression, which could support such assertions of primacy. Rather, the diverse dimensions of subordination, exploitation and oppression are contingently 'entangled' in ways that depend on the variable historical circumstances of particular societies. In Northern Ireland there are complex relationships between religious denominations and socio-economic opportunities, which create particular possibilities for alliance and conflict. Similarly, ecological issues play a different role in developing as opposed to developed economies: there are evidently divergent relationships between subsistence and consumption, conservation and development, resources and risks in these different settings.

At the same time, the authority of experience can never be totally self-enclosed either. Once it is constituted (or is able to represent itself) as a distinct constituency and 'subject position', no movement can simply act in isolation according to its own particular perspective without relating to the broader society. Or, more precisely, to do so would be to abandon politics for the sake of separatism. Political action involves acting to change society and institutions, which inevitably depends on engaging in relationships with those who do not share and may even oppose the movement's interests. To follow the path of separatism by confining one's action to an autonomous or autarkic community of like-minded people is to make political action in that sense impossible. Separatism cannot even provide a microcosm of genuine liberation, which might serve as an example or prototype for the wider society. As we have seen, specific movement discourses do not account for all of the interests and potential liberation of movement members. Individuals have their own unique experiences and may have multiple, cross-cutting and even conflicting identities; they have corresponding allegiances to diverse movements and discourses. Any

[20] On Laclau and Mouffe's concept of articulation, see above, p. 116.
[21] See above, chapter 3.

single movement's discourse is thus inevitably both partial and pro-visional in relation to its members and, as a result, always subject to criticism and revision.

The political effectiveness of any movement thus always depends on its engagement with a broader framework of values, interests and related discourses. The authority of personal experience and suffering must be mediated with more general orders of value, with some gen-eralizable framework of norms and laws, if the movement is to achieve its goals in the broader society. The varied claims of social movements inevitably both resemble and conflict with analogous claims by other constituencies. Parallels and synergies between them offer the possibil-ity of co-operation and sometimes alliances with other movements in pursuit of these generalizable norms and rights. At the same time, if conflicting demands and rights-claims are to be resolved, they must be able to be calibrated against some common standard. One contribu-tion to resolving these differences is through recourse to discursive resources – for example, discourses of rights and autonomy or equality and solidarity – developed by earlier movements. Movements some-times generate new normative structures and institutional designs; sometimes they give novel interpretations to ones inherited from earlier waves of activism. Discourses of equality, freedom, rights and social justice developed by liberal, democratic and socialist movements have been extended to constituencies that were, until recently, ignored or rejected by them. Gay and lesbian movements have succeeded in extending notions of privacy, freedom and equality to formerly prohibited sexual acts and relationships. The women's movement has successfully extended to women a norm of equal citizenship previously confined to men – and originally only wealthy or property-owning men at that.

At the same time, movements also need to determine those 'enemies' who can never belong to any mutually advantageous alliance or coali-tion and whose demands can never be accepted or accommodated. Fascism, racism and religious bigotry are surely incompatible with any defensible alliance of emancipatory social movements, not least because these ideologies pride themselves precisely on opposing the demands of women, sexual, ethnic and religious minorities. This does not mean, however, that people who support such 'reactionary' move-ments should simply be ignored. An emancipatory alliance should be able to offer alternative interpretations of the situation and needs of people who may suffer genuine hardships, albeit not for the reasons they put forward. Poor whites are indeed deprived, even if their depri-vation has nothing to do with their fantasies of privileged black people.

Alliance and co-operation around a common framework of values is also essential for the institutionalization of movement goals. Social movements cannot afford to ignore altogether the institutionalized domain of politics, including both the nation-state and global institutions of governance. We have sought to understand extra-institutional politics as the formative or creative dimension of politics. But this perspective captures only one essential dimension of politics. The fact that social movements are extra- and often anti-institutional surely means that they can only be understood by reference to the institutional order. Extra-institutional politics is usually anti-institutional in the sense of opposing and attempting to change existing institutions. But only a minority of extra-institutional activists are against institutions as such. Some radical anarchists, for example, reject all forms of authority on the unlikely assumption that, in the absence of state oppression and capitalist exploitation, spontaneous human sociability would guarantee a peaceful and harmonious society. In fact, even most anarchists assume that, in the absence of state authority, social life would be regulated in some way by informal social norms and authority. And, as critics of anarchism have pointed out, informal norms can be just as oppressive as formal ones.

The institutionalization of movement goals – whether through laws and core state institutions or more broadly through societal norms – requires some form of shared normative or ideological framework. Different constituencies and interests may 'agree to differ' about some things – for example, religious beliefs, dietary practices and cultural values – as long as they do not have a negative impact on others. But these differences in 'private' or 'self-regarding' affairs still leave substantial public matters over which agreement must be reached.[22] What is more, in an era of intensified globalization, the institutional domain is no longer confined to the national context, which raises issues of cosmopolitan justice as well. The need for some degree of unity or articulation is particularly apparent at the level of electoral politics. Political parties seek majority electoral support by means of platforms or programmes of broad appeal, whether these are based on a party ideology or some more pragmatic rationale. By contrast, most social movements represent only a minority of the electorate. Short of abandoning the sphere of state and electoral politics altogether, movements must seek both some kind of alliance with other constituencies and some basis for appeal to the broader electorate. In these terms, green parties can be understood as attempts to ground broad electoral appeal in the concerns of a range of new and alter-globalization movements.

In addition to these normative and ideological issues, contemporary social movements also depend on shared knowledge of the world. Modern science and technology, with associated 'manufactured risks' of nuclear war, environmental collapse and global warming, raise

---

[22] A classic formulation of this distinction in the liberal tradition is J. S. Mill's *On Liberty*.

factual as well as moral issues. We share a common world, which determines both possibilities and limits for human activity. Perhaps nature is no longer an absolute given, in the sense that natural processes are now increasingly subject to human intervention, but there is little doubt that there are objective requirements for human survival, even if we cannot always know with certainty what they are.[23] Once again, the value of a sceptical awareness of the limits of scientific expertise should not be confused with radical scepticism (recently associated with postmodernism) about the value of scientific method as such. Radical scepticism undermines the more useful distinction between well-established and merely speculative or tendentious scientific claims. As past debates about the dangers of smoking and current debates over the reality of anthropogenic climate change make clear, a generalized scepticism about science simply leaves more space for self-serving campaigns of disinformation by affected commercial interests. A more focused scepticism, on the other hand, relies on concrete ways of differentiating between scientific claims by assessing the *relative* strength of competing theories and their supporting evidence. Evidently, we can only decide between the science of climate change and those who deny it on the basis of concrete empirical evidence.

Problematic as the science of climate change may have become, the difficulties raised by the *social* sciences are even more complex. The social sciences of individual and social psychology, sociology, political science, history and economics are no less essential sources of common knowledge for political agents, but they are undoubtedly more controversial and disputed than any natural sciences. The previous section outlined the limits to any predictive knowledge of society, which rule out both a predictive social science modelled on the natural sciences and determinist versions of Marxism.[24] At the same time, there is no reason to abandon the epistemological standard of objectivity altogether. In this context, Roy Bhaskar's critical realism and critical naturalism, where the latter emphasizes the more fluid and complex nature of the social, represent promising approaches to the philosophy of social science.[25] From the perspective of political actors, knowledge of society is never purely disinterested; and partial knowledge is always potentially misleading. The accumulated wisdom of tradition may be a better guide than disconnected empirical observations which, as in the case of nutrition and the findings of medical science, are often contradicted by other research and, taken by themselves, imply

[23]   See Giddens, *Beyond Left and Right*, esp. ch. 8.
[24]   See above, pp. 207–9.
[25]   See R. Bhaskar, *Scientific Realism and Human Emancipation* (London, Verso, 1986), and cf. A. Collier, *Critical Realism: An Introduction to Roy Bhaskar's Philosophy* (London, Verso, 1994).

misleading advice. But such criticisms presuppose the possibility of judging – rather than simply dismissing – any social scientific claims to knowledge.

Social movements thus need both a shared normative framework (albeit one that incorporates considerable diversity) and a shared but similarly differentiated and self-critical knowledge of physical and social reality. Both normative framework and factual knowledge may well be contentious, but that is precisely because 'agreeing to differ' cannot go 'all the way down'. If the commonness of our shared world did not matter, then it might be just a matter of relative values and rival cognitive frames – although it would then no longer be obvious why we still insist on talking of values rather than preferences, and cognitive frames rather than imaginative fictions. Because our shared world is indispensable, we have no choice but to strive for some kind of agreement around normative framework and knowledge of reality. This is a feasible goal, as long as the limits to both normative and factual agreement are understood as contingent and concrete rather than as the general consequences of an abstract philosophy and epistemology.

9.4 Ideology Through the Looking-Glass

In the modern period, the function of a common framework for social movements has been fulfilled by a variety of ideologies, which fuse values, norms and beliefs with commitment to specific political goals and strategies. Some of the most familiar and persistent of these have been liberalism, socialism, Marxism, conservatism and democracy. However, all of these ideologies share a common feature, which is no longer tenable, namely a fundamental assumption that history has an inbuilt direction of progress and that progress involves economic growth. Both liberalism and socialism, in their different ways, affirm this anticipated direction of development and adjust their political claims and strategies accordingly. As we shall see briefly in what follows, they differ mainly over the role of the state, their interpretation of values of freedom and equality and their view of the ultimate destination of development.

Liberal democrats welcome progress and think it best secured by avoiding excessive state interference whilst subjecting the state to democratic accountability. They look forward to the inevitable spread of freedom and democracy, sometimes disagreeing amongst themselves about the relative importance of these values. Freedom is interpreted mainly in negative terms as being left alone. Equality is understood as equality before the law and, more recently, as equality of opportunity. These positions imply a limited role for the state. Socialists agree that progress is inevitable but anticipate a different destination. Socialists think that progress will eventually lead (either abruptly through revolution or gradually through a series of reforms) to a socialist state, which will administer the economy in the interests of all workers. The socialist ideal reflects different basic values. Freedom is understood more positively to involve access to material and sometimes cultural resources. More than equal citizenship and equality before the law, equality for socialists requires either greater material equality or a more radical version of equality of opportunity.[26] Both imply a more extensive role for the state. Of the major modern ideologies, conservatism is obviously less favourable to modernity. But still, like other modern ideologies, conservatism also assumes a given direction of history or development, albeit one that must be resisted or slowed down. An influential formulation of conservative ideas was penned by Edmund Burke in response to the French Revolution. Far from being an unthinking avoidance of political ideas – the source of descriptions of Conservatives as the 'stupid party' – Burke's conservatism was a self-conscious attempt to preserve what he saw as valuable and even sacred in the 'old order' (or *ancien régime*) that was being obliterated by the revolution. In contrast to 'pre-modern' societies, where traditional values and institutions are largely accepted without serious question or challenge, conservatism responds to the perception that society is changing and traditional values are in danger. Traditional society is something that must be actively preserved.[27]

However, a common framework for contemporary social movements can no longer be premised on the direction of history posited by the familiar ideologies of liberalism, socialism and even conservatism. The material expansion of human civilization is now surely coming to an end and, as a result, ideological assumptions of progress are no longer plausible. As environmentalists and climate change scientists argue, human society is rapidly approaching material limits, which constrain the further expansion of both the human population and its use of natural resources. These material limits do not signal the end of history, in the sense of continuing and significant changes to human society, culture and life. The narrative of humanity will (it is to be hoped) continue for some time. But these limits do imply that our material civilization cannot continue to expand indefinitely according to an internal logic of unconstrained, rapid and even accelerating growth,

---

[26] A classic discussion of alternative conceptions of freedom or liberty is I. Berlin, 'Two Concepts of Liberty' in *Four Essays on Liberty* (Oxford and New York, Oxford University Press, 1969).

[27] Cf. Burke, *Reflections on the Revolution in France*. For a review of major modern ideologies including liberalism, socialism and conservatism, see A. Heywood, *Political Ideologies: An Introduction* (Houndmills, Basingstoke and New York, Palgrave Macmillan, 2007), 4th edn.

consumption and waste. By the same token, political ideologies can no longer afford to conceive of the state and politics as mere regulators (more or less intrusive) of an essentially unquestionable and unstoppable engine of growth. As we shall see, though limits to the material expansion of human civilization do not imply a retreat from radicalism. On the contrary, considerable radicalism is required if we are to reconfigure politics, economy and society so as to live within them.

If history, understood as an inevitable process of development, can no longer be the source of a common ideological framework, then perhaps the concept of nature can fulfil that role? The obvious candidate for a shared framework might seem to be ecology or green ideology. Green ideology certainly has some obvious advantages, not least because ecology directly addresses the relationship between nature and society, which is an unavoidable issue in the contemporary context. The success of green parties in a number of countries testifies to the appeal of green ideas, particularly for activists of new social and alter-globalization movements. Crucially, though, the general appeal of green ideas is the result of contingent historical factors; there is nothing in the concept of nature itself that provides an adequate basis for a common ideological framework.[28] The preservation of nature is obviously essential, in the sense that human survival depends on basic natural processes and resources. But, as Giddens emphasizes, nature can no longer be treated as a fixed, external horizon of human life.[29] For one thing, there is no reason why we should preserve every aspect of the non-human world, which includes harmful substances and processes. It is, in any case, much too late, since there is little remaining wilderness or 'nature' in the sense of ecosystems entirely unaffected by human intervention. Human beings have already transformed nature through their ability to manipulate chemical, physical and atomic processes. We have an increasing ability to transform nature further by means of genetic and nano-technologies. It does not obviously make sense actively to preserve harmful viruses and bacteria simply because they are there; of course, we may wish to preserve them for the sake of their genetic material, which might contribute to new pharmaceuticals or antibiotics. Human beings have no choice but to exercise independent judgements in their interactions with nature.

Even more clearly, the concept of nature does not provide the basis for unambiguous moral and political norms and values, which might govern relations between human beings or even between human beings and the rest of nature. Natural examples of complex interdependence, stability and harmony offer only one side of nature which, from another perspective, is 'red in tooth and claw'. Many species that

---

[28] See above, chapter 5.
[29] Giddens, *Beyond Left and Right*, pp. 47–50 and 202–8.

human beings should certainly aim to preserve only exist by preying on other animals. Social Darwinists have derived harsh norms of 'survival of the fittest' and elimination of the weak with as much justification (that is to say, with no justification) as more benign derivations from the concept of nature.[30] And if the concept of nature does not provide a philosophical basis for a common ideological framework, there is no guarantee that problems resulting from our mistreatment of nature will serve to promote a benign, green ideology. There is no guarantee, in other words, that, however urgent and disruptive ecological problems may become, they will automatically generate support for benign green values of social justice, gender equality, sexual diversity and grassroots democracy. If anything, environmental collapse is more likely to lead to some kind of authoritarian or elitist response.

A number of thinkers have suggested another possibility, namely a reformed version of conservatism. Conservative ideology does indeed resonate with central environmental concerns, not least the value of conservation; conservatives did, as we saw earlier, resist the Enlightenment's uncritical enthusiasm for progress. But eighteenth-century conservatives who wished to preserve the 'old order' were defending social hierarchy and property rights, inherited religion and traditional values concerning the family and sexuality. What is more, whilst the ideological heirs of these conservatives remain committed to those values, they have in the meantime become wedded to the neoliberal project of unfettered capitalism and unending economic growth. They have abandoned the original meaning of conservatism with its defining ethos of resistance to change. Put another way, progress and development have become almost sacred values that contemporary conservatives seek to preserve. Self-styled (capital-C) Conservatives are no longer really conservative in the broader or original sense.[31] Conversely and paradoxically, the (in some sense) conservative goal of conserving the material and cultural achievements of human civilization now requires substantial and even radical changes to the prevailing societal model. Radicalism is now necessary if we are to preserve what is valuable in society, institutions and the natural world. It is in that sense – and in that sense alone – that contemporary radicals should adopt a conservative stance. We must take the radical step of abandoning assumptions of unending material progress and limitless economic growth in order to have a chance of preserving our common world. A conservative stance of this kind does not mean that we should preserve existing inequalities of wealth and privilege, status and hier-

---

[30] See M. Hawkins, *Social Darwinism in European and American Thought: 1860–1945* (Cambridge and New York, Cambridge University Press, 1997).

[31] See J. Gray, *Enlightenment's Wake: Politics and Culture at the Close of the Modern Age* (London and New York, Routledge, 1995).

archy. On the contrary, these traditionally right-wing commitments make even less sense in the current situation which, as we shall see in the next section, demands instead a revival of egalitarian values and the ideal of social justice.

9.5 Towards A Common Framework for Contemporary Social Movements

Once the untenable commitment to an unending process of material progress is given up, the values traditionally associated with modern ideologies can be reconsidered. Freed of their now obsolete developmental baggage, they can be combined or articulated in new ways more suitable to our present situation. What follows are a few speculative and sketchy remarks on one possible basis of a common ideological framework.

In the first place, the era of unconditional individualism is now surely over. Individualism was initially justified as the socially beneficial unleashing of selfish wants. Liberal economists take Adam Smith to have argued, in effect, that the individual's unfettered pursuit of private interests would result in greater public benefit thanks to an 'invisible hand', which leads him 'to promote an end which was no part of his intention'. A burgeoning 'wealth of nations' would improve everyone's economic position, even if some would benefit much more than others.[32] In the present situation, however, the unlimited pursuit of self-interest understood in this way has become dangerous, threatening to degrade nature and disrupt social harmony. The endless expansion of wants in today's affluent societies belies Marx's expectation that the burgeoning productivity of the economy would eventually be able to satisfy every need and so put an end to both scarcity and class struggle. We now have no reason to believe that there is any absolute limit to the creation of new wants, once existing wants have been satisfied. In any case, individualism as pursued in a consumerist society is a dubious form of individualism. Far from being encouraged to develop and express their individual selves, people are persuaded to want products promoted by advertising, to seek status by acquiring products that others have already obtained.

A further implication of approaching limits to growth is the need to abandon the increasingly invasive culture of materialism. The dominant conception of progress, shared by both liberal, socialist and social

---

[32] See A. Smith, *An Inquiry into the Nature and Causes of the Wealth of Nations* (Oxford, Clarendon Press, 1976), Glasgow Edition of the Works and Correspondence, Vol. 2A, Bk IV, ch. 2, ¶9, p. 456.

democratic traditions, has largely relied on a definition of happiness or 'welfare' as the satisfaction of material wants. This connection is made explicit by utilitarianism and welfare economics, which assume that increasing material wealth translates reliably into happiness. Accordingly, success in contemporary institutional politics is judged largely by the ability of governments to promote growth of the Gross Domestic Product (GDP). But the materialist account of welfare rests on shaky foundations. Ideological claims that a growing economy always benefits the poor are questionable. The increasing gap between rich and poor leaves the poor worse-off in terms of relative (rather than absolute) poverty. In any case, ecological limits to growth mean that even if the poor do slowly become better-off with increasing GDP, they are unlikely to be able to reach a decent level of material well-being.[33] At the global level, the ever-increasing consumption of affluent societies is possible only at the expense of the world's poor, who are unlikely to be able to achieve western levels of affluence within currently projected ecological limits. Individual happiness can be combined with social harmony – both within and between countries – only if happiness is detached from the competitive pursuit of material goods. Material security is, of course, still an urgent goal for the majority of the world's population, which lives in relative and often absolute poverty, as well as for a minority in the West. But this only reinforces the need to abandon a materialist and consumerist outlook. Given the fact of limited resources, the poor will only be able to escape from poverty on a global scale if the rich are prepared to give up their never-ending pursuit of wealth. Absolute poverty can certainly be addressed within current ecological limits: it is possible to supply every human being with the basic means of survival. But the increasing wealth of the affluent continues to generate relative poverty and so spur further competition for scarce resources.

There is, in any case, mounting psychological and sociological evidence that material wealth leads to greater happiness only up to a certain threshold, one that the majority of people in rich societies have now passed. Not only are reported levels of happiness no longer increasing, but some of the least satisfied people are the most well-off. Finally, and paradoxically, the nature of consumerism itself tends to contradict materialist assumptions about human happiness. The consumerist pleasures offered by more and more goods – and not only luxury ones – are not really material at all. They depend instead on the consumption of symbols, images and fantasies, which are produced by the designers and advertisers of products. The 'discreet charm' of many consumer goods derives more from their ability to convey status or to

---

[33] Cf. T. Jackson, *Prosperity Without Growth: Economics for a Finite Planet* (London and Sterling, Earthscan, 2009).

exude an aura of freedom or transgression than from any satisfaction of strictly material needs.[34]

The compatibility of individual happiness with social harmony depends on reviving values of social justice and equality, which were regarded as redundant by the major ideological traditions of modernity. The liberal tradition is hostile to the ideals of social justice and material equality, because redistributive measures are seen to violate property rights and encourage a potentially authoritarian expansion of the state. Even social democrats have accepted that there is no need to adjust the gap between rich and poor, because an expanding economy would increase everyone's wealth (even if some will become much wealthier than others). As a result, for social democrats the value of equality of opportunity – memorably described as an equal opportunity to become unequal – has largely displaced the value of material equality. A similar intuition underlies Rawls's 'difference principle', which regards material inequalities as justified provided they are part of a scheme of incentives that improves the productivity of society and hence the wealth of even the worst-off.[35]

Now that an endless expansion of material consumption is no longer an option, both liberal and social democratic assumptions cease to be persuasive. The most likely outcome of unfettered economic growth is increasing inequality between rich and poor and the growing dissatisfaction of those who see themselves as permanently impoverished. The values of material equality and social justice must be seriously considered once again. Social movements should promote a genuinely autonomous formation of needs for the sake of real happiness and human flourishing. The pursuit of these goals depends on the revival of an ethical discourse, which need not claim universal truth or absolute authenticity. There are many ways to combine genuine happiness with a small ecological footprint. The Slow Food movement rejects the emphasis on the quantity of food and its speed of delivery, focusing instead on its quality, enjoyment and the social conditions in which it is enjoyed. Less well known is the fact that the slow movement advocates slowness in other activities as well, including sex, walking, reading and conversation. These and other forms of pleasure are – unlike the competition for status and positional goods – not zero-sum enjoyments but rather activities that are enhanced by the participation and enjoyment of other people.[36]

---

[34] See J. Baudrillard, *The Consumer Society: Myths and Structures* (London and Thousand Oaks, CA, Sage, 1998); R. Layard, *Happiness: Lessons from a New Science* (New York, Penguin, 2005).

[35] Rawls, *Theory of Justice*.

[36] For an overview, see C. Honoré, *In Praise of Slow: How a Worldwide Movement is Challenging the Cult of Speed* (London, Orion, 2005).

The replacement of self-interested materialism and individualism with a just social order would favour – and be made more likely by – a shift to a more activist and responsible, or what is sometimes described as a republican conception of politics, citizenship and freedom. The individual freedom and rights championed by liberals and social democrats, which are taken to include the freedom not to participate in politics, should be supplemented by values of civic engagement and responsibility for our common world. We should take action, in Arendt's republican terms, for the sake of *amor mundi* or 'love of the world'. She associates this commitment with a richer and, above all, more public conception of both the self and its happiness. She points to the experience of the American and French revolutions and other episodes of political activism, in which actors are able to identify with their public selves and enjoy, as a result, a more enduring public happiness. Psychological studies confirm that happiness is best achieved through identification with something larger than one's self, whether this is a community, a cause, an institution or a movement.[37] Significantly, the value of civic engagement supplements but does not replace liberal freedoms. Republican liberty is compatible with the negative liberty of citizens, who can still choose to pursue their private concerns without interference from the state. But such private freedoms are only likely to survive if we are able to regain control of the material development of our civilization; and that goal evidently depends on concerted and responsible political action. The republican turn from the private to the public world has, once again, some affinities with a Burkean conservatism, which values social order and the continuity of tradition either in preference to, or as the necessary conditions for, individual freedoms and rights. But recognition of the value of tradition does not, let us repeat, imply commitment to hierarchy and inequality.

If impending environmental crisis requires us to abandon our commitment to unending material progress, we should also abandon the related optimism that, come what may, things will in the end turn out well. To the extent that it encourages complacency, faith in progress discourages action. Exposing the dangerous illusion of automatic progress leaves us, on the other hand, with the challenge of improving society through a deliberate and, it must be said, difficult course of action. In the end, we have no alternative but to engage in widespread, continuing and inventive political action for the sake of our common world. In the absence of appropriate steps from governments and other institutions, we must turn to the extra-institutional action of social movements. It would of course be naïve to assume that social movements will inevitably succeed where institutions have failed. But pessimism about our future prospects is equally misplaced. Pessimism

---

[37] See Arendt, *On Revolution*, and Layard, *Happiness*.

discourages action that is deemed futile when, as we have seen in previous chapters, action to change the future is always possible even if its outcome is necessarily uncertain. Both optimism and pessimism are inappropriate reactions to our current situation because the future depends on what we now collectively decide to do.

Further Reading

Raymond Geuss provides a clear and concise analysis of critical theory in *The Idea of a Critical Theory: Habermas and the Frankfurt School*. The preceding outline of a critical theory of social movements draws on my earlier book, *Authenticity and Empowerment: A Theory of Liberation*. Readings for the related approaches of Offe, Habermas, Touraine and Melucci can be found in chapter 8 above. Hannah Arendt's ideas are lucidly presented in Margaret Canovan, *Hannah Arendt: A Reinterpretation of her Political Thought*. The epistemological approach adopted in this chapter reflects the ideas of Roy Bhaskar, *Scientific Realism and Human Emancipation*. Bhaskar's ideas are explained in Andrew Collier's *Critical Realism: An Introduction to Roy Bhaskar's Philosophy*. Some helpful attempts to understand the intellectual, ideological and political implications of environmental crisis include John Gray, *Enlightenment's Wake: Politics and Culture at the Close of the Modern Age*; Anthony Giddens, *Beyond Left and Right: The Future of Radical Politics* and *The Politics of Climate Change*; and Colin Crouch, *Post-Democracy*.

Bibliography

Alexander, K. and Thompson, E. P., eds.: *Out of Apathy* (London, Stevens, 1960).

Altman, D.: 'What Changed in the 70s?' in *Homosexuality, Power and Politics*, ed. Gay Left Collective (London, Allison and Busby, 1980).

Altman, D.: *Global Sex* (Chicago, University of Chicago Press, 2001).

Anderson, B.: *Imagined Communities: Reflections on the Origins and Spread of Nationalism* (London, Verso, 1983).

Anderson, D. L., ed.: *The Columbia History of the Vietnam War* (New York, Columbia University Press, 2011).

Anderson, K. B.: *Marx at the Margins: On Nationalism, Ethnicity, and Non-Western Societies* (Chicago, University of Chicago Press, 2010).

Archibugi, D. and Held, D., eds.: *Cosmopolitan Democracy: An Agenda for a New World Order* (Cambridge, Polity Press, 1995).

Arendt, H.: *The Origins of Totalitarianism* (London, Allen & Unwin, 1967), 3rd edn.

Arendt, H.: *On Revolution* (Harmondsworth, Penguin, 1973).

Arendt, H.: *Between Past and Future: Eight Exercises in Political Thought* (London and New York, Penguin, 1977).

Arendt, H.: *The Human Condition* (Chicago, University of Chicago Press, 1998), 2nd edn.

Arnold, R.: *Ecoterror: The Violent Agenda to Save Nature: The World of the Unabomber* (Bellevue, WA, Free Enterprise Press, 1997).

Ashton, O., Fyson, R. and Roberts, S., eds.: *The Chartist Legacy* (Woodbridge, Suffolk, Merlin Press, 1999).

Bacchi, C. L.: *Same Difference: Feminism and Sexual Difference* (Sydney, Allen and Unwin, 1990).

Bacon, F.: *The Advancement of Learning* (London, Dent, 1915).

Bahro, R.: *The Alternative in Eastern Europe* (London, New Left Books, 1978), trans. D. Fernbach.

Bailey, B.: *The Luddite Rebellion* (Stroud, Sutton Publishing, 1998).

Bakan, J.: *The Corporation: The Pathological Pursuit of Profit and Power* (New York, Free Press, 2004).

Banks, O.: *Becoming a Feminist: The Social Origins of 'First Wave' Feminism* (Brighton, Wheatsheaf, 1986).

Barber, B. R.: *Jihad vs. Mc World* (New York, Ballantine Books, 1996).

Barber, B. R.: *Strong Democracy: Participatory Politics for a New Age* (Berkeley and London, University of California Press, 2003), 2nd edn.

Barbour, F. B., ed.: *The Black Power Revolt: A Collection of Essays* (Boston, MA, Sargent, 1968).

Barnard, F. M.: *Herder's Social and Political Thought: From Enlightenment to Nationalism* (Oxford, Clarendon Press, 1965).

Baudrillard, J.: *The Consumer Society: Myths and Structures* (London and Thousand Oaks, CA, Sage, 1998).

Bauman, Y. and Rose, E.: 'Selection or Indoctrination: Why Do Economics Students Donate Less than the Rest?' *Journal of Economic Behavior and Organization*, 79, 2011, pp. 318–27.

Beauvoir, S. de: *The Ethics of Ambiguity* (Secaucus, NJ, Citadel Press, 1972), trans. B. Frechtman.

Beauvoir, S. de: *The Second Sex* (1949) (New York, Knopf, 2010), trans. C. Borde and S. Malovany-Chevallier.

Beckett, J. R., ed.: *Past and Present: The Construction of Aboriginality* (Canberra, Aboriginal Studies Press, 1988).

Bell, D.: *The End of Ideology: On the Exhaustion of Political Ideas in the Fifties* (Glencoe, IL, Free Press, 1960).

Bell, D.: *The Coming of Post-Industrial Society: A Venture in Social Forecasting* (New York, Basic Books, 1978).

Benford, R. D. and Snow, D. A.: 'Framing Processes and Social Movements: An Overview and Assessment', *Annual Review of Sociology*, 26, 2000, pp. 611–39.

Benton, T.: *Natural Relations: Ecology, Animal Rights, and Social Justice* (London, Verso, 1993).

Berlin, I.: 'Two Concepts of Liberty' in *Four Essays on Liberty* (Oxford and New York, Oxford University Press, 1969).

Bhaskar, R.: *Scientific Realism and Human Emancipation* (London, Verso, 1986).

Blackburn, R.: *The American Crucible: Slavery, Emancipation and Human Rights* (London and New York, Verso, 2011).

Blake, W.: *Poems and Prophecies* (London and New York, Dent and Dutton, 1972).

Bloch, E.: *The Principle of Hope* (Blackwell, Oxford, 1986), 3 vols.

Bloxham, D. and Gerwarth, R., eds.: *Political Violence in Twentieth-Century Europe* (Cambridge and New York, Cambridge University Press, 2011).

Boggs, C.: *Social Movements and Political Power: Emerging Forms of*

Radicalism in the West (Philadelphia, Temple University Press, 1986).

Böll, H.: *Die Verlorene Ehre der Katherina Blum* (Munich, DTV, 1976).

Bookchin, M.: *Post-Scarcity Anarchism* (Palo Alto, CA, Ramparts Press, 1971).

Bookchin, M.: *The Ecology of Freedom: The Emergence and Dissolution of Hierarchy* (Palo Alto, CA, Cheshire Books, 1982).

Bramwell, A.: *Ecology in the Twentieth Century: A History* (New Haven, Yale University Press, 1989).

Brand, K.-W., Büsser, D. and Rucht, D.: *Aufbruch in eine andere Gesellschaft: Neue soziale Bewegungen in der Bundesrepublik* (Frankfurt and New York, Campus, 1986), 3rd rev. edn.

Brecht, B.: *The Life of Galileo* (London, Methuen, 1964), trans. D. I. Vesey.

Brown, B. and Singer, P.: *The Greens* (Melbourne, Text Publishing, 1996).

Brown, W.: *States of Injury: Power and Freedom in Late Modernity* (Princeton, NJ, Princeton University Press, 1995).

Burgmann, M. and Burgmann, V.: *Green Bans, Red Union: Environmental Activism and the New South Wales Builders Labourers' Federation* (Sydney, UNSW Press, 1998).

Burgmann, V.: *Power, Profit and Protest: Australian Social Movements and Globalisation* (Crows Nest, NSW, Allen and Unwin, 2003).

Burke, E.: *Reflections on the Revolution in France* (New Haven, Yale University Press, 2003), ed. F. M. Turner.

Burnham, J.: *The Coming Defeat of Communism* (London, Cape, 1950).

Burns, J. M.: *Leadership* (New York and London, Harper & Row, 1978).

Butler, J.: *Gender Trouble: Feminism and Subversion of Identity* (New York and London, Routledge, 1990).

Butterfield, H.: *The Whig Interpretation of History* (London, George Bell, 1950).

Canadian Security Intelligence Service, Archived Report No. 2000/08, 'Anti-Globalization: A Spreading Phenomenon' (accessed at www. csis-scrs.gc.ca/pblctns/prspctvs/200008–eng.asp).

Canovan, M.: *Hannah Arendt: A Reinterpretation of her Political Thought* (Cambridge and New York, Cambridge University Press, 1994).

Carson, R.: *Silent Spring* (Boston, MA, Houghton Mifflin, 1962).

Carter, A.: *Peace Movements: International Protest and World Politics since 1945* (London and New York, Longman, 1992).

Carter, N.: *The Politics of the Environment: Ideas, Activism, Policy* (Cambridge and New York, Cambridge University Press, 2001).

Castells, M.: *The Rise of the Network Society* (Oxford and Malden, MA, Blackwell, 2000), 2nd edn.

Clarke, P.: *The Keynesian Revolution and its Economic Consequences: Selected Essays* (Cheltenham, Edward Elgar, 1998).

Cohen, J. L.: 'Between Crisis Management and Social Movements: The Place of Institutional Reform', *Telos*, 54, Summer 1982, pp. 21–40.

Cohen, J. L.: 'Strategy or Identity: New Theoretical Paradigms and Contemporary Social Movements', *Social Research*, 52:4, 1985, pp. 663–717.

Cohen, J. L. and Arato, A.: *Civil Society and Political Theory* (Cambridge, MA, MIT Press, 1992).

Collier, A.: *Critical Realism: An Introduction to Roy Bhaskar's Philosophy* (London, Verso, 1994).

Conkin, P. K.: *The State of the Earth: Environmental Challenges on the Road to 2100* (Lexington, University Press of Kentucky, 2007).

Connolly, W. E.: *The Ethos of Pluralization* (Minneapolis, University of Minnesota Press, 1995).

Cotgrove, S.: *Catastrophe or Cornucopia* (London, Wiley, 1982).

Crick, B. R.: *The American Science of Politics: Its Origins and Conditions* (London, Routledge & Kegan Paul, 1959).

Crick, B. R.: *In Defence of Politics* (New York and London, Continuum, 2000), 5th edn.

Crouch, C.: *Post-Democracy* (Cambridge and Malden, MA, Polity Press, 2004).

Curtin, J.: 'Houses Too Big, Say Greens', *Sydney Morning Herald*, 1 December 2009.

Dahl, R. A.: *Who Governs? Democracy and Power in an American City* (New Haven, Yale University Press, 1961).

Daly, H. E. and Farley, J.: *Ecological Economics: Principles and Applications* (Washington, Island Press, 2010), 2nd edn.

Danius, S., Jonsson, S. and Spivak, G. C.: 'An Interview with Gayatri Chakravorty Spivak', *Boundary 2*, 20:2, 1993, pp. 24–50.

Dean, J. C. and Diani, M., eds.: *Alain Touraine* (New York and London, Routledge, 1996).

Della Porta, D. and Diani, M.: *Social Movements: An Introduction* (Oxford and Malden, MA, Blackwell, 1999).

D'Emilio, J. and Freedman, E. B.: *Intimate Matters: A History of Sexuality in America* (New York, Harper & Row, 1988).

Djilas, M.: *The New Class: An Analysis of the Communist System* (New York, Praeger, 1957).

Dobson, A.: *Green Political Thought* (London and New York, Routledge, 2000), 3rd edn.

Dryzek, J. S.: *Deliberative Global Politics: Discourse and Democracy in a Divided World* (Cambridge and Malden, MA, Polity Press, 2006).

Dunant, S.: *The War of the Words: The Political Correctness Debate* (London, Virago, 1994).

Durkheim, E.: *Suicide: A Study in Sociology* [*Le Suicide: étude de sociologie*] (1897) (London, Routledge and Kegan Paul, 1952), trans. J. A. Spaulding and G. Simpson.

Easton, D.: *The Political System: An Inquiry into the State of Political Science* (New York, Knopf, 1971), 2nd edn.

Eden, D.: *Autonomy: Capitalism, Class and Politics* (Farnham and Burlington, VT, Ashgate, 2012).

Eder, K.: 'The "New Social Movements": Moral Crusades, Political Pressure Groups, or Social Movements?', *Social Research*, 52:4, 1985, pp. 869–91.

Eder, K.: 'The Rise of Counter-culture Movements against Modernity: Nature as a New Field of Class Struggle', *Theory, Culture and Society*, 7:4, 1990, pp. 28–32.

Edwards, B. and McCarthy, J. D.: 'Resources and Social Movement Mobilization' in *The Blackwell Companion to Social Movements*, ed. D. A. Snow, S. A. Soule and H. Kriesi (Oxford, Blackwell, 2004).

Ehrlich, P.: *The Population Bomb* (New York, Ballantine Books, 1968).

Eisenstein, H.: *Contemporary Feminist Thought* (London, Unwin, 1984).

Ekins, P., ed.: *The Living Economy: A New Economy in the Making* (London and New York, Routledge and Kegan Paul, 1986).

Elliott, L.: *The Global Politics of the Environment* (London, Macmillan, 1998).

Engels, F.: *Socialism: Utopian and Scientific* (London, Allen & Unwin, 1920), trans. E. Aveling.

Engels, F.: *The Peasant War in Germany* (1850) (London, Allen & Unwin, 1927), trans. M. J. Olgin.

Esping-Andersen, G.: *The Three Worlds of Welfare Capitalism* (Princeton, NJ, Princeton University Press, 1990).

Evans, R. J.: *The Feminists: Women's Emancipation Movements in Europe, America, and Australasia: 1840–1920* (New York, Croom Helm, 1977).

Eyerman, R. and Jamison, A.: *Social Movements: A Cognitive Approach* (University Park, PA, Pennsylvania State University Press, 1991).

Feenberg, A.: *When Poetry Ruled the Streets: The French May Events of 1968* (Albany, NY, State University of New York Press, 2001).

Ferguson, N.: *Empire: How Britain Made the Modern World* (London, Allen Lane, 2003).

Foster, W. Z.: *Outline History of the World Trade Union Movement* (New York, International Publishers, 1956).

Foucault, M.: *Society Must Be Defended: Lectures at the Collège de France, 1975–76* (London, Penguin, 2004), trans. D. Macey.

Foucault, M. and Deleuze, G.: 'Intellectuals and Power' in *Language, Counter-Memory, Practice* (Ithaca, NY, Cornell University Press, 1977), trans. D. F. Bouchard and S. Simon.

Franklin, J. H. and Moss, A.: *From Slavery to Freedom: A History of African Americans* (New York, Knopf, 2000).

Freeman, J.: 'Origins of the Women's Liberation Movement', *American Journal of Sociology*, 78:4, 1973.

Freire, P.: *Education for Critical Consciousness* (New York, Continuum, 1973).

Friedman, T. L.: *The World is Flat: A Brief History of the Twenty-First Century* (New York, Farrar, Straus and Giroux, 2005).

Fukuyama, F.: *The End of History and the Last Man* (New York, Free Press, 1992).

Gaggi, S.: *Modern/Postmodern: A Study in Twentieth-Century Arts and Ideas* (Philadelphia: University of Pennsylvania Press, 1989).

Gamble, A.: *The Conservative Nation* (London and Boston, MA, Routledge & Kegan Paul, 1974).

Gandhi, M.: *The Essential Writings of Mahatma Gandhi* (Delhi and Oxford, Oxford University Press, 1991), ed. R. N. Iyer.

Gandhi, M.: *Hind Swaraj and Other Writings* (Cambridge and New York, Cambridge University Press, 1997), ed. A. J. Parel.

Geuss, R.: *The Idea of a Critical Theory: Habermas and the Frankfurt School* (Cambridge, Cambridge University Press, 1981).

Giddens, A.: *Beyond Left and Right: The Future of Radical Politics* (Cambridge, Polity Press, 1994)

Giddens, A.: *The Politics of Climate Change* (Cambridge and Malden, MA, Polity Press, 2009).

Gladstone, D.: *The Twentieth-Century Welfare State* (New York, St Martin's Press, 1999).

Gleick, J.: *Chaos: Making a New Science* (London, Heinemann, 1987).

Goffman, E.: *Frame Analysis: An Essay on the Organization of Experience* (New York, Harper and Row, 1974).

Goodell, J.: *How to Cool the Planet* (Boston, MA and New York, Houghton Mifflin Harcourt, 2010).

Goodwin, J., Jasper, J. M. and Polletta, F., eds.: *Passionate Politics: Emotions and Social Movements* (Chicago and London, University of Chicago Press, 2001).

Gorz, A.: *Paths to Paradise: On the Liberation from Work* (London, Pluto, 1985).

Gorz, A.: *Capitalism, Socialism, Ecology* (London and New York, Verso, 1994), trans. C. Turner.

Gosse, V.: *Rethinking the New Left: An Interpretative History* (New York, Palgrave Macmillan, 2005).

Gramsci, A.: *Selections from the Prison Notebooks* (London, Lawrence & Wishart, 1971), ed. Q. Hoare and G. Nowell Smith.

Gray, J.: *Enlightenment's Wake: Politics and Culture at the Close of the Modern Age* (London and New York, Routledge, 1995).

Gunew, S. and Yeatman, A.: *Feminism and the Politics of Difference* (St Leonards, NSW, Allen and Unwin, 1993).

Haas, A. P., Eliason, M., Mays, V. M., et al.: 'Suicide and Suicide Risk in Lesbian, Gay, Bisexual, and Transgender Populations: Review and Recommendations', *Journal of Homosexuality*, 58:1, 2011, pp. 10–51.

Habermas, J.: 'Wahrheitstheorien' in *Wirklichkeit und Reflexion: Walter Schulz zum 60. Geburtstag* (Pfullingen, Neske, 1973).

Habermas, J.: *Theory and Practice* (London, Heinemann, 1974).

Habermas, J.: *Legitimation Crisis* (London, Heinemann, 1976), trans. T. McCarthy.

Habermas, J.: 'New Social Movements', *Telos*, 49, 1981, pp. 33–7.

Habermas, J.: *The Theory of Communicative Action*, Vol. I, *Reason and the Rationalization of Society* (Cambridge, Polity Press, 1984), trans. T. McCarthy.

Habermas, J.: *The Theory of Communicative Action*, Vol. II, *Lifeworld and System: A Critique of Functionalist Reason* (Cambridge, Polity Press, 1987), trans. T. McCarthy.

Habermas, J.: *The Structural Transformation of the Public Sphere: An Inquiry into a Category of Bourgeois Society* (1962) (Cambridge, MA, MIT Press, 1989), trans. T. Burger.

Habermas, J.: *Moral Consciousness and Communicative Action* (Cambridge, MA, MIT Press, 1990), trans. C. Lenhardt and S. W. Nicholsen.

Habermas, J.: *The Postnational Constellation: Political Essays* (Cambridge, MA, MIT Press, 2001).

Halévy, E.: *The Growth of Philosophic Radicalism* (London, Faber, 1949), 2nd edn, trans. M. Morris.

Halperin, D. M.: *Foucault: Towards A Gay Hagiography* (Oxford and New York, Oxford University Press, 1995).

Hamilton, C. and Dennis, R.: *Affluenza: When Too Much is Never Enough* (Crows Nest, NSW, Allen and Unwin, 2005).

Hardin, G. J.: 'The Tragedy of the Commons', *Science*, 162:3859, 1968, pp. 1243–8.

Hardt, M. and Negri, A.: *Empire* (Cambridge, MA and London, Harvard University Press, 2000).

Harrison, J. F. C.: *Robert Owen and the Owenites in Britain and America: The Quest for the New Moral World* (London, Routledge and Kegan Paul, 1969).

Harvey, D.: *The Condition of Postmodernity: An Enquiry into the Origins of Cultural Change* (Oxford and Cambridge, MA, Blackwell, 1990).

Hatzenbuehler, M.: 'The Social Environment and Suicide Attempts in Lesbian, Gay, and Bisexual Youth', *Pediatrics*, 127:5, 2011, pp. 896–903.

Haughney, D.: *Neoliberal Economics, Democratic Transition, and Mapuche Demands for Rights in Chile* (Gainesville, University Press of Florida, 2006).

Hawkins, M.: *Social Darwinism in European and American Thought: 1860–1945* (Cambridge and New York, Cambridge University Press, 1997).

Hay, C.: *Why We Hate Politics* (Cambridge and Malden, MA, Polity Press, 2007).

Hayek, F. A. von: *The Constitution of Liberty* (London, Routledge and Kegan Paul, 1976).

Hegel, G. W. F.: *The Philosophy of History* (New York, Prometheus, 1991), trans. J. Sibree.

Held, D.: *Models of Democracy* (Cambridge, Polity Press, 1987).

Held, D.: *Introduction to Critical Theory: Horkheimer to Habermas* (Cambridge, Polity Press, 1990).

Hewitt, C.: 'The Socioeconomic Position of Gay Men: A Review of the Evidence', *American Journal of Economics and Sociology*, 54:4, October 1995, pp. 461–79.

Heywood, A.: *Political Ideologies: An Introduction* (Houndmills, Basingstoke and New York, Palgrave Macmillan, 2007), 4th edn.

Hindess, B.: *Choice, Rationality, and Social Theory* (London and Boston, MA, Unwin Hyman, 1988).

Hobson, J. M.: *The Eastern Origins of Western Civilization* (Cambridge and New York, Cambridge University Press, 2004).

Holub, R. C.: *Jürgen Habermas: Critic in the Public Sphere* (London and New York, Routledge, 1991).

Honneth, A.: *The Struggle for Recognition: The Moral Grammar of Social Conflicts* (Cambridge, MA, MIT Press, 1995).

Honoré, C.: *In Praise of Slow: How a Worldwide Movement is Challenging the Cult of Speed* (London, Orion, 2005).

Hülsberg, W.: *The German Greens: A Social and Political Profile* (London and New York, Verso, 1988).

Hume, D.: *A Treatise of Human Nature* (1739–40) (Oxford, Clarendon Press, 1888), ed. L. A. Selby-Bigge.

Hume, D.: *An Enquiry Concerning the Principles of Morals* in *Enquiries Concerning the Human Understanding and Concerning the Principles of Morals* (Oxford, Clarendon Press, 1902), 2nd edn, ed. L. A. Selby-Bigge.

Huntington, S. P.: 'The United States' in M. Crozier, S. P. Huntington and J. Watanuki, *The Crisis of Democracy* (New York, New York University Press, 1975).

Inglehart, R.: *The Silent Revolution: Changing Values and Political Styles among Western Publics* (Princeton, NJ, Princeton University Press, 1977).

Inglehart, R.: *Culture Shift in Advanced Industrial Society* (Princeton, NJ, Princeton University Press, 1990).

Jackson, T.: *Prosperity Without Growth: Economics for a Finite Planet* (London and Sterling, Earthscan, 2009).

Jacques, M. and Mulhern, F.: *The Forward March of Labour Halted?* (London, NLB, 1981).

Jagose, A.: *Queer Theory* (Melbourne, Melbourne University Press, 1996).

Jakopovich, D.: 'Uniting to Win: Labour–Environmental Alliances', *Capitalism, Nature, Socialism*, 20:2, 2009, pp. 74–96.

James, C. L. R.: *The Black Jacobins: Toussaint L'Ouverture and the San Domingo Revolution* (London, Allison and Busby, 1980).

Jansson, B. S.: *The Reluctant Welfare State: A History of American Social Welfare Policies* (Belmont, CA, Wadsworth, 1988).

Jasper, J. M.: *The Art of Moral Protest: Culture, Biography, and Creativity in Social Movements* (Chicago and London, University of Chicago Press, 1997).

Jasper, J. M. and Polletta, F., eds.: *Passionate Politics: Emotions and Social Movements* (Chicago, University of Chicago Press, 2001).

Jennett, C. and Stewart, R. G.: *Politics of the Future: The Role of Social Movements* (South Melbourne, Macmillan, 1989).

Johnston, H. and Klandermans, B., eds.: *Social Movements and Culture* (Minneapolis, University of Minnesota Press, 1995).

Joseph, P. E., ed.: *The Black Power Movement: Rethinking the Civil Rights – Black Power Era* (New York and London, Routledge, 2006).

Judt, T.: *Postwar: A History of Europe since 1945* (London, Pimlico, 2007).

Kane, J.: *The Politics of Moral Capital* (Cambridge and New York, Cambridge University Press, 2001).

Keane, J.: *Democracy and Civil Society* (London, Verso, 1988).

Keane, J.: *Global Civil Society?* (Cambridge and New York, Cambridge University Press, 2003).

Keane, J.: *The Life and Death of Democracy* (New York and London, Simon & Schuster, 2009).

Keane, J.: 'Monitory Democracy and Media-Saturated Societies', *Griffith Review*, 24, 2009, accessed at https://griffithreview.com/edition-24–participation-society/monitory-democracy-and-media-saturated-societies.

Killian, L. M.: 'Social Movements' in *Handbook of Modern Sociology*, ed. R. E. L. Faris (Chicago, Rand McNally, 1964).

Kinealy, C.: *A Death-dealing Famine: The Great Hunger in Ireland* (London, Pluto Press, 1997).

Kirchheimer, O.: 'The Transformation of the Western European Party Systems' in *Political Parties and Political Development*, ed. J. La Palombara and M. Weiner (Princeton, NJ, Princeton University Press, 1966).

Klein, N.: *No Logo: Taking Aim at the Brand Bullies* (New York, Picador, 1999).

Klein, N.: *The Shock Doctrine: The Rise of Disaster Capitalism* (New York, Henry Holt, 2007).

Klingberg, F.: *The Anti-Slavery Movement in England: A Study in English Humanitarianism* (Hamden, CN, Archon, 1968).

Kornhauser, W. A.: *The Politics of Mass Society* (Glencoe, IL, Free Press, 1959).

Kriesi, H., Koopmans, R., Dyvendak, J. W. and Giugni, M. G.: *New Social Movements in Western Europe: A Comparative Analysis* (Minneapolis, University of Minnesota Press, 1995).

Krugman, P. R., Obstfeld, M. and Melitz, M. J.: *International Economics: Theory and Policy* (Boston, MA and London, Pearson Education, 2012), 9th edn.

Laclau, E. and Mouffe, C.: *Hegemony and Socialist Strategy: Towards a Radical Democratic Politics* (London, Verso, 1985).

Lash, S. and Urry, J.: *The End of Organized Capitalism* (Cambridge, Polity Press, 1987).

Lasswell, H. D.: *Politics: Who Gets What, When, How* (1936) (New York, P. Smith, 1950).

Layard, R.: *Happiness: Lessons from a New Science* (New York, Penguin, 2005).

Le Bon, G.: *The Crowd: A Study of the Popular Mind* (1896) (London, Benn, 1947).

Leftwich, A., ed.: *What is Politics? The Activity and its Study* (Oxford, Polity Press, 2004).

Lenin, V. I.: *What Is To Be Done?* (Harmondsworth, Penguin, 1988), ed. R. Service.

Little, G.: *Political Ensembles: A Psychosocial Approach to Politics and Leadership* (Oxford and New York, Oxford University Press, 1985).

Locke, J.: *An Essay Concerning Toleration, and Other Writings on Law and Politics* (Oxford, Clarendon Press; New York, Oxford University Press, 2006), ed. J. R. Milton and P. Milton.

Lotringer, S. and Marazzi, C., eds.: *Autonomia: Post-Political Politics* (New York, Semiotext(e), 2007), 2nd edn.

Lovelock, J. E.: *Gaia: A New Look at Life on Earth* (Oxford, Oxford University Press, 1987), rev. edn.

Lovelock, J. E.: *The Revenge of Gaia: Why the Earth is Fighting Back – and How We Can Still Save Humanity* (New York and London, Allen Lane, 2006).

Lukács, G.: *History and Class Consciousness: Studies in Marxist Dialectics* (London, Merlin Press, 1971), trans. R. Livingstone.

Luxemburg, R.: *Selected Political Writings* (London, Cape, 1972), ed. R. Looker.

Lyotard, J. F.: *The Postmodern Condition: A Report on Knowledge* (Manchester, Manchester University Press, 1984), trans. B. Massumi.

Macey, M. and Carling, A.: *Ethnic, Racial and Religious Inequalities: The Perils of Subjectivity* (Houndmills, Basingstoke and New York, Palgrave Macmillan, 2011).

Macpherson, C. B.: *The Life and Times of Liberal Democracy* (Oxford and New York, Oxford University Press, 1977).

Maddison, S. and Scalmer, S.: *Activist Wisdom: Practical Knowledge and Creative Tension in Social Movements* (Sydney, UNSW Press, 2006).

Mandela, N.: *Long Walk to Freedom: The Autobiography of Nelson Mandela* (London, Abacus, 1995).

Marcuse, H.: *One-Dimensional Man: Studies in the Ideology of Advanced Industrial Society* (London, Routledge and Kegan Paul, 1964).

Marcuse, H.: *Eros and Civilization: A Philosophical Inquiry into Freud* (London, Allen Lane, 1969).

Marcuse, H.: *Five Lectures: Psychoanalysis, Politics and Utopia* (London, Allen Lane, 1970), trans. J. J. Shapiro and S. M. Weber.

Marx, K. and Engels, F.: *The Communist Manifesto* (Harmondsworth, Penguin, 1967), trans. S. Moore.

Maslow, A. H.: 'A Theory of Human Motivation', *Psychological Review*, 50:4, 1943.

McAdam, D.: *Freedom Summer* (Oxford and New York, Oxford University Press, 1988).

McGuiness, S. B.: 'Black Power in Australia' in *Racism: The Australian Experience*, ed. F. S. Stevens (Sydney, Australia and New Zealand Book Company, 1977), 2nd edn, Vol. II.

McNay, L.: *Against Recognition* (Cambridge, Polity Press, 2008).

Meadows, D. H. and Meadows, D. L.: *Limits to Growth: A Report for the Club of Rome's Project on the Predicament of Mankind* (New York, Universe Books, 1972).

Melucci, A.: 'The Symbolic Challenge of Contemporary Movements', *Social Research*, 52:4, 1985, pp. 789–815.

Melucci, A.: *Nomads of the Present: Social Movements and Individual Needs in Contemporary Society* (London, Hutchinson Radius, 1989).

Melucci, A.: 'A Strange Kind of Newness: What's "New" in the New Social Movements' in *New Social Movements: From Ideology to Identity*, ed. E. Larana, H. Johnston and J. R. Gusfield (Philadelphia, Temple University Press, 1994).

Melucci, A.: *Challenging Codes: Collective Action in the Information Age* (Cambridge and New York, Cambridge University Press, 1996).

Meredith, M.: *Mandela: A Biography* (New York, St Martin's Press, 1998).

Micklethwait, J. and Wooldridge, A.: *The Company: A Short History of a Revolutionary Idea* (New York, Modern Library, 2003).

Mies, M. and Shiva, V.: *Ecofeminism* (London, Fernwood Publications, 1993).

Miliband, R.: *The State in Capitalist Society* (London, Weidenfeld & Nicolson, 1969).

Miliband, R.: *Capitalist Democracy in Britain* (Oxford and New York, Oxford University Press, 1982).

Mill, J. S.: *On Liberty, and Considerations on Representative Government* (Oxford, Basil Blackwell, 1946).

Moghiss, H., ed.: *Women and Islam: Critical Concepts in Sociology* (London and New York, Routledge, 2005).

Montesquieu: *De L'esprit des lois* in *Montesquieu: Oeuvres complètes* (Paris, Éditions du Seuil, 1964).

More, T.: *Utopia* (Cambridge and New York, Cambridge University Press, 1989), trans. R. M. Adams, ed. G. M. Logan and R. M. Adams.

Morris. A. D. and Mueller, C. M., eds.: *Frontiers in Social Movement Theory* (New Haven and London, Yale University Press, 1992).

Mouffe, C.: *The Return of the Political* (London and New York, Verso, 2005).

Mulgan, G. J.: *Politics in an Antipolitical Age* (Cambridge and Malden, MA, Polity Press, 1994).

Munck, R.: *Marx @ 2000: Late Marxist Perspectives* (London and New York, Zed Books, 2000).

Naess, A.: *Ecology, Community, and Lifestyle: Outline of an Ecosophy* (Cambridge and New York, Cambridge University Press, 1989), trans. D. Rothenberg.

Narula, R. and Dunning, J. H.: 'Industrial Development, Globalization and Multinational Enterprises: New Realities for Developing Countries', *Oxford Development Studies*, 28:2, 2000, pp. 141–67.

Nicholson, L. and Seidman, S., eds.: *Social Postmodernism: Beyond Identity Politics* (Cambridge and New York, Cambridge University Press, 1995).

Novelli, M. and Ferus-Comelo, A., eds.: *Globalization, Knowledge and Labour: Education for Solidarity within Spaces of Resistance* (London and New York, Routledge, 2010).

Nozick, R.: *Anarchy, State, and Utopia* (New York, Basic Books, 1974).

Nussbaum, M. C.: 'Justice for Women!', review of Susan M. Okin, *Justice, Gender, and the Family*, *New York Review of Books*, 8 Oct. 1992, pp. 43–8.

Oberschall, A.: *Social Conflict and Social Movements* (Englewood Cliffs, NJ, Prentice Hall, 1973).

Offe, C.: 'New Social Movements: Challenging the Boundaries of Institutional Politics', *Social Research*, 52:4, 1985, pp. 817–68.

Offe, C.: *Contradictions of the Welfare State* (Cambridge, MA, MIT Press, 1987), ed. J. Keane.

Okin, S. M.: *Justice, Gender, and the Family* (New York, Basic Books, 1989).

Olson, M.: *The Logic of Collective Action* (Cambridge, MA, Harvard University Press, 1965).

Pakulski, J.: *Social Movements: The Politics of Moral Protest* (Melbourne, Longman Cheshire, 1991).

Parfit, D.: *Reasons and Persons* (Oxford, Clarendon Press, 1984).

Parkin, F.: *Middle Class Radicalism: The Social Bases of the British Campaign for Nuclear Disarmament* (Manchester, Manchester University Press, 1968).

Parry, M. L., Canziani, O. F., Palutikof, J. P., van der Linden, P. J. and Hanson, C. E., eds.: *Contribution of Working Group II to the Fourth Assessment Report of the Intergovernmental Panel on Climate Change* (Cambridge and New York, Cambridge University Press, 2007).

Pateman, C.: *Participation and Democratic Theory* (Cambridge, Cambridge University Press, 1970).

Patton, P.: *Deleuze and the Political* (London and New York, Routledge, 2000).

Pepper, D.: *Eco-Socialism: From Deep Ecology to Social Justice* (London and New York, Routledge, 1993).

Pleyers, G.: *Alter-Globalization: Becoming Actors in the Global Age* (Cambridge and Malden, MA, Polity Press, 2010).

Popper, K. R.: *The Poverty of Historicism* (London, Routledge & Kegan Paul, 1961), 2nd edn.

Popper, K. R.: *The Open Society and its Enemies* (London, Routledge & Kegan Paul, 1966), 2 vols.

Proust, M.: *In Search of Lost Time* (New York, Modern Library, 2003), 6 vols., trans. D. J. Enright, C. K. Scott-Moncrieff and T. Kilmartin.

Pusey, M.: *Jürgen Habermas* (London and New York, Tavistock, 1976).

Pusey, M.: *Economic Rationalism in Canberra: A Nation-building State Changes its Mind* (Cambridge and New York, Cambridge University Press, 1991).

Rawls, J.: *A Theory of Justice* (Cambridge, MA, Belknap Press, 1971).

Riall, N.: *The Italian Risorgimento: State, Society and National Unification* (London and New York, Routledge, 1994).

Roberts, M. W.: 'Emergence of Gay Identity and Gay Social Movements in Developing Countries: The AIDS Crisis as Catalyst', *Alternatives: Global, Local, Political*, 20:2, 1995, pp. 243–64.

Rorty, R.: *Philosophy and the Mirror of Nature* (Princeton, NJ, Princeton University Press, 1980).

Roszak, T.: *The Making of a Counter-culture: Reflections on the Technocratic Society and its Youthful Opposition* (London, Faber, 1970).

Rowbotham, S., Segal, L. and Wainwright, H.: *Beyond the Fragments: Feminism and the Making of Socialism* (London, Merlin Press, 1979), 2nd rev. edn.

Rucht, D., ed.: *Research on Social Movements: The State of the Art in Western Europe and the USA* (Frankfurt, Campus; Boulder, CO, Westview Press, 1991).

Ryle, M.: *Ecology and Socialism* (London, Century Hutchinson, 1988).

Sarah, E., ed.: *Reassessments of 'First Wave' Feminism* (Oxford and New York, Pergamon, 1983).

Sartre, J.-P.: *Critique of Dialectical Reason* (London, New Left Books, 1991), trans. A. Sheridan-Smith.

Sartre, J.-P.: *Being and Nothingness: A Phenomenological Essay on Ontology* (Routledge, London, 2003), trans. H. E. Barnes.

Sawer, M.: 'Wearing your Politics on your Sleeve: The Role of Political Colours in Social Movements', *Social Movement Studies*, 6:1, 2007, pp. 39–56.

Scalmer, S.: *Gandhi in the West: The Mahatma and the Rise of Radical Protest* (Cambridge University Press, Cambridge and New York, 2011).

Scharf, T.: *The German Greens: Challenging the Consensus* (Berg, Oxford and Providence, USA, 1994).

Scholte, J. A.: *Globalization: A Critical Introduction* (Palgrave, Houndmills, Basingstoke and New York, 2000).

Seidman, S.: *The Postmodern Turn: New Perspectives on Social Theory* (Cambridge University Press, Cambridge and New York, 1994).

Singer, P.: *Democracy and Disobedience* (Oxford, Clarendon Press, 1973).

Skinner, Q.: *The Foundations of Modern Political Thought* (Cambridge, Cambridge University Press, 1978), 2 vols.: Vol. I, *The Renaissance*, and Vol. II, *The Age of Reformation*.

Smelser, N. J.: *Theory of Collective Behavior* (New York, Free Press, 1962).

Smelser, N. J.: *The Faces of Terrorism: Social and Psychological Dimensions* (Princeton, NJ, Princeton University Press, 2007).

Smith, A.: *An Inquiry into the Nature and Causes of the Wealth of Nations* (Oxford, Clarendon Press, 1976), Glasgow Edition of the Works and Correspondence.

Spender, D.: *Man-Made Language* (London, Pandora, 1990).

Spretnak, C. and Capra, F.: *Green Politics: The Global Promise* (New York, E. P. Dutton; London, Hutchinson, 1984).

Srivastava, H. S.: *The History of Indian Famines and Development of Famine Policy, 1858–1918* (Agra, Sri Ram Mehra, 1968).

Staggenborg, S.: *Social Movements* (Oxford and New York, Oxford University Press, 2011).

Stalin, J.: *Problems of Leninism* (Moscow, Foreign Languages Publishing House, 1947), 11th edn.

Steakley, J. D.: *The Homosexual Emancipation Movement in Germany* (Salem, NH, Ayer, 1993).

Steger, M. B.: *The Quest for Evolutionary Socialism: Eduard Bernstein and Social Democracy* (Cambridge and New York, Cambridge University Press, 1997).

Steger, M. B.: *Globalization: A Very Short Introduction* (Oxford and New York, Oxford University Press, 2009), 2nd edn.

Tarrow, S.: *Power in Movement: Collective Action, Social Movements and Politics* (Cambridge and New York, Cambridge University Press, 1998).

Taylor, M.: *Rationality and Revolution* (Cambridge University Press, Cambridge and New York, 1987).

Taylor, M.: *Rationality and Revolutionary Collective Action* (Cambridge and New York, Cambridge University Press, 1988).

Taylor, R. K. S.: *Against the Bomb: The British Peace Movement 1958–65* (Oxford, Clarendon Press; New York, Oxford University Press, 1988).

Thompson, E. P.: *The Making of the English Working Class* (1963) (London, Gollancz, 1980).

Thoreau, H. D.: *Walden* (1854) (Princeton, NJ, Princeton University Press, 1971), ed. J. L. Shanley.

Tilly, C.: *From Mobilization to Revolution* (Reading, MA, Addison-Wesley, 1978).

Tilly, C.: 'Models and Realities of Popular Collective Action', *Social Research*, 52:4, 1985, pp. 717–48.

Tilly, C.: *Contention and Democracy in Europe: 1650–2000* (New York and Cambridge, Cambridge University Press, 2004).

Tilly, C.: *Social Movements, 1768–2004* (Boulder and London, Paradigm Publishers, 2004).

Tong, R. P.: *Feminist Thought: A More Comprehensive Introduction* (Boulder, CO, Westview Press, 2008), 3rd edn.

Touraine, A.: *Conscience ouvrière* (Paris, Éditions du Seuil, 1966).

Touraine, A.: *The May Movement: Revolt and Reform* (New York, Random House, 1971), trans. L. F. X. Mayhew.

Touraine, A.: *The Self-Production of Society* (Chicago and London, University of Chicago Press, 1977), trans. D. Coltman.

Touraine, A.: *The Voice and the Eye: An Analysis of Social Movements* (Cambridge and New York, Cambridge University Press, 1981), trans. A. Duff.

Touraine, A.: 'An Introduction to the Study of Social Movements', *Social Research*, 52:4, 1985, pp. 749–88.

Touraine, A.: *Beyond Neoliberalism* (Malden, MA and Cambridge, Polity Press, 2001), trans. D. Macey.

Touraine, A.: *A New Paradigm for Understanding Today's World* (Malden, MA and Cambridge, Polity Press, 2007), trans. G. Elliott.

Touraine, A., Hegedus, Z., Dubet, F. and Wieviorka, M.: *Anti-Nuclear Protest: The Opposition to Nuclear Energy in France* (Cambridge and New York, Cambridge University Press, 1983), trans. P. Fawcett.

Urry, J.: *Global Complexity* (Malden, MA and Cambridge, Polity Press, 2003).

Urwin, D. W.: *A Political History of Western Europe since 1945* (London, Longman, 1997).

Verney, K.: *Black Civil Rights in America* (London and New York, Routledge, 2000).

Vidal, J.: *McLibel* (London, Macmillan, 1997).

Vincent, A.: *Modern Political Ideologies* (Chichester and Malden, MA, Wiley-Blackwell, 2010), 3rd edn.

Walzer, M.: *Obligations: Essays on Disobedience, War, and Citizenship* (Cambridge, MA, Harvard University Press, 1970).

Warren, K. J., ed.: *Ecofeminism: Women, Culture, Nature* (Bloomington, Indiana University Press, 1997).

Waterman, P.: 'Social-movement Unionism: A New Union Model for a New World Order?' *Review (Fernand Braudel Center)*, 16:3, 1993, pp. 245–78.

Weber, M.: 'The Profession and Vocation of Politics' ['Politik als Beruf'] (1919), in *Max Weber: Political Writings*, ed. P. Lassman and R. Speirs

(Cambridge and New York, Cambridge University Press, 1994), pp. 309–69.

Weber, M.: *The Protestant Ethic and the Spirit of Capitalism* (Los Angeles, Roxbury, 2002), trans. S. Kalberg.

West, D.: *Authenticity and Empowerment: A Theory of Liberation* (Brighton, Harvester Wheatsheaf, 1990).

West, D.: 'New Social Movements' in *Handbook of Political Theory*, ed. G. F. Gaus and C. Kukathas (London & Thousand Oaks, CA, Sage, 2004), ch. 20, pp. 265–76.

Wiesenthal, H.: *Realism in Green Politics: Social Movements and Ecological Reform in Germany* (Manchester and New York, Manchester University Press, 1993).

Wilkinson, P.: *Social Movement* (London, Macmillan, 1971).

Williams, R.: *Keywords: A Vocabulary of Culture and Society* (London, Fontana, 1976).

Woodham Smith, C.: *The Great Hunger: Ireland 1845–49* (London and New York, Penguin, 1992).

Wotherspoon, G.: *City of the Plain: History of a Gay Sub-Culture* (Sydney, Hale & Iremonger, 1991).

Young, I. M.: *Justice and the Politics of Difference* (Princeton, NJ, Princeton University Press, 1990).

Young, I. M.: 'Together in Difference: Transforming the Logic of Group Political Conflict' in *The Rights of Minority Cultures*, ed. W. Kymlicka (Oxford and New York, Oxford University Press, 1995), pp. 155–76.

Young, R.: '"Monkeywrenching" and the Processes of Democracy', *Environmental Politics*, 4:4, 1995, pp. 199–214.

Zald, M. N. and McCarthy, J.: *Social Movements in an Organizational Society* (New Brunswick, NJ, Transaction, 1987).

Index